skyline

Advanced Level Ausgabe C

Peter Bruck
Sabine Kranz
Petra Schmidt
Friedhold Schmidt
Anja Johannvordersielhorst
Thomas Tepe
T. Lothar Wullen

Ernst Klett Verlag
Stuttgart Düsseldorf Leipzig

skyline

Advanced Level Ausgabe C

Herausgegeben von
Professor Dr. Peter Bruck, Lüdinghausen,
OStR Sabine Kranz, Köln,
StD' Petra Schmidt, Bottrop,
StD Friedhold Schmidt, Thèze,
StR' Anja Johannvordersielhorst, Lüdenscheid,
StD Thomas Tepe, Münster,
StD T. Lothar Wullen, Bergisch-Gladbach

Begleitmaterialien zu Skyline: Advanced Level Ausgabe C:
CD mit ausgewählten Texten und Liedern und Hörverstehenstexten,
ISBN 3-12-510472-6
Video ISBN 3-12-510473-4
DVD ISBN 3-12-510474-2
Angela (Roman) 3-12-578160-4

1. Auflage 1 7 6 5 4 | 2009 08 07 06

Alle Drucke dieser Auflage können im Unterricht
nebeneinander benutzt werden, sie sind untereinander
unverändert. Die letzte Zahl bezeichnet das Jahr dieses Druckes.

Internetadresse: http://www.klett.de

Redaktion: Helen Smyth

Gestaltung: Bettina Herrmann (**beluga**design), Ulrike Wollenberg, Marion Köster
Umschlaggestaltung: Nikolaus Keller, Stuttgart
Christian Dekelver, Weingarten
Reproduktion: Meyle + Müller Medien-Management, Pforzheim
Druck: Stürtz GmbH, Würzburg
Printed in Germany.
ISBN 3-12-510470-X

9 783125 104709

Living the Dream

Cultural mix and clash – UK

First peoples

Focus on The Matrix

Barriers and bridges

Contents

Index

Abbreviations and symbols in this book

AE	American English
AusE	Australian English
b.	born
BE	British English
cf.	compare
col.	column
e.g.	for example
esp.	especially
etc.	etcetera, and so on
exclam.	exclamation
fig.	figurative
GB	refers to a specifically British phenomenon
i.e.	that is
l.; ll.	line; lines
opp.	*of* opposite of
o.s.	oneself
p.; pp.	page; pages
s.o.	someone
s.th.	something
US	refers to a specifically American phenomenon
usu.	usually

text / listening comprehension on CD

sequence on video

false friend

possible activity

Over to you – you decide what to do with the text

talk about a photo, cartoon, etc.

Living the Dream

The immigrant story

Looking and thinking

- Speculate about the expectations of the immigrants in the photos below. To what extent do you think their expectations differ/are the same?
- As you work through the chapter collect new vocabulary. Then reorganise the vocabulary in a way which will help you to memorise it, e.g. in a word field or mind map.

Hispanic migrant workers harvest lettuce in California (1989)

Immigrant family looking at the New York skyline from Ellis Island (1925)

Before you read

- Look at the pie charts below showing social conditions in US households around 1900 and 2000. Match the following headings with the most suitable pair of charts: living alone – households headed by a married couple – people living in big households (six or more people) – share of income spent on food.

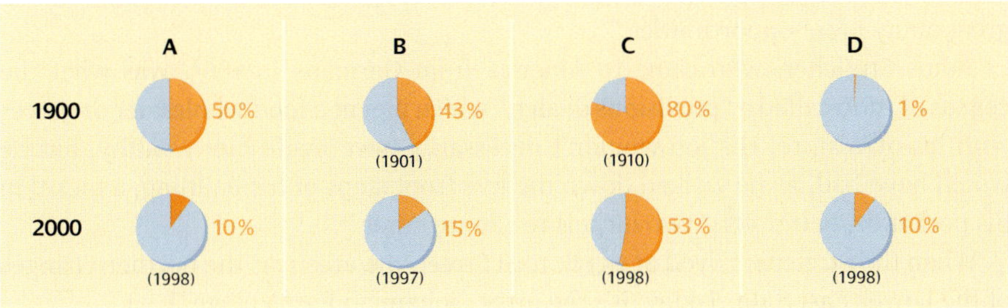

An Amazing Journey

To understand who we are – how life in America has changed and how it has remained the same – *U.S. News* compared the story of one family who lived at a New York address in 1900 with those who live there today and tracked the changes recorded by the U.S. census. The picture that emerges is one of a nation that continues to be defined, in many ways, by its immigrants, even though today's are of decidedly different origin from those of a century ago. America is more diverse, with nearly 7 million people saying they belong to more than one race. Most of us live in metropolitan areas today, not in the countryside. Far more of us own our own homes today, but families are smaller, if we have them at all. We are putting off marriage and kids. More of us, straight and gay, are simply living together. The number of single parents, both fathers and mothers, is on the rise. Millions are living alone. We earn vastly more money and are better educated. We are healthier and live longer. And most of us who work work less.

The 10-hour day and six-day workweek were the norm in 1900. "People started working when they were young; they worked long hours and then they died," says John Logan, a sociology professor at the State University of New York-Albany who dug through the 1900 and 1920 censuses to study the experience of various New York families. […]

There is an important thread, however, connecting 1900 and 2000. The beginning and end of the century were both marked by huge numbers of immigrants flocking to the United States, separated from old communities and old ways in search of better opportunities or refuge from political turmoil or religious strife. As Pulitzer-Prize-winning Harvard historian Oscar Handlin wrote, "Once I thought to write a history of the immigrants in America. Then, I discovered that the immigrants were American History." A century ago, the newcomers were from Europe. Today, they're from Mexico, Central and South America, China, the Philippines, Africa, and the Caribbean. During the 1990s, the number of Vietnamese swelled by 83 percent, Chinese increased by 48 percent, and Indians rose by 26 percent. The number of Mexicans grew by 53 percent during the decade. Gateway cities, such as New York, which topped a record 8 million in the 2000 census, are booming in population because of rising numbers of Hispanics and Asians. Immigrants then and now share

10 **straight** *here:* heterosexual
19 **thread** *here:* link between two things
20 **to flock** to go somewhere in large numbers
22 **Pulitzer Prize** annual prize for achievements in journalism or literature
29 **gateway city** city which immigrants use as port of entry into the US

common dreams and aspirations: to build a new life and better themselves. “Doing well [in 1900] was if everyone survived and the children could get jobs and they could pool their incomes, and they had enough to get by,” says Logan. “Doing superwell was that someone could go to school and 20 years later had a better future. Not everyone managed that. There was a lot of lean-on-me within families and ethnic communities. Many immigrants do that today. Most of the rest of us have a great many more opportunities.”

Julius Streicher, who came to America from Germany in 1885, was what the census of 1900 called a “provisions dealer,” which meant a food wholesaler or grocer with his own store. His job wouldn’t necessarily have made him wealthy, but he would have had, as he walked down the five front steps of his building, a nickel in his pocket or, better yet, “two nickels to rub together.”

When the Streichers lived at 253 E. 10th Street, the area was the northern fringes of the Lower East Side. Today, it’s the artsy, bohemian East Village. [...]

Today, some of the windows at 253 E. 10th Street have bars on them, which would have been unlikely 100 years ago. There are four apartments to a floor – 20 in all. But it’s no longer a building of immigrants. For almost $900 a month, Harvey Weissman, 30, who grew up in Connecticut, has a small, one-bedroom apartment in the building without central air but with great views of majestic skyscrapers. At first, Weissman didn’t feel he fit into the neighborhood. With an economics and Spanish degree from Clark University, he pursued a career as an accountant. But he decided that wasn’t who he really was. Eventually, he chucked the corporate job. Today, he’s trying to build an acting career. “Now I feel very happy to be here; the creative energy is very strong,” he says. “It gives me courage to see other people doing it.” [...]

Unlike their counterparts in 1900, most of today’s residents of 253 E. 10th Street live alone – and love it. “It’s liberating to know that I have my own private respite from the city,” says Harvey Weissman. But he’s honest about the downside too: “It gets lonely.” [...] Weissman once thought his life would be conventional: a regular job, a house in the ’burbs, wife, kids. But he doesn’t have that neat picture anymore. “Coming to New York opened up my eyes to so many different paths,” he says. He’d like to find a life partner, he says, but he’s still learning to enjoy his own company. He’s not so sure about kids anymore either. “Some people would say it’s selfish not to get married and have children,” he says, “but it may be more selfish to have children just to fit into expectations.” [...]

[In 1900] most Americans had little trouble distinguishing themselves from most other people in the world by their sense of unquenchable optimism. The term “American Dream” would not be coined until the 1930s, but Americans in 1900 knew what it was: Grab it now, grab it all, grab it fast. (They were the dot-commers of their time.) [...]

Not all made it. Not all wanted to. Though it is often little noted, many immigrants gave up on America. Roughly a fourth to a third who came to this country left again. According to Thomas Schlereth, between 1899 and 1924 about “half the Italians, Hungarians and Slovaks; about 12 percent of the Irish; and about 23 percent of the Scandinavians” went back to Europe. Life could be lonely and hard in America.

It certainly turned out to be for the Streichers. By 1920, Julius was a widower, living in his sister’s rented house in Brooklyn. He was no longer a grocer but was

36 **lean-on-me** dependence
44 **fringe** outer edge
45 **artsy** *(informal)* giving the impression of being interested in the arts
50 **central air** air conditioning
53 **to chuck** *(informal) here:* to give up
58 **respite** place of rest
61 **’burb** *short for* suburb
68 **unquenchable** never ending
70 **to grab** *here:* to take an opportunity
70 **dot-commer** s.o. who sets up an internet company

now listed in the census as an unskilled factory worker. In 1900, he had begun the process of becoming a citizen. By 1920, he had not become one. Today, we don't know what became of Julius Streicher or his family. Like the American experience, some stories are not yet ended.

By Roger Simon and Angie Cannon, US News & World Report, *August 6, 2001.*

Exploring the text

1 a) According to the text, what were the signs that an immigrant had 'made it' in the US in 1900?
b) What information does the text give about immigrants who did not make it?
2 How do the writers of the article define 'being an American today'?
3 How have Harvey Weissman's expectations in life changed?

Close-up: statistics

- a) Look at the bar charts below showing the origins of US immigrants a hundred years ago and in the more recent past. What strikes you about the statistics?

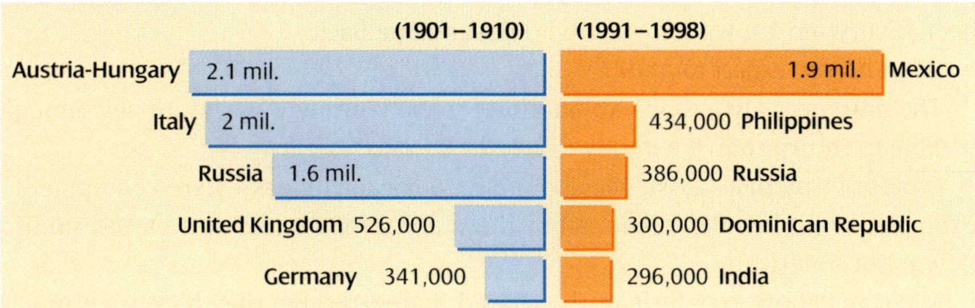

b) Compare the modern US immigrant experience with that of immigrants in Germany.

A step further

- How would you describe Harvey Weissman's attitude to life?

Being illegal in the US

The film Bread and Roses *(2000) narrates the experiences of Maya, a Mexican in California, who works illegally for a non-union cleaning service. Maya gets to know a union representative, Sam Shapiro, who tries to organize the cleaners. Following a secret meeting the supervisor, Perez, finds a union flyer and fires one of the cleaners, Berta. Maya goes to see Sam.*

Exploring the scene

Watch the scene twice and take notes to help you answer these questions.

1 What does Maya mean when she asks Sam "What do you risk"?
2 What do we learn about Berta and her family?
3 How is Maya's emotional state underlined by the camera work?
4 How does the scene end? What impression is conveyed by the camera work at the end of the scene? Refer to the glossary on page 184 for ideas.

A step further

- Imagine Maya meets Berta and tells her about her talk with Sam. Act out the scene.

Before you read

- In what ways has the US influenced the culture and way of life in countries around the world? Which aspects of American culture do you have contact with?

Mexico is memory

Second generation Mexican-American Richard Rodriguez looks at Mexican-American relations and the effect the US has had on Mexico and Mexican immigrants in the US.

VETE PERO NO ME OLVIDES.

Go, but do not forget me, someone has written on the side of a building near the border in Tijuana.

Mexicans may know their souls are imperiled in America but they do not recognize the risk by its proper name.

Two Mexican teenagers say they are going to *los Estados Unidos* for a job. Nothing more.

For three or four generations now, Mexican villages have lived under the rumor of America, a rumor vaguer than paradise. America exists in thousands of maternal prayers and in thousands of pubescent dreams. Everyone knows someone who has been. Everyone knows someone who never came back.

What do you expect to find?

The answer is always an explanation for the journey: "I want money enough to be able to return to live with my family in Mexico."

Proofs of America's existence abound in Mexican villages – stereo equipment, for example, or broken-down cars – but these are things Americans picked up or put down, not America.

Mexicans know very little of the United States, though they have seen America, the TV show, and America, the movie. […]

Mexican teenagers waiting along the levee in Tijuana are bound to be fooled by the United States because they do not yet realize the future will be as binding as the past. The American job will introduce the Mexican to an industry, an optimism, a solitude nowhere described in Mexico's theology.

How can two Mexican teenagers know this, clutching the paper bags their mamas packed for them this morning? The past is already the future, for the bags contain only a change of underwear. These two may have seen *Dallas* on TV and they may think they are privy to the logic and locution of America. But that is not the same thing as having twenty American dollars in their own pockets.

Mexico, mad mother. She still does not know what to make of our leaving. For most of this century Mexico has seen her children flee the house of memory. During the Revolution 10 percent of the population picked up and moved to the United States; in the decades following the Revolution, Mexico has watched many more of her children cast their lots with the future; head north for work, for wages; north for life. Bad enough that so many left, worse that so many left her for the gringo.

America wanted cheap labor. American contractors reached down into Mexico for men to build America. Sons followed fathers north. It became a rite of passage for the poor Mexican male.

I will send for you or I will come home rich. […]

Mexicans crossing the border are secret agents of matriarchy. Mexicans have slipped America a darker beer, a cuisine of *tú*. Mexicans have invaded American privacy to

3 **Tijuana** [tɪˈhwɑːnə] Mexican city on the US border
10 **pubescent** [pjuːˈbesənt] of a child who is developing into an adult
21 **binding** limiting
22 **industry** *here:* quality of working hard
27 **privy** [prɪvɪ] **to s.th.** *(formal)* sharing secrets
27 **locution** *(formal)* way of speaking
31 **Revolution** the Mexican Revolution (1910)
33 **to cast one's … future** *here:* to risk their futures by deciding to go to the US
39 **to slip** to give secretly
40 ***tú*** refers to the Mexican culture

babysit or to watch the dying or to wash lipstick off the cocktail glasses. Mexicans have forced Southwestern Americans to speak Spanish whenever they want their eggs fried or their roses pruned. Mexicans have overwhelmed the Church – eleven o'clock masses in most Valley towns are Spanish masses. By force of numbers, Mexicans have taken over grammar-school classrooms. The Southwest is besotted with the culture of *tú*.

But Mexico was fooled by her own tragic knowledge of relationship. The desert is a tide. How could Mexico not have realized that tragedy would wash back on her, polluted with gringo optimism?

A young man leaves his Mexican village for Los Angeles in 1923. He returns one rainy night in 1925. He tells his family, next day he tells the village, that it is okay up there. The following spring, four village men accompany him back to L.A. They send money home. Mothers keep their sons' dollars in airtight jars, opening the jars only when someone is sick or someone is dying. The money is saturated with rumor.

Thus have Mexicans from America undermined the tranquillity of Mexican villages they thought only to preserve. The Mexican American became a revolutionary figure, more subversive than a Chichimeca, more subversive than Pancho Villa.

In the 1970s, President Luis Echeverría invited planeloads of "Chicano leaders" to visit Mexico with the apparent goal of creating a lobby for the interests of Mexico modeled on the Israeli lobby. Perhaps the Chicano was the key to Mexico's future? The Chicano, after all, defied assimilation in the United States, or said he did. The Chicano sought to retain his culture, his mother tongue. In the 1980s, the government ministry in Mexico City announced a policy of reconciliation *(acercamiento)* regarding Mexican Americans.

By the 1980s, Mexican Americans were, on average, older, wealthier, better educated than the average Mexican; we also had fewer children. In the 1980s, the proud house of Mexico was crumbling, the economy was folding, the wealthy of Mexico had begun their exodus, following the peasant's route north. Along the border, Mexican towns inclined toward America and away from Mexico City. And from the North came unclean enchantments of the gringo – the black music, the blond breasts, the drugged eyes of tourists.

How much is the gum?

Mexico worried about her own. What influence shall she have? The village is international now. Most of the men have been north; many of the women, too. Have seen. Everyone has heard stories.

Mexico cannot hold the attention of her children. The average age of the country descends into adolescence. More than half of Mexico is under fifteen years of age. What is the prognosis for memory in a country so young?

For Mexico is memory …

From Days of Obligation. An Argument with My Mexican Father by *Richard Rodriguez, New York: Penguin Books 1993, pp. 50–52, 72–73.*

57 **Chichimeca** nomadic people in the North of Mexico
58 **Pancho Villa** leader in the Mexican Revolution
68 **to fold** *(informal here)* to go bankrupt
71 **gringo** *(slang, negative)* a foreigner in a Latin American country

Exploring the text

1 List the positive and negative effects the US has had on the lives of Mexicans.
2 How is the US characterized in the text?
3 Find examples of *personification* in the text and explain their function.
4 How does Richard Rodriguez view the future of Mexico?

Personification
a kind of metaphor in which human characteristics are given to an object.

Before you read

- a) What difficulties might second-generation immigrants in the US have compared to the problems their parents had to face?
  b) How do you think their parents might feel about their children's integration into American society, especially on a day like their high school graduation?

Stuck in the middle

A third-generation Amerasian still feels in-between

In 1871 my great-grandfather Fong See, an illiterate peasant, left his village in southern China for Sacramento, California, in search of his father, who had disappeared during the building of the transcontinental railroad. At about the same time, Letticie Pruett's family crossed America in a covered wagon and homesteaded in Oregon. By the late 1890s, after years of manual labor, Fong See owned the Curiosity Bizarre, which manufactured underwear for brothels. Letticie had run away from home and ended up in Sacramento. When no one would hire a single, uneducated woman, she drifted into Chinatown and the Curiosity Bizarre, where she begged Fong See for a job. He hired her, one thing led to another, and they decided to get married.

It was against the law in California and many other states for Chinese and Caucasians to marry. It was also against the law for Chinese to own property in California, and unlawful at the federal level for Chinese to become naturalized citizens. These laws had grown out of the so-called "Driving Out", when Chinese had literally been driven from Western towns – when they weren't hung, shot, burned or stabbed by members of the white community, who had no fear of retribution because Chinese could not testify in court against Caucasians. What started as informal harassment was formalized with the Exclusion Act of 1882, which barred the immigration of Chinese laborers and led to even more institutionalized racism.

But with a contract marriage drawn up by a lawyer, my great-grandparents set out to achieve the American Dream. Fong See and Letticie raised five mixed-race children and ran five antique stores in southern California. Fong See became the patriarch of Los Angeles Chinatown. He was the first Chinese in the U.S. to own an automobile and was one of the few Chinese to do business with the white community

4 **transcontinental railroad** railway linking New York and San Francisco
5 **to homestead** *(old, AE)* to settle on a piece of land and farm it
9 **to drift** to go somewhere without having a plan
22 **contract marriage** a marriage on paper only

by selling props to the nascent film industry and antiques to customers like Frank Lloyd Wright. Despite these successes, Fong See's four sons – all American-born citizens – had to go to Mexico to marry their Caucasian fiancées.

Drop down another two generations. I am only one-eighth Chinese, with red hair and freckles. People often ask me where I fit in and how I define myself. My answer has to do with where I grew up and what I saw around me. Fong See had four wives, as Chinese traditional codes dictate for men with great wealth and prowess, so the Chinese side of my family in Los Angeles numbers close to 400, with only a handful that look like me. It's been 130 years since my great-great-grandfather left China, and we've become educated, changed our way of dress and lost our Cantonese. But there's a deep core that connects to our peasant ancestors.

Many small rituals in my daily life mirror what I experienced as a child. I tell my sons to put only what they're going to eat on their plates, and I still pick at their discarded chicken bones. When they want comfort food, I cook them rice. (Shortly after going to college, my older son called to announce happily that the girls next door had a rice cooker.) When my younger son boasted that he'd told his chemistry teacher to stop checking her e-mail during class, I made him go back the next day with a gift of a perfect orange and an apology.

I do look different, and nothing will ever change that or people's reactions. At my baby shower, some friends mistook my father, a professor, for a Chinese waiter. I've had Chinese Americans and Chinese-in-China talk about me as though I weren't there: "I had a cousin from the south who looked like her, but her hair is disgusting." On book tours, Caucasians will often ask point-blank, "Why would you choose to be Chinese when you have all the privileges of being white?" Given my family and the era in which I grew up, I don't know that I had a choice.

The last of America's miscegenation laws were overturned in 1965. Intermarriage is common, and if you walk into a classroom today, it's impossible to tell a child's exact race, or what race or ethnicity he or she may identify with. You certainly can't with my own sons, who are only one-sixteenth Chinese and otherwise Irish, English, Scottish, Spanish, Russian, German, Austrian and Polish. I tell them it's up to them to choose their own identities – just so long as they marry nice Chinese girls. They think I'm kidding. I'm not, really. Who, I wonder, is going to cook them their rice?

By Lisa See, TIME Asia, *September 4, 2001.*

27 **Frank Lloyd Wright** (1869–1959) famous American architect
37 **core** innermost part
46 **baby shower** *(AE)* party given before a baby is born
50 **given** in view of
52 **miscegenation** [ˌmɪsɪdʒɪˈneɪʃn] which forbids interracial marriages
56 **to be up to s.o.** to be s.o.'s own decision

Exploring the text

1 How were Chinese immigrants treated in the US at the end of the 19th and beginning of the 20th centuries?

2 a) Describe Lisa See's family background. In what way is her ancestry unusual?
b) Why, do you think, does she give so much detail about her family history?

3 To what extent has Lisa See been assimilated into mainstream America?

A step further

- Do you think that it would be possible to create a society in Germany where people can choose their own cultural identities, or not?
- Read the text "Mexico is memory" on pages 10–11. Compare the Chinese experience of immigration with the Mexican one. What similarities and differences do you notice?

Before you read

- What advice would you give to someone who wants to change careers?
- Think of five people in the US who have become successful. Try to list the factors which contributed to their success.

Making it Big in America

In many countries, success is like royalty: you must be born to it. In sharp contrast, here your dreams are within your grasp. Why? This country has traditionally invited every citizen to exploit five basic American attributes that distinguish the U.S. from virtually every other country in the world: our willingness to give women the same educational opportunities as men; our unrivaled history of openness to immigrants, who remain an endless source of economic vitality; our easy access to higher education, as opposed to such nations as Japan and Germany, where teenage students must pass vigorous exams to qualify for college; our tradition of upward mobility which – more so than in the class-conscious societies of Europe and Asia – allows children to escape the circumstances of their birth; and our uncommon acceptance of career change, which lets people reinvent themselves again and again until they unleash their full potential. […]

Overcome your upbringing José Gaitán, attorney

Americans and foreigners alike are justly horrified by the deprivation and violence in our nation's ghettos. What is often overlooked, though, is that most Americans who are born in the ghetto aren't destined to die there. According to researchers at the University of Michigan, 56 % of teenagers whose family income put them in the nation's lowest fifth of all families in the 1970s had climbed out of the basement a decade later. Indeed, 12 % were among the country's top 40 % of earners. Seattle attorney José Gaitán, 39, was one of them.

Gaitán grew up in the city's rough central neighborhood, the son of an illegal Salvadoran immigrant father who was deported when José was five and an American-born, heroin-addicted mother. Today Gaitán is co-owner of the law firm Gaitán & Cusack and an adjunct professor at the University of Washington's law school. He earns more than $ 100,000 a year and lives in a $ 225,000 house with his wife Olive, 40, and her two children from a previous marriage. […]

Growing up on welfare, Gaitán remembers that food was so scarce that he shared two turkey TV dinners with his mother and younger brother one Thanksgiving. He found the path to a better life at Seattle First Baptist Church, where a minister, a Boy Scout leader and a Boeing engineer encouraged him to work hard in school. "They took the time to nurture me and show me that I could change my life," Gaitán says.

His grades won him scholarships at private Linfield College in McMinnville, Ore. After graduating with a bachelor's degree in political science and history in 1973, he returned to Seattle and worked his way through the University of Washington's School of Law, in part by scraping barnacles off ships. He stayed in Seattle and worked as a county and federal prosecutor until 1982, when he and a partner opened a private practice.

Today his firm counts Nabisco and the Federal Deposit Insurance Corporation among its clients, grosses more than $ 2 million a year and employs 13 lawyers. Says

2 **within your grasp** which you can achieve
4 **virtually** ∇ almost
16 **destined** when one's future has been planned
24 **adjunct professor** university teacher who is not a member of the teaching staff
33 **Ore.** *short for* Oregon

Gaitán: "Social and economic mobility is a function of hard work, a 'can do' attitude and being good to people."

Risk reinventing yourself Mike Hernacki, author

In Europe and Japan, the career you choose in your teens or twenties – and often the employer – is usually what you're stuck with for life. But not here. Every year, one in 10 U.S. workers changes occupations. This license to be restless allows Americans to keep switching careers until they maximize their productivity and happiness. One such striver is San Diego's Mike Hernacki, 46, who shed his professional skin five times in 14 years before finally finding his calling as a freelance business writer. Now he brings in $100,000 a year working out of a comfortable home office [...] that he impishly describes as a "Victorian bordello".

As the son of Polish immigrants growing up in Detroit, Hernacki dreamed of becoming a writer, but his parents, who ran a small grocery store, pressured him to pursue a more practical career choice. So after earning a bachelor's degree from Michigan State in 1965, he bounced from teaching elementary school in suburban Detroit for $5,000 a year to copywriting at a small advertising agency for $10,000 before going on to earn a law degree at Detroit College of Law. Though he was making $30,000 a year as an attorney in a Detroit suburb, he abandoned that profession too after only 18 months. "I dreaded going to court," he says. "All that conflict really got me down." In 1977, seeking a sunnier climate, he left Michigan for San Diego. Over the next 18 months, he earned $25,000 as a stockbroker. "But I didn't want to be a stockbroker for 30 years," he says. "It didn't excite me."

In 1979, Hernacki's wife Wanda, now 45, encouraged him to quit the brokerage business and pursue his long-deferred dream of writing. For the first eight months he earned a mere $5,000. "But for the first time in my life," he recalls, "I loved what I was doing." The next year he began writing annual reports for brokerage houses and other corporations. His take: $31,000.

Inspired by his own successful career change, Hernacki expanded his repertoire to include self-help books such as *The Ultimate Secret to Getting Absolutely Everything You Want* (Berkley, $3.50), which has sold 100,000 copies. Repeating the advice in his book, Hernacki says: "Changing careers is a leap into the unknown, but if you love your work, the money will follow."

By Mary Granfield, Money, *October 1991.*

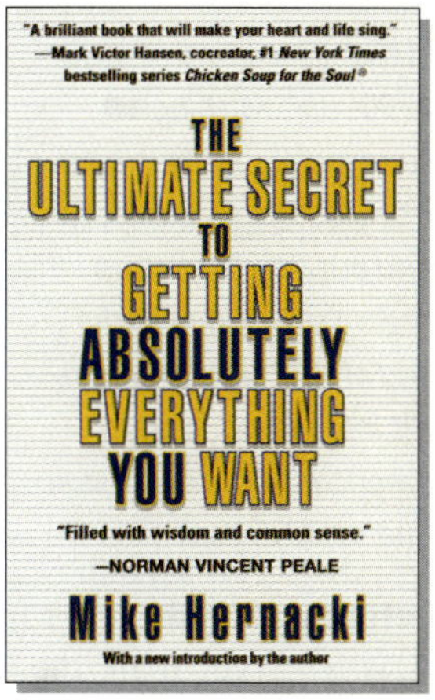

45 **to be stuck with s.th.** *(informal) here:* to be unable to change s.th.
46 **license** *here:* freedom
48 **to shed one's professional skin** *(fig.)* to change careers
55 **to bounce** *here:* to move quickly
61 **stockbroker** *Wertpapierhändler*
67 **take** *(informal)* money earned

Exploring the text

1 Look at the three headings in the text and sum up the message in your own words.

2 a) Outline the careers of the two men profiled in the text.
b) In what kind of publication would you expect to find this kind of profile?

3 According to Mary Granfield, why would these men's careers not be possible in Europe, for example? Do you agree with her point of view, or not?

A step further

- Rank the factors contributing to success mentioned in ll. 4–12 in order of importance. Then compare your list with another student's.
- Write an introduction to *The Ultimate Secret to Getting ...* (ll. 69–70) as if you were Mike Hernacki. Highlight your experiences and encourage readers to take action.

In the second half of the 1990s BBC Washington correspondent Gavin Esler travelled across the US, to find out if the American Dream still existed at the end of the old millennium. His interviews included Americans from every state and social class.

Before you read

- Why, do you think, did Gavin Esler call his book about the US *The United States of Anger*? How might the American Dream have gone wrong for some Americans?

The United States of Anger

My appointment with the American Dream is five miles out of town. I smell it first, wood smoke rising above the snowy fields. The Morin family have built their own log cabin in two acres, surrounded by forests of white birch, oak and pine.

Claude Morin is a thickset man of thirty-two with a walrus moustache and wiry hair like a pot scourer. When he shakes your hand, it stays shook. Your body bounces. His wife, Ann Marie, is an articulate physiotherapist who works in a small local hospital. They have one daughter, Mary, aged three, who peeps out shyly from behind her mother's legs, and a dog, Bayley, who stands accused of gross moral turpitude. Instead of breeding as planned with another thoroughbred spaniel to produce a litter which would make the Morins $250 a head in much needed cash, Bayley has been sleeping around, giving birth to nine mongrel pups. Little Mary shows off the pups anyway.

Claude says he was laid off by the paper-mill last October. He speaks slowly and deliberately, trying to hide his anger. He has spent three months as a house-husband looking after his daughter while his wife is the sole breadwinner, and he knows he is running out of options. He admits with restrained panic that yet another job he applied for told him today that he had not been hired. As a machine operator at the paper-mill he used to work twelve-hour shifts at $13 an hour. Hard work, good money. Now all the jobs are around $7 an hour, even if he could get one. Stacking shelves in a supermarket. Dreary. Dead end. Dismal. He says he might lose the log cabin, and the big man is almost in tears because this really is his American Dream, the home the family built themselves in the forest. The Morins' desperation is part of a pattern which suggests this may become the generation in which – for many average Americans – the venerable cliché of the Dream finally crumbles. […]

"We were always raised with the ideals that if we wanted something we had to work for it," Ann Marie says of the basic rules of her life, the social contract which guided generations of Americans to prosperity. "That was not a problem for us. We want to work … We *have* lived the American Dream. We would like to have another child –"

"But not right now," Claude breaks in. Another child can typically cost $10,000 or more in hospital fees for a normal delivery, plus all the dislocation to the mother's career. Europeans rarely understand this American anxiety.

To lose a job in the United States usually means to lose health insurance, possibly for an entire family. Every industrial society is experiencing 'downsizing' by corporate bosses anxious to boost profits and maximize efficiency. But the United States is the only industrialized country without a health insurance system for all its citizens. […]

We walked outside with the spaniel Bayley barking and running crazily in the snow. With the enthusiasm of a pioneer, Claude explained how he chose the land, cleared the trees, then sank the foundations. They bought logs in a kit but cut every joint themselves, varnished the wood with the help of brothers, sisters, mothers, fathers and cousins. "I told them I'd get the beer and the food," he laughed, "if they helped with the work."

Then he talked about the pain of selling up and moving away to where the jobs are. The sunbelt, maybe. Texas, the south or south-west, Montana, Wyoming. He

19 **to stack** *here:* to fill with products
25 **to raise s.o.** *here:* to teach s.o. as a child
31 **dislocation** interruption
34 **downsizing** reduction in the number of workers
40 **to sink the foundations** to prepare the concrete base of a building

did not know where. He and Ann Marie still dared to believe that they might do better than their parents and that three-year old Mary could do even better still, maybe becoming a doctor – though opinion polls suggest half of all Americans do *not* think the next generation will be better off. In Britain and Europe there are similar worries about the future, but nowhere is there such a sense that the Dream is fading as there is for middle-class Americans. They fear that the sun is setting on a way of life and that able, skilled workers will no longer be able to make it as their parents did.

In October 1996 the *Washington Post* reported that three out of five Americans claimed they did not make enough money to save. One in four had problems with bill collectors. And in 1996 there were a record 1 million bankruptcies. At the height of the supposed boom more citizens were filing for personal bankruptcy than the 900,000 total bankruptcies recorded at the end of the recession in 1992. The prosperity of America in the aggregate was not filtering through to most of its citizens, except those who were already well off.

The Morins and I said farewell. I drove back to my hotel in the darkness hoping they would be lucky. Theirs was the perennial dilemma at the core of American life since the first immigrants left Europe: do you stay among friends and family or do you sacrifice and uproot for the promise that thousands of miles away there really is a better life? The Morins would uproot, I decided, to pursue the Dream. Americans always did.

From The United States of Anger. The People and the American Dream *by Gavin Esler, London: Michael Joseph, 1997, pp. 28–32.*

49 **well / better off** having more money
54 ***Washington Post*** *(US)* national newspaper
56 **bill collector** person employed to obtain money that s.o. owes
57 **to file for personal bankruptcy** to officially declare that you cannot pay back money you owe

Imagine how one of the people in the unemployment exchange would reply to the question: What is your American Dream?"

Exploring the text

1 a) How does the writer use the term "American Dream" in the text?
b) What does the term mean to the family he interviews?

2 How does the writer describe Claude Morin?

3 Compare the Morins' situation with the success stories described in "Making it Big in the US" (pp. 14–15). What makes the Morins' situation different? How significant are these differences?

4 The writer mentions a number of differences between the US and Europe. Work out these differences and comment on them.

Close-up: vocabulary

Find and make a list of phrases in the text relating to 'making it' and 'not making it' in the US.

A step further

- Imagine and act out a conversation in which Claude and Ann Marie discuss their future and come to a decision about what they should do.

The dawning of a new millennium

Listen to the recording of the speech made by President Bill Clinton on New Year's Eve, 1999. What message do you think he had for the people of America?

Before you read

- In the days following the terrorist attacks on the World Trade Center on September 11, 2001, New York City firefighters became a symbol of hope for the people of New York. Speculate as to why this was the case.

The darkest day

The following speech was made by Rudolph Giuliani, Mayor of New York at the Citywide Prayer Service on September 23, 2001, a week after the terrorist attacks on targets in the US.

On September 11th, New York City suffered the darkest day in our history. It is now up to us to make this our finest hour.

Today we come together in the Capital of the World, as a united City. We're accompanied by religious leaders of every faith, to offer a prayer for the families of those who have been lost, to offer a prayer for our City and to offer a prayer for America.

The proud Twin Towers that once crowned our famous skyline – no longer stand. But our skyline will rise again.

In the words of President George W. Bush, "we will rebuild New York City."

To those who say that our City will never be the same, I say you are right. It will be better.

Now we understand much more clearly why people from all over the globe want to come to New York, and to America ... why they always have, and why they always will.

It's called freedom, equal protection under law, respect for human life, and the promise of opportunity.

All of the victims of this tragedy were innocent.

All of them were heroes.

The Bible says [John 15:13] "Greater love hath no man than this, that a man lay down his life for his friends." Our brave New York City Firefighters ... New York City Police Officers ... Port Authority Police Officers ... EMS workers ... health care workers ... court officers ... and uniformed service members...

They laid down their lives for strangers. They were inspired by their sense of duty and their love for humanity. As they raced into the Twin Towers and the other buildings to save lives, they didn't stop to ask how rich or poor the person was, they didn't stop to ask what religion, what race, what nationality. They just raced in to save their fellow human beings.

They are the best example of love that we have in our society.

The people they were trying to rescue – the people who worked in the World Trade Center and the buildings around it – were each engaged in the quiet heroism of supporting their families, pursuing their dreams and playing their own meaningful part in a diverse, dynamic and free society. They represented more than 60 different nations. They will also occupy a permanent and sacred place in our history and in our hearts.

Even in the midst of the darkest tragedy there are miracles that help our faith to go on. I would like to share one miracle of September 11th with you.

St. Paul's Chapel is one of the oldest and most historic buildings in the City of New York. It was built in 1766, when the surrounding area was still countryside. The Chapel survived our war of independence – including seven years of wartime occupation.

After George Washington was inaugurated the first President of the United States, in New York City on April 30th, 1789, he walked to St. Paul's, and he kneeled down to pray. The pew where he worshipped is still there. Framed on the wall beside it is

New York City firefighters in action following the terrorist attack on the World Trade Centre on September 11, 2001

19 **hath** *(old)* has
19 **to lay down one's life** to be prepared to die to save others
21 **EMS** emergency medical service
22 **court officer** official who works at a courthouse
22 **service member** member of the armed forces

the oldest known representation of the Great Seal of the United States of America – it's a majestic eagle, holding in one talon an olive branch, proclaiming our abiding desire for peace … and in the other, a cluster of arrows, a forewarning of our determination to defend our liberty. On a banner above the Eagle is written *E Pluribus Unum*, "Out of Many, One."

For the past 25 years, the chapel stood directly in the shadow of the World Trade Center Towers. When the Towers fell, more than a dozen modern buildings were destroyed and damaged. Yet somehow, amid all the destruction and devastation, St. Paul's Chapel still stands … without so much as a broken window.

It's a small miracle in some ways, but the presence of that chapel standing defiant and serene amid the ruins of war sends an eloquent message about the strength and resilience of the people of New York City, and the people of America.

We unite under the banner of *E Pluribus Unum*. We find strength in our diversity. We're a city where people look different, talk different, think different. But we're a City at one with all of the people at the World Trade Center, and with all of America. We love our diversity, and we love our freedom.

Like our founding fathers who fought and died for freedom … like our ancestors who fought and died to preserve our union and to end the sin of slavery … like our fathers and grandfathers who fought and died to liberate the world from Nazism, and Fascism, and Communism … the cluster of arrows to defend our freedom, and the olive branch of peace have now been handed to us.

We will hold them firmly in our hands, honor their memory, and lift them up toward heaven to light the world.

In the days since this attack, we have met the worst of humanity with the best of humanity.

We pray for our President, George W. Bush … and for our Governor George Pataki … who have provided us with such inspiring leadership during these very, very difficult times. We pray for all of those whose loved ones are lost or missing … we pray for our children, and we say to them: "Do not be afraid. It's safe to live your life." Finally, we pray for America … and for all of those who join us in defending freedom, law, and humanity.

We humbly bow our heads and we ask God to bless the City of New York, and we ask God to bless the United States of America.

Thank you.

What attitude towards the attacks in New York does the cartoonist convey?

53 **defiant** *here:* refusing to give up
75 **humbly** *opp. of* proudly

Exploring the text

1. According to Rudolph Giuliani, what makes America attractive to people around the world?
2. Keeping in mind the occasion on which the speech was delivered, which part(s) do you find most remarkable?

Close-up: rhetorical devices

Identify the rhetorical devices the speaker uses and explain their function. You can refer to the box on the right for ideas.

A step further

- What kind of memorial could the city erect to the heroes of September 11, 2001?

Talking about rhetorical devices

Rhetorical devices are used to persuade, the most common being: *alliteration, anecdotes, assonance, hyperbole, irony, sarcasm* and *understatement.* Other devices include quotations and proverbs, the personal pronoun 'we' and 'you', repetition of key words, rhetorical questions and a personal appeal to the audience.

Before you read

a) The photo on the left was taken on the American national holiday, the 4th of July. How do you think the young man would answer the question: "Why are you wearing the American flag on your T-shirt?"
b) What does the 4th of July celebrate? Why, do you think, is the holiday significant for Americans today?
c) Could you imagine wearing a T-shirt with the flag of your country, or not? Give reasons for your answer.

A time to celebrate

Italian-Americans are often heard to say on a wonderful occasion *"Hai trovato l'America!"* – You have found America. And so have we all. The Fourth of July is a genuine celebration, the least commercial of our national days. The star-spangled banner is raised on millions of flagpoles, and every Main Street has its parade. New York had the spectacular tall ships in its harbor, a reminder of how this country came to be found and settled nearly 400 years ago. What an extraordinary affirmation of the faith that we and our forebears put in the Founding Fathers. "The happy Union of these states is a wonder; their constitution a miracle: their example the hope of Liberty throughout the world." So wrote James Madison in 1829 and so it has proved. One nation under God dedicated to freedom, justice and equality of opportunity. This is our heritage.

The goal of Americans new and old is to participate in the American dream. You don't hear much about the French dream, or the British dream, or the Russian dream. It is the American dream that is the magnet to millions all over the world. It is a dream built on individual effort – talent, ambition, risk-taking, readiness to change, and just plain hard work – qualities that count more in America than social background or luck. We celebrate individualism over conformity, entrepreneurialism over bureaucracy, pragmatism over ideology, and innovation over tradition. We nourish our mavericks, cherish our young, welcome newcomers, and encourage the rise of talent.

Unencumbered by a feudal past, we are more egalitarian, more meritocratic, and more individualistic than any other country in the world. Americans look to what they can do for themselves and others, not what government may do for them. It is the liberation of individual energies that has enabled America to flourish despite so many predictions that the experiment was bound to fail. How could so many races, colors, and creeds work and live together in a spirit of mutual tolerance? Our forefathers were prescient in providing a framework of order, a bill of rights, and a separation of powers. Power in our Constitution resides with the people, who delegate it to the government, rather than the other way around.

As we begin the 21st century, America is once again the image of the future. After the angst of a decade ago, America has established a position of surpassing dominance in the world, but it's a dominance that results as much from our values and culture as from our economic and military power. It is truly the American age.

Opportunity abounds. And the bounty is shared. All but the very poor live better than all but the very rich of a century ago. Anybody who wishes to work has the

9 **James Madison** president of the US from 1809–1817
17 **entrepreneurialism** spirit which encourages one to start a new business
19 **maverick** s.o. who acts differently to the rest
21 **unencumbered** *opp. of* limited
21 **egalitarian** believing in equal rights
34 **bounty** *here:* rewards

opportunity to move from the bottom of the ladder to a middle-class standard of life, or even higher. A majority of the poorest 20 percent of the population in 1975 made it to the top three fifths of the income distribution by the 1990s, i.e. to middle class or better, with almost 3 out of 10 making it to the top quintile.

Two economists, W. Michael Cox and Richard Alm, have noted that if you measure American living standards by what people own, what they buy, and how they live – and not simply by incomes – Americans are living better and better. The rich have gotten richer, but so have the poor. Yes, there is inequality. But inequality is not necessarily inequity. We are less troubled by differences in wealth because equal opportunity, not egalitarianism, fires the engines of achievement.

Some may decry our ambitions in the pursuit of happiness. A recent poll showed that the level of income needed to fulfill our dreams doubled between 1986 and 1994 and is currently more than twice the median household income. But if today's abundance feels inadequate, it is only because Americans today view as essential many things that used to be considered luxuries.

Today, education is the key to upward mobility. In this age of information, it is heartening that the proportion of the population graduating from high school and attaining college degrees has soared to record levels. More than 80 percent of Americans graduate from high school, and almost 50 percent of high school graduates between the ages of 18 and 24 attend college. We have led the world in the proportion of our citizens graduating from public elementary school, then from high school, and more recently attending college and graduate school.

America will continue to change as a response to new challenges. It must. It is no static utopia. But this is July. Let us take a moment to celebrate.

By Mortimer B. Zuckerman, U.S. NEWS & WORLD REPORT, July 17, 2000.

39 **quintile** one-fifth
44 **inequity** unfairness
48 **median** average
51 **upward mobility** ability to move to a higher social position

Exploring the text

1 Which aspects of the American Dream does Mortimer Zuckerman emphasize?

2 a) Which aspects of American society are criticized in the text?
  b) How does Mortimer Zuckerman deal with this criticism?

3 a) What does he mean in ll. 58–59 when he says that America "is no static utopia"?
  b) What consequences could this claim have for the American Dream?

A step further

- Mortimer Zuckermann claims in line 30 that "America is ... the image of the future". To what extent do you agree / disagree with him?

The essence of the American Dream

Listen to the extract from a radio programme which deals with aspects of the American Dream.

Los Vendidos

Characters

Honest Sancho | Farm Worker | Johnny
Secretary | Revolucionario | Mexican-American

Scene: Honest Sancho's Used Mexican Lot and Mexican Curio Shop. Three models are on display in Honest Sancho's shop: to the right, there is a Revolucionario, complete with sombrero, carrilleras, and carabina 30-30. At center, on the floor, there is the Farm Worker, under a broad straw sombrero. At stage left is the Pachuco, filero in hand.

(Honest Sancho is moving among his models, dusting them off and preparing for another day of business.)

Sancho Bueno, bueno, mis monos, vamos a ver a quien vendemos ahora, ¿no? *(To audience.)* ¡Quihubo! I'm Honest Sancho and this is my shop. Antes fui contratista pero ahora logré tener mi negocito. All I need now is a customer. *(A bell rings offstage.)* Ay, a customer!

Secretary *(entering)* Good morning, I'm Miss Jiménez from –

Sancho ¡Ah, una chicana! Welcome, welcome Señorita Jiménez.

Secretary *(Anglo pronunciation)* JIM-enez.

Sancho ¿Qué?

Secretary My name is Miss JIM-enez. Don't you speak English? What's wrong with you?

Sancho Oh, nothing, Señorita JIM-enez. I'm here to help you.

Secretary That's better. As I was starting to say, I'm a secretary from Governor Reagan's office, and we're looking for a Mexican type for the administration.

Sancho Well, you come to the right place, lady. This is Honest Sancho's Used Mexican lot, and we got all types here. Any particular type you want?

Secretary Yes, we were looking for somebody suave –

Sancho Suave.

Secretary Debonair.

Sancho De buen aire.

Secretary Dark.

Sancho Prieto.

Secretary But of course not too dark.

Sancho No muy prieto.

Secretary Perhaps, beige.

Sancho Beige, just the tone. Así como cafecito con leche, ¿no?

Secretary One more thing. He must be hard-working.

Sancho That could only be one model. Step right over here to the center of the shop, lady. *(They cross to the Farm Worker.)* This is our standard farm worker model. As you can see, in the words of our beloved Senator George Murphy, he is "built close to the ground." Also take special notice of his four-ply Goodyear huaraches, made from the rain tire. This wide-brimmed sombrero is an extra added feature – keeps off the sun, rain, and dust.

Secretary Yes, it does look durable.

Sancho And our farm-worker model is friendly. Muy amable. Watch. *(Snaps his fingers.)*

---

0 **vendido** s.o. who will do anything for money
3 **revolucionario** revolutionary (cf. photo, page 25)
4 **lot** *(AE) here:* land on which a building is located
6 **carrillera** cartridge (= *Patrone*) belt
7 **Pachuco** *(1940's Chicano slang)* s.o. wearing a jacket with wide shoulders and baggy trousers
7 **filero** knife
11 **Bueno … Quihubo!** Good, good my cute ones, let's see who we can sell something to, O.K.?
12 **Antes … negocito** I used to be a contractor (= s.o. who is paid a certain rate), but now I have succeeded in starting my little business
16 **chicana** American woman of Mexican origin
18 **qué?** What?
22 **Governor Reagan** Ronald Reagan who later became US president
26 **suave** [swɑːv] s.o. who is polite and confident
31 **prieto** *(Spanish)* black
35 **Así como …** Like coffee with milk?
41 **huaraches** leather sandals
44 **muy amable** very friendly

Farm Worker *(lifts up head)* Buenos días, señorita. *(His head drops.)*

Secretary My, he's friendly.

Sancho Didn't I tell you? Loves his patrones! But his most attractive feature is that he's hard-working. Let me show you. *(Snaps fingers. Farm Worker stands.)*

Farm Worker ¡El jale! *(He begins to work.)*

Sancho As you can see, he is cutting grapes.

Secretary Oh, I wouldn't know.

Sancho He also picks cotton. *(Snap. Farm Worker begins to pick cotton.)*

Secretary Versatile, isn't he?

Sancho He also picks melons. *(Snap. Farm Worker picks melons.)* That's his slow speed for late in the season. Here's his fast speed. *(Snap. Farm Worker picks faster.)*

Secretary ¡Chihuahua! … I mean, goodness, he sure is a hard worker.

Sancho *(pulls the Farm Worker to his feet)* And that isn't the half of it. Do you see these little holes on his arms that appear to be pores? During those hot sluggish days in the field, when the vines or the branches get so entangled, it's almost impossible to move; these holes emit a certain grease that allow our model to slip and slide right through the crop with no trouble at all.

Secretary Wonderful. But is he economical?

Sancho Economical? Señorita, you are looking at the Volkswagen of Mexicans. Pennies a day is all it takes. One plate of beans and tortillas will keep him going all day. That, and chile. Plenty of chile. Chile jalapenos, chile verde, chile colorado. But, of course, if you do give him chile *(Snap. Farm Worker turns left face. Snap. Farm Worker bends over.)* then you have to change his oil filter once a week.

Secretary What about storage?

Sancho No problem. You know these new farm labor camps our Honorable Governor Reagan has built out by Parlier or Raisin City? They were designed with our model in mind. Five, six, seven, even ten in one of those shacks will give you no trouble at all. You can also put him in old barns, old cars, river banks. You can even leave him out in the field overnight with no worry!

Secretary Remarkable.

Sancho And here's an added feature: every year at the end of the season, this model goes back to Mexico and doesn't return, automatically, until next Spring.

Secretary How about that. But tell me: does he speak English?

Sancho Another outstanding feature is that last year this model was programmed to go out on STRIKE! *(Snap)*.

Farm Worker ¡HUELGA! ¡HUELGA! Hermanos, sálganse de esos files. *(Snap. He stops.)*

Secretary No! Oh no, we can't strike in the State Capitol.

Sancho Well, he also scabs. *(Snap.)*

Farm Worker Me vendo barato, ¿y qué? *(Snap.)*

Secretary That's much better, but you didn't answer my question. Does he speak English?

48 **patron** boss
50 **el jale** the job
83 **outstanding** very good
85 **¡Huelga! … esos files** Strike! Strike! Brothers, leave those rows!
88 **to scab** *(negative)* to work when others are on strike
89 **Me vendo … qué?** I come cheap, so what?

Sancho Bueno … no, pero he has other –

Secretary No.

Sancho Other features.

Secretary NO! He just won't do!

Sancho Okay, okay pues. We have other models.

Secretary I hope so. What we need is something a little more sophisticated.

Sancho Sophisti – ¿qué?

Secretary An urban model.

Sancho Ah, from the city! Step right back. Over here in this corner of the shop is exactly what you're looking for. Introducing our new 1969 JOHNNY PACHUCO model! This is our fast-back model. Streamlined. Built for speed, low-riding, city life. Take a look at some of these features. Mag shoes, dual exhausts, green chartreuse paint-job, dark-tint windshield, a little poof on top. Let me just turn him on. *(Snap. Johnny walks to stage center with a pachuco bounce.)*

Secretary What was that?

Sancho That, señorita, was the Chicano shuffle.

Secretary Okay, what does he do?

Sancho Anything and everything necessary for city life. For instance, survival: he knife fights. *(Snap. Johnny pulls out switch blade and swings at Secretary). (Secretary screams.)*

Sancho He dances. *(Snap.)*

Johnny *(singing)* "Angel Baby, my Angel Baby …" *(Snap.)*

Sancho And here's a feature no city model can be without. He gets arrested, but not without resisting, of course. *(Snap.)*

Johnny ¡En la madre, la placa! I didn't do it! I didn't do it! *(Johnny turns and stands up against an imaginary wall, legs spread out, arms behind his back.)*

Secretary Oh no, we can't have arrests! We must maintain law and order.

Sancho But he's bilingual!

Secretary Bilingual?

Sancho Simón que yes. He speaks English! Johnny, give us some English. *(Snap.)*

Johnny *(comes downstage)* Fuck you!

Secretary *(gasps)* Oh! I've never been so insulted in my whole life!

Sancho Well, he learned it in your school.

Secretary I don't care where he learned it.

Sancho But he's economical!

Secretary Economical?

Sancho Nickels and dimes. You can keep Johnny running on hamburgers, Taco Bell tacos, Lucky Lager beer, Thunderbird wine, yesca –

Secretary Yesca?

Sancho Mota.

Secretary Mota?

Sancho Leños … Marijuana. *(Snap; Johnny inhales on an imaginary joint.)*

Secretary That's against the law!

Johnny *(big smile, holding his breath)* Yeah.

Sancho He also sniffs glue. *(Snap. Johnny inhales glue, big smile.)*

Johnny Tha's too much man, ése.

Secretary No, Mr. Sancho, I don't think this –

92 **Bueno … no, pero** well … no, but
96 **pues** then
97 **sophisticated** complex, cultured
102 **fast-back** refers to cars which form an unbroken curve from front to back
104 **poof** *here:* piece of hair which stands up
116 **¡En la madre, la placa!** Oh no, the police!
121 **Simón que yes** yes, sure
133 **leños** joints of marijuana

Sancho Wait a minute, he has other qualities I know you'll love. For example, an inferiority complex. *(Snap.)*

Johnny *(to Sancho)* You think you're better than me, huh ése? *(Swings switch blade.)*

Sancho He can also be beaten and he bruises, cut him and he bleeds; kick him and he – *(He beats, bruises, and kicks Pachuco.)* would you like to try it?

Secretary Oh, I couldn't

Sancho Be my guest. He's a great scapegoat.

Secretary No, really.

Sancho Please.

Secretary Well, all right. Just once. *(She kicks Pachuco.)* Oh, he's so soft.

Sancho Wasn't that good? Try again.

Secretary *(kicks Pachuco)* Oh, he's so wonderful! *(She kicks him again.)*

Sancho Okay, that's enough, lady. You ruin the merchandise. Yes, our Johnny Pachuco model can give you many hours of pleasure. Why, the L.A.P.D. just bought twenty of these to train their rookie cops on. And talk about maintenance. Señorita, you are looking at an entirely self-supporting machine. You're never going to find our Johnny Pachuco model on the relief rolls. No, sir, this model knows how to liberate.

Secretary Liberate?

Sancho He steals. *(Snap. Johnny rushes the Secretary and steals her purse.)*

Johnny ¡Dame esa bolsa, vieja! *(He grabs the purse and runs. Snap by Sancho. He stops.)*

(Secretary runs after Johnny and grabs purse away from him, kicking him as she goes.)

Secretary No, no, no! We can't have any *more* thieves in the State Administration. Put him back.

Sancho Okay, we still got other models. Come on, Johnny, we'll sell you to some old lady. *(Sancho takes Johnny back to his place.)*

Secretary Mr. Sancho, I don't think you quite understand what we need. What we need is something that will attract the women voters. Something more traditional, more romantic.

Sancho Ah, a lover. *(He smiles meaningfully.)* Step right over here, señorita. Introducing our standard Revolucionario and/or Early California Bandit type. As you can see he is well-built, sturdy, durable. This is the International Harvester of Mexicans.

Secretary What does he do?

Sancho You name it, he does it. He rides horses, stays in the mountains, crosses deserts, plains, rivers, leads revolutions, follows revolutions, kills, can be killed, serves as a martyr, hero, movie star – did I say movie star? Did you ever see *Viva Zapata*? *Viva Villa*? *Villa Rides*? *Pancho Villa Returns*? *Pancho Villa Goes Back*? *Pancho Villa Meets Abbott and Costello* –

Secretary I've never seen any of those.

Sancho Well, he was in all of them. Listen to this. *(Snap.)*

Revolucionario *(scream)* ¡VIVA VILLAAAAA!

Secretary That's awfully loud.

Sancho He has a volume control. *(He adjusts volume. Snap.)*

Revolucionario *(mousey voice)* ¡Viva Villa!

Secretary That's better.

142 **to bruise** to have a mark on the skin where one was hit

145 **scapegoat** s.o. who is made responsible for s.th. he / she did not do

152 **L.A.P.D.** Los Angeles Police Department

155 **on the relief rolls** registered as s.o. who receives financial help from the state

159 **dame esa bolsa, vieja** give me that bag, old lady

170 **Early California Bandit** refers to Tiburcio Vasquez who terrorized California from the mid 19th. century until his hanging in 1875

171 **International Harvester** *(fig. here)* an antique that people collect

Sancho And even if you didn't see him in the movies, perhaps you saw him on TV. He makes commercials. *(Snap.)*

Revolucionario Is there a Frito Bandito in your house?

Secretary Oh yes, I've seen that one!

Sancho Another feature about this one is that he is economical. He runs on raw horsemeat and tequila!

Secretary Isn't that rather savage?

Sancho Al contrario, it makes him a lover. *(Snap.)*

Revolucionario *(to Secretary)* ¡Ay, mamasota, cochota, ven pa'ca! *(He grabs Secretary and folds her back – Latin-Lover style.)*

Sancho *(Snap. Revolucionario goes back upright.)* Now wasn't that nice?

Secretary Well, it was rather nice.

Sancho And finally, there is one outstanding feature about this model I KNOW the ladies are going to love: He's a GENUINE antique! He was made in Mexico in 1910!

Secretary Made in Mexico?

Sancho That's right. Once in Tijuana, twice in Guadalajara, three times in Cuernavaca.

Secretary Mr. Sancho, I thought he was an American product.

Sancho No, but –

Secretary No, I'm sorry. We can't buy anything but American-made products. He just won't do.

Sancho But he's an antique!

Secretary I don't care. You still don't understand what we need. It's true we need Mexican models such as these, but it's more important that he be *American.*

Sancho American?

Secretary That's right, and judging from what you've shown me, I don't think you have what we want. Well, my lunch hour's almost over; I better –

Sancho Wait a minute! Mexican but American?

Secretary That's correct.

Sancho Mexican but … *(A sudden flash.)* AMERICAN! Yeah, I think we've got exactly what you want. He just came in today! Give me a minute. *(He exits. Talks from backstage.)* Here he is in the shop. Let me just get some papers off. There. Introducing our new 1970 Mexican-American! Ta-ra-ra-ra-ra-ra-RA-RAAA! *(Sancho brings out the Mexican-American model, a clean-shaven middle-class type in a business suit, with glasses.)*

Secretary *(impressed)* Where have you been hiding this one?

Sancho He just came in this morning. Ain't he a beauty? Feast your eyes on him! Sturdy US STEEL frame, streamlined, modern. As a matter of fact, he is built exactly like our Anglo models except that he comes in a variety of darker shades: Naugahyde, leather, or Leaterette.

Secretary Naugahyde.

Sancho Well, we'll just write that down. Yes, señorita, this model represents the apex of American engineering! He is bilingual, college educated, ambitious! Say the word "acculturate" and he accelerates. He is intelligent, well-mannered, clean – did I say clean? *(Snap. Mexican-American raises his arm.)* Smell.

Secretary *(smells)* Old Sobaco, my favorite.

193 **al contrario** on the contrary
194 **¡Ay, mamasota, cochota, ven pa'ca!** Hey, lady, let's go for a ride!
225 **Naugahyde** *(trademark)* man-made material made to look like leather
225 **Leaterette** paper or cloth made to look like leather
229 **to acculturate** to adopt the cultural behaviour of another group

Sancho *(Snap. Mexican-American turns toward Sancho)* Eric! *(To Secretary.)* We call him Eric García. *(To Eric.)* I want you to meet Miss JIM-enez, Eric.

Mexican-American Miss JIM-enez, I am delighted to make your acquaintance. *(He kisses her hand.)*

Secretary Oh, my, how charming!

Sancho Did you feel the suction? He has seven especially engineered suction cups right behind his lips. He's a charmer all right!

Secretary How about boards? Does he function on boards?

Sancho You name them, he is on them. Parole boards, draft boards, school boards, taco quality control boards, surf boards, two-by-fours.

Secretary Does he function in politics?

Sancho Señorita, you are looking at a political MACHINE. Have you ever heard of the OEO, EOC, COD, WAR ON POVERTY? That's our model! Not only that, he makes political speeches.

Secretary May I hear one?

Sancho With pleasure. *(Snap.)* Eric, give us a speech.

Mexican-American Mr. Congressman, Mr. Chairman, members of the board, honored guests, ladies and gentlemen. *(Sancho and Secretary applaud.)* Please, please. I come before you as a Mexican-American to tell you about the problems of the Mexican. The problems of the Mexican stem from one thing and one thing alone: he's stupid. He's uneducated. He needs to stay in school. He needs to be ambitious, forward-looking, harder-working. He needs to think American, American, American, AMERICAN, AMERICAN, AMERICAN. GOD BLESS AMERICA! GOD BLESS AMERICA! GOD BLESS AMERICA!! *(He goes out of control.)* *(Sancho snaps frantically and the Mexican-American finally slumps forward, bending at the waist.)*

Secretary Oh my, he's patriotic too!

Sancho Sí, señorita, he loves his country. Let me just make a little adjustment here. *(Stands Mexican-American up.)*

Secretary What about upkeep? Is he economical?

Sancho Well, no, I won't lie to you. The Mexican-American costs a little bit more, but you get what you pay for. He's worth every extra cent. You can keep him running on dry Martinis, Langendorf bread.

Secretary Apple pie?

Sancho Only Mom's. Of course, he's also programmed to eat Mexican food at ceremonial functions, but I must warn you: an overdose of beans will plug up his exhaust.

Secretary Fine! There's just one more question: HOW MUCH DO YOU WANT FOR HIM?

Sancho Well, I tell you what I'm gonna do. Today and today only, because you've been so sweet, I'm gonna let you steal this model from me! I'm gonna let you drive him off the lot for the simple price of – let's see taxes and license included – $15,000.

Secretary Fifteen thousand DOLLARS? For a MEXICAN!

Sancho Mexican? What are you talking, lady? This is a Mexican-AMERICAN! We had to melt down two pachucos, a farm worker, and three gabachos to make this model! You want quality, but you gotta pay for it! This is no cheap run-about. He's got class!

Secretary Okay, I'll take him.

239 **board** *here:* committee
240 **draft board** *(US)* committee which selects people for military service
241 **two-by-four** piece of wood (= a board) measuring two inches by four inches
244 **OEO** *(US, old)* **Office of Economic Opportunity**; body which provides services in the community
244 **EOC Equal Opportunity Commission**
244 **COD** *(business term) short for* **cash on delivery**
276 **gabacho** *(negative, Chicano term)* white American
277 **run-about** usu. small car one uses for short journeys

Sancho You will?

Secretary Here's your money.

Sancho You mind if I count it?

Secretary Go right ahead.

Sancho Well, you'll get your pink slip in the mail. Oh, do you want me to wrap him up for you? We have a box in the back.

Secretary No, thank you. The Governor is having a luncheon this afternoon, and we need a brown face in the crowd. How do I drive him?

Sancho Just snap your fingers. He'll do anything you want.

(Secretary snaps. Mexican-American steps forward.)

Mexican-American RAZA QUERIDA, ¡VAMOS LEVANTANDO ARMAS PARA LIBERARNOS DE ESTOS DESGRACIADOS GABACHOS QUE NOS EXPLOTAN! VAMOS.

Secretary What did he say?

Sancho Something about lifting arms, killing white people, etc.

Secretary But he's not supposed to say that!

Sancho Look, lady, don't blame me for bugs from the factory. He's your Mexican-American; you bought him, now drive him off the lot!

Secretary But he's broken!

Sancho Try snapping another finger.

(Secretary snaps. Mexican-American comes to life again.)

Mexican-American ¡ESTA GRAN HUMANIDAD HA DICHO BASTA! Y SE HA PUESTO EN MARCHA! ¡BASTA! ¡BASTA! ¡VIVA LA RAZA! ¡VIVA LA CAUSA! ¡VIVA LA HUELGA! ¡VIVAN LOS BROWN BERETS! ¡VIVAN LOS ESTUDIANTES! ¡CHICANO POWER!

(The Mexican-American turns toward the Secretary, who gasps and backs up. He keeps turning toward the Pachuco, Farm Worker, and Revolucionario, snapping his fingers and turning each of them on, one by one.)

Pachuco *(Snap. To Secretary)* I'm going to get you, baby! ¡Viva la Raza!

Farm Worker *(Snap. To Secretary)* ¡Viva la huelga! ¡Viva la Huelga! ¡VIVA LA HUELGA!

Revolucionario *(Snap. To Secretary)* ¡Viva la revolución! ¡VIVA LA REVOLUCION!

(The three models join together and advance toward the Secretary who backs up and runs out of the shop screaming. Sancho is at the other end of the shop holding his money in his hand. All freeze. After a few seconds of silence, the Pachuco moves and stretches, shaking his arms and loosening up. The Farm Worker and Revolucionario do the same. Sancho stays where he is, frozen to his spot.)

Johnny Man, that was a long one, ése. *(Others agree with him.)*

Farm Worker How did we do?

Johnny Perty good, look all that lana, man! *(He goes over to Sancho and removes the money from his hand. Sancho stays where he is.)*

Revolucionario En la madre, look at all the money.

Johnny We keep this up, we're going to be rich.

Farm Worker They think we're machines.

Revolucionario Burros.

Johnny Puppets.

284 **pink slip** note telling one that one has been fired
290 **Raza querida … vamos.** Beloved people, let's take up arms to free ourselves from those damned whites who exploit us! Let's go.
301 **¡Esta gran … Chicano Power!** This great mass of humanity has said enough! And it begins to march! Enough! Enough! Long live La Raza! Long live the cause! Long live the strike! Long live the Brown Berets! Long live the students! Chicano Power!
303 **Brown Berets** militant Chicano organization of the late 1960s and early 1970s
318 **ése** *here:* that one
320 **perty** pretty, i.e. quite
320 **lana** wool, *here:* money
325 **burro** donkey

Mexican-American The only thing I don't like is – how come I always got to play the goddamn Mexican-American?
Johnny That's what you get for finishing high school.
Farm Worker How about our wages, ése?
Johnny Here it comes right now. $ 3,000 for you, $ 3,000 for you, $ 3,000 for you, and $ 3,000 for me. The rest we put back into the business.
Mexican-American Too much, man. Heh, where you vatos going tonight?
Farm Worker I'm going over to Concha's. There's a party.
Johnny Wait a minute, vatos. What about our salesman? I think he needs an oil job.
Revolucionario Leave him to me.
(The Pachuco, Farm Worker, and Mexican-American exit, talking loudly about their plans for the night. The Revolucionario goes over to Sancho, removes his derby hat and cigar, lifts him up, and throws him over his shoulder. Sancho hangs loose, lifeless.)
Revolucionario *(to audience)* He's the best model we got! ¡Ajúa! *(Exit.)*
(End.)

By Luis M. Valdez, "Los Vendidos", from Rereading America, *ed. Gary Colombo et al, Bedford Books of St. Martin's Press: Boston, 1992, pp. 375–385.*

333 **vatos** guys
342 **¡ajua!** *(Mexican Spanish)* hurray!

Exploring the text

1 a) In small groups, think of five questions about the short play as regards the theme, the characters, the order of events and the message. Make sure you know the answers to your questions.
b) Put the questions to the rest of the class and discuss the answers you get.
2 a) At what points in the short play do the actors speak Spanish?
b) Why, do you think, does the playwright include Spanish dialogues? What effect do they probably have on an English-speaking audience?
3 What attitudes does Luis Valdez criticize in his play? What means does he use to voice this criticism?

Close-up: short plays

1 Read through the information in the box on the right. What typical features of a short play do you notice in *Los Vendidos*? Find as many examples of these features as possible.
2 Examine the importance of the dialogue in the short play. Identify key speeches which:
- add to character and plot development;
- show the relationship between characters;
- set the tone of the play;
- provoke a particular reaction among the audience.

Talking about short plays

short in length – action happens in one place in a specific time period – no subplots – situation more important than plot – concentration on critical situations – few characters – characters reduced to most important characteristics – short dialogues

A step further

- Working in small groups, think of one immigrant group in your country which is often subject to stereotyping. What qualities and characteristics are often applied to this group? In what ways are these stereotypes oversimplifed or incorrect? Present your ideas in class.

Using your skills

Forrest Gump

Getting started

- Scene profile

a) Analyse the first four and a half minutes of *Forrest Gump* in detail. Watch the opening *credits* and first scene at least twice. In groups, focus on and make notes about **one** of the following aspects: the characters, the action, camera operations, visual symbols, film music, special effects.

b) Form new groups. Each new group should have a representative from each of the first set of groups. Share your ideas and make a one-page scene profile as follows:

Credits
the list of actors and others involved in the film shown at the beginning and / or end

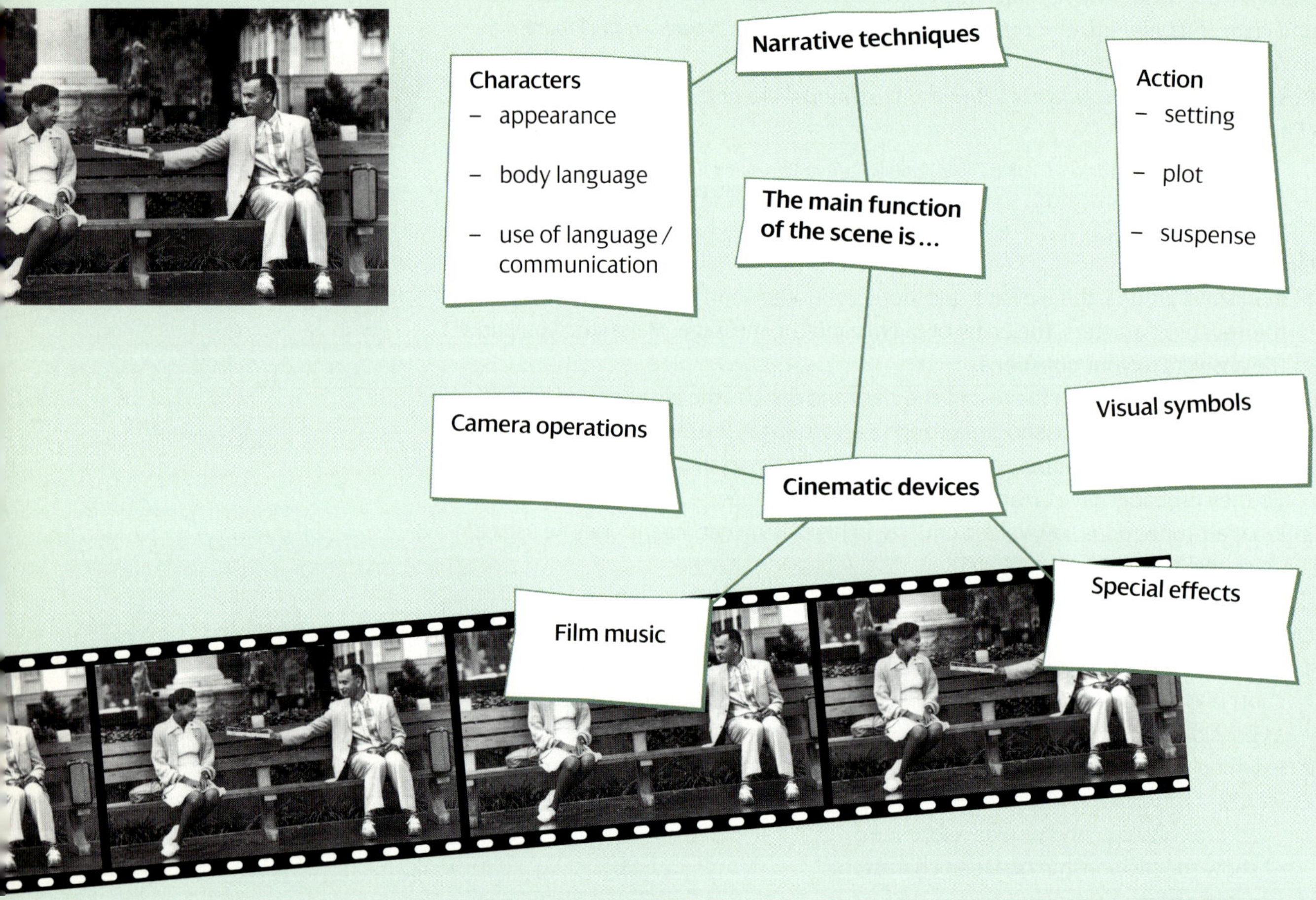

c) Now try to complete the sentence in the middle of the above scene profile: "The main function of the scene is ..." How do the cinematic devices used in the scene serve this function?

d) The *Forrest Gump* DVD includes a commentary on the introductory scene by the director Robert Zemeckis. Write this commentary. You could start like this:
"It took me a long time to come up with an effective beginning. In fact, some people may argue that it is a fairly conventional beginning, but let me explain some of the ideas behind it..."

Using your skills

Watching and thinking

- Key scenes
When viewing the whole film, identify key scenes for detailed analysis and develop further scene profiles based on the model on the opposite page.
- Viewing log
Turn your notes and materials from classwork and homework into a 'viewing log'. Your log should include the following elements:
  - stills (Search for pictures in the internet using a search engine such as www.yahoo.com or www.google.com.);
  - profiles of key scenes (cf. viewing exercise above);
  - a plot summary;
  - a profile of the protagonist and an analysis of his relationship with Mrs Gump, Jenny, Bubba and Lieutenant Dan;
  - a collection of memorable quotes;
  - a table showing how Forrest's life reflects events in American history (cf. box on the right for key terms. You can choose **one** person / aspect which you would like to research and write a glossary entry for your subject. Be prepared to provide background information for the rest of the class when it is featured in the film.);
  - a detailed analysis of **one** of the following minor characters: Forrest's mother, Jenny, Bubba or Lieutenant Dan;
  - **one** major theme, e.g. love and friendship, success and happiness, moving on and coming home, destiny and God, running and floating, and its significance for the plot and characters;
  - **one** specific analytic focus, e.g. humour, *narrative structure* (cf. box below), music, camera operations, computer-generated imaging (cf. photo below right), the American Dream;

Narrative structure
refers to the order in which events are presented: the writer may start at the beginning, end or even in the middle. He / she may use flashbacks or flashforwards. He / she may offer a conclusive or an open ending.

  - your own review of the film (cf. skills file, page 189).

Forrest Gump's America

Armstrong, Neil
Baez, Joan
Black Panther Party
Kennedy, John F.
Kennedy, Robert
Ku-Klux-Klan
Lennon, John
Monroe, Marilyn
Nixon-Watergate scandal
Presley, Elvis
Slavery
US colleges: sports and scholarships
US-Chinese relations
Vietnam War
Wallace, George

A step further

- Trailer
a) Film companies use 'trailers' to advertise new films and videos. List the characteristics of a trailer and then write a definition based on your ideas.
b) Use the information in your viewing log to develop ideas for a trailer for *Forrest Gump*. Which clips from the film would you include? Write the text for a voice-over to go with the sequence of scenes you have chosen.

Cultural mix and clash – UK

Britain as a multicultural society

Looking and thinking

- Look at the photos and statistics below. What impression do you get of Britain as a multicultural society?
- What factors may have produced the survey results below right?
- Think of the benefits and problems of "immigration". Collect your ideas in a mind map which you can add to as you work through the chapter.

Knocking on Britain's Door: Asylum applications in 2001

	UK	Germany	France
New applications	92,000	88,287	47,291
Allowed to remain	39,990	19,942	7,323
Deported	9,285	27,902	*

** The French government does not release deportation figures. Sources: UNHCR Statistical Yearbook 2001; Asylum Statistics United Kingdom 2001, www.bundesgrenzschutz.de*

Riots involving young Asians in Bradford, England in 2001

"43 % of black Britons believe Britain has benefited from immigration.

47 % of white Britons believe the country has been damaged by immigration over the past 50 years."

BBC/ICM May 2002
(Published in Time, June 24, 2002)

A market scene in urban England

Before you read

- Imagine you are going to live in another country for a period of time.
  a) What difficulties might you have in adjusting to life there?
  b) How would you deal with these difficulties?
- What factors motivate, or force, people to emigrate to another country?

England was a peculiar-tasting smoked fish

Young Salahuddin, garlanded and warned, boarded a Douglas DC-8 and journeyed into the west. Ahead of him, England; beside him, his father, Changez Chamchawala; below him, home and beauty. Like Nasreen, the future Saladin had never found it easy to cry.

On that first aeroplane he read science fiction tales of interplanetary migration: Asimov's *Foundation*, Ray Bradbury's *Martian Chronicles*. He imagined the DC-8 was the mother ship, bearing the Chosen, the Elect of God and man, across unthinkable distances, travelling for generations, breeding eugenically, that their seed might one day take root somewhere in a brave new world beneath a yellow sun. He corrected himself: not the mother but the father ship, because there he was, after all, the great man, Abbu, Dad. Thirteen-year-old Salahuddin, setting aside recent doubts and grievances, entered once again his childish adoration of his father, because he had, had, had worshipped him, he was a great father until you started growing a mind of your own, and then to argue with him was called a betrayal of his love, but never mind that now, *I accuse him of becoming my supreme being, so that what happened was like a loss of faith* ... yes, the father ship, an aircraft was not a flying womb but a metal phallus, and the passengers were spermatozoa waiting to be spilt.

Five and a half hours of time zones; turn your watch upside down in Bombay and you see the time in London. *My father*, Chamcha would think, years later, in the midst of his bitterness. *I accuse him of inverting Time.*

How far did they fly? Five and a half thousand as the crow. Or: from Indianness to Englishness, an immeasurable distance. Or, not very far at all, because they rose from one great city, fell to another. The distance between cities is always small; a villager, travelling a hundred miles to town, traverses emptier, darker, more terrifying space.

What Changez Chamchawala did when the aeroplane took off: trying not to let his son see him doing it, he crossed two pairs of fingers on each hand, and rotated both his thumbs.

And when they were installed in a hotel within a few feet of the ancient location of the Tyburn tree, Changez said to his son: "Take. This belongs to you." And held out, at arm's length, a black billfold about whose identity there could be no mistake. "You are a man now. Take."

The return of the confiscated wallet, complete with all its currency, proved to be one of Changez Chamchawala's little traps. Salahuddin had been deceived by these all his life. Whenever his father wanted to punish him, he would offer him a present, a bar of imported chocolate or a tin of Kraft cheese, and would then grab him when he came to get it. "Donkey," Changez scorned his infant son. "Always, always, the carrot leads you to my stick."

3 **Nasreen** Salahuddin's mother
8 **eugenically** [juːˈdjenɪklɪ] selectively to improve the quality of the human race
11 **Abbu** *(Hindi)* father
21 **as the crow (flies)** in a straight line (**crow** = *Krähe*)
30 **the Tyburn tree** *(historical, London)* wooden structure used to hang criminals
31 **billfold** *(AE)* wallet
33 **confiscated** Salahuddin found the wallet in the street. His father took it away.

Salahuddin in London took the proffered wallet, accepting the gift of manhood; whereupon his father said: "Now that you are a man, it is for you to look after your old father while we are in London town. You pay all the bills."

January, 1961. A year you could turn upside down and it would still, unlike your watch, tell the same time. It was winter; but when Salahuddin Chamchawala began to shiver in his hotel room, it was because he was scared halfway out of his wits; his crock of gold had turned, suddenly, into a sorcerer's curse.

Those two weeks in London before he went to his boarding school turned into a nightmare of cash-tills and calculations, because Changez had meant exactly what he said and never put his hand into his own pocket once. Salahuddin had to buy his own clothes, such as a double-breasted blue serge mackintosh and seven blue-and-white striped Van Heusen shirts with detachable semi-stiff collars which Changez made him wear every day, to get used to the studs, and Salahuddin felt as if a blunt knife were being pushed in just beneath his newly broken Adam's-apple; and he had to make sure there would be enough for the hotel room, and everything, so that he was too nervous to ask his father if they could go to a movie, not even one, not even *The Pure Hell of St Trinians*, or to eat out, not a single Chinese meal, and in later years, he would remember nothing of his first fortnight in his beloved Ellowen Deeowen except pounds shillings pence, like the disciple of the philosopher-king Chanakya who asked the great man what he meant by saying one could live in the world and also not live in it, and who was told to carry a brim-full pitcher of water through a holiday crowd without spilling a drop, on pain of death, so that when he returned he was unable to describe the day's festivities, having been like a blind man, seeing only the jug on his head.

Changez Chamchawala became very still in those days, seeming not to care if he ate or drank or did any damn thing, he was happy sitting in the hotel room watching television, especially when the Flintstones were on, because, he told his son, that Wilma bibi reminded him of Nasreen. Salahuddin tried to prove he was a man by fasting right along with his father, trying to outlast him, but he never managed it, and when the pangs got too strong he went out of the hotel to the cheap joint nearby where you could buy take-away roast chickens that hung greasily in the window, turning slowly on their spits. When he brought the chicken into the hotel lobby he became embarrassed, not wanting the staff to see, so he stuffed it inside double-breasted serge and went up in the lift reeking of spit-roast, his mackintosh bulging, his face turning red. Chicken-breasted beneath the gaze of dowagers and liftwallahs he felt the birth of that implacable rage which would burn within him, undiminished, for over a quarter of a century; which would boil away his childhood father-worship and make him a secular man, who would do his best, thereafter, to live without a god of any type; which would fuel, perhaps, his determination to become the thing his father was-not-could-never-be, that is, a goodandproper Englishman. Yes, an English, even if his mother had been right all along, even if there was only paper in the toilets and tepid, used water full of mud and soap to step into after taking exercise, even if it meant a lifetime spent amongst winter-naked trees whose fingers clutched despairingly at the few, pale hours of watery, filtered light. On winter nights he, who had never slept beneath more than a sheet, lay beneath mountains of wool and felt like a figure in an ancient myth, condemned by the gods to have a boulder pressing down upon his chest; but never mind, he would be English, even

45 **crock** an earthenware pot
47 **cash-till** drawer where money is kept in a shop
50 **detachable** which one can take off
51 **stud** *auswechselbarer Kragenknopf*
56 **Ellowen Deeowen** L-O-N-D-O-N, London
59 **brim-full** full to the top
66 **bibi** *(Hindi)* woman, girl
68 **joint** *(slang) here:* a cheap restaurant
73 **dowager** ['daʊədʒə] *(informal)* an elegant elderly woman
73 **wallah** ['wɒlə] *(Hindi)* person responsible for s.th. *here:* the lift
76 **secular** ['sekjələ] *opp. of* religious
80 **to take exercise** to do sport
82 **to clutch** to try to catch

if his classmates giggled at his voice and excluded him from their secrets, because these exclusions only increased his determination, and that was when he began to act, to find masks that these fellows would recognize, paleface masks, clown-masks, until he fooled them into thinking he was *okay*, he was *people-like-us*. He fooled them the way a sensitive human being can persuade gorillas to accept him into their family, to fondle and caress and stuff bananas in his mouth. [...]

One day soon after he started at the school he came down to breakfast to find a kipper on his plate. He sat there staring at it, not knowing where to begin. Then he cut into it, and got a mouthful of tiny bones. And after extracting them all, another mouthful, more bones. His fellow-pupils watched him suffer in silence; not one of them said, here, let me show you, you eat it in this way. It took him ninety minutes to eat the fish and he was not permitted to rise from the table until it was done. By that time he was shaking, and if he had been able to cry he would have done so. Then the thought occurred to him that he had been taught an important lesson. England was a peculiar-tasting smoked fish full of spikes and bones, and nobody would ever tell him how to eat it. He discovered that he was a bloody-minded person. "I'll show them all," he swore. "You see if I don't." The eaten kipper was his first victory, the first step in his conquest of England.

William the Conqueror, it is said, began by eating a mouthful of English sand.

From The Satanic Verses *by Salman Rushdie, London: Viking Penguin Inc. 1988, pp. 40–44.*

101 **bloody-minded** *(BE informal)* deliberately unreasonable

Exploring the text

1 a) Describe your first reaction to the text. What did you like most / least about it?
b) What point, do you think, is the writer trying to convey?

2 How does Salahuddin feel about leaving his country? Describe his feelings, thoughts and anxieties.

3 What are the boy's memories of his first two weeks in England?

4 Why is he determined to become "a goodandproper Englishman" (l. 78)?

5 a) What impression of England and the English is conveyed by Salahuddin's memories?
b) What light is thrown on his life in India before he came to England?

6 a) Describe the structure of the extract.
b) From which *point of view* is the story told? How does this affect the way we see the characters?

Close-up: language

- Salman Rushdie is often praised for his vibrant *images* and *allusions.* Find examples in the text which you find particularly striking and say what effect they have.

A step further

- Comment on the following quotation from the extract:
"The distance between cities is always small; a villager travelling a hundred miles to town, traverses emptier, darker, more terrifying space." (ll. 23–25)

Point of view
the perspective from which the *narrator* presents a story to the reader

Images (figures of speech)
express a thought indirectly, i.e. figuratively, using pictures which have to be interpreted

Allusion
a reference to historical or fictional characters, places or events or works which the reader may recognise.

Before you read

- a) How would you react if someone spoke to you in broken German?
  b) How do you feel when you have to express yourself in a foreign language, e.g. when you have to give a talk in English in class or communicate when you are on holiday abroad?

Talking about poetry

The poem is about / deals with …
It consists of … stanzas.
The poet uses free verse / an (ir)regular rhythm to …
It makes allusions to …
It uses repetition / symbols / metaphors / similes to create a … effect
The images evoke associations with …

Close-up: language

- Based on examples in the poem, make a list of the features of West Indian English. Classify the features according to pronunciation, vocabulary and grammar.

Exploring the text

1. Who is the speaker in the poem and how does he characterize himself?
2. Sum up the message of the poem in your own words. Refer to the box on the left for ideas.
3. How does the poet manage to combine humour with serious issues?
4. Do you think that people like the speaker are really dangerous? Give reasons for your answer.

Dub poetry
is a form of Caribbean oral poetry which originated in Jamaica and Britain in the 1970s.

A step further

- Rewrite the poem as a standard English prose text.
- *Listen Mr Oxford Don* is an example of 'dub poetry'. Find out more about this type of poetry and how it gave a voice to a particular ethnic group in Britain. You could use the names of some famous dub poets such as John Agard, Linton Kwesi Johnson and Benjamin Zephaniah as key words for a web search. Then present your findings to the rest of the class.
- Look at the following statistics on immigration in Europe. Then answer the following questions.
  a) Compare attitudes to immigration in the UK with those in other European countries.
  b) What patterns, if any, do you notice in the statistics?

Talking about statistics

The statistics show / suggest / prove…
The figures support / back up the claim that …
There is no evidence that …
Compared to X the number of people in Y who …

European country	Population in millions	unemploy-ment rate April 2002	Total immigration in 2001 (thousands)	Legal immigrants % of population	% believing immigrants increase insecurity
Belgium	10.2	6.8	1.8	8.3	62
Germany	82.2	8.1	180	9.0	58
France	59.0	9.2	60	5.5	55
Finland	5.1	9.1	6.1	1.7	34
Portugal	10.2	4.0	50	1.8	51
Sweden	8.8	5.3	30	5.4	26
UK	59.8	5.1	155	3.8	38

Source: based on El Pais *16.06.2002 with data from Eurostat, EU, OCDE and ONU.*

Listen Mr Oxford Don

Me not no Oxford don
me a simple immigrant
from Clapham Common
I didn't graduate
I immigrate

But listen Mr Oxford don
I'm a man on de run
and a man on de run
is a dangerous one

I ent have no gun
I ent have no knife
but mugging de Queen's English
is the story of my life

I dont need no axe
to split/up yu syntax
I dont need no hammer
to mash up yu grammar

I warning you Mr Oxford don
I'm a wanted man
and a wanted man
is a dangerous one

Dem accuse me of assault
on de Oxford dictionary/
imagin a concise peaceful man like me/
dem want me serve time
for inciting rhyme to riot
but I tekking it quiet
down here in Clapham Common

I'm not a violent man Mr Oxford don
I only armed wit muh human breath
but human breath
is a dangerous weapon

So mek dem send one big word after me
I ent serving no jail sentence
I slashing suffix in self-defence
I bashing future wit present tense
and if necessary

I making de Queen's English accessory/to my offence

By John Agard, Voiceprint: an anthology of oral and related poetry from the Caribbean (Longman Caribbean Writers), *Harlow: Longman, 1989, p. 109.*

0 **don** *here:* tutor in an English university
3 **Clapham Common** district in southwest London
4 **to graduate** *(BE)* to receive a degree or diploma
12 **to mug** *(informal)* to attack, usu. to rob
17 **to mash up** usu. to beat up; *here:* to use incorrectly
24 **concise** [kən'saɪs] *here:* only using a few words
25 **to serve time** to spend time in prison
26 **to incite to riot** to arouse to public violence
35 **to slash** to cut with a sweeping stroke
36 **to bash** *(informal)* to strike violently
38 **accessory** *(legal term here)* s.o. who helps another in a crime

John Agard, Jamaica
(b. 1949, Georgetown, Guyana)

Before you read

- a) Think of ways in which people can be discriminated against.
  b) Describe a case of discrimination you have heard about.
  c) What measures could be taken to prevent discrimination?

Telephone conversation

The price seemed reasonable, location
Indifferent. The landlady swore she lived
Off premises. Nothing remained
But self-confession. "Madam," I warned,
"I hate a wasted journey – I am African."
Silence. Silenced transmission of
Pressurized good-breeding. Voice, when it came,
Lipstick coated, long gold-rolled
Cigarette-holder pipped. Caught I was, foully.
"HOW DARK?" … I had not misheard … "ARE YOU LIGHT
OR VERY DARK?" Button B. Button A. Stench
Of rancid breath of public hide-and-speak.
Red booth. Red pillar-box. Red double-tiered
Omnibus squelching tar. It *was* real! Shamed
By ill-mannered silence, surrender
Pushed dumbfounded to beg simplification.
Considerate she was, varying the emphasis –
"ARE YOU DARK? OR VERY LIGHT?" Revelation came.
"You mean – like plain or milk chocolate?
Her assent was clinical, crushing in its light
Impersonality. Rapidly, wave-length adjusted,
I chose. "West African sepia" – and as afterthought,
"Down in my passport." Silence for spectroscopic
Flight of fancy, till truthfulness clanged her accent
Hard on the mouthpiece. "WHAT'S THAT?" conceding

"DON'T KNOW WHAT THAT IS." "Like brunette."
"THAT'S DARK, ISN'T IT?" "Not altogether.
Facially, I am brunette, but madam, you should see
The rest of me. Palm of my hand, soles of my feet
Are a peroxide blonde. Friction, caused –
Foolishly madam – by sitting down, has turned
My bottom raven black – One moment madam!" – sensing
Her receiver rearing on the thunderclap
About my ears – "Madam," I pleaded, "wouldn't you rather
See for yourself?"

By Wole Soyinka, Seven Themes in Modern Verse, *M. Wollman, ed. Harrap, 1975.*

3 **premises** ['premɪsɪz] *here:* in the same building
7 **good-breeding** good behaviour learnt as a young person
9 **to pip** to make a short, high-pitched noise
9 **foully** [aʊ] *here:* badly
11 **Button B, Button A** *(old British public telephones)* one pressed Button A to hear the person at the other end and B to get one's money back
12 **hide-and-speak** *pun on* hide-and-seek *(Versteckspiel)*
13 **double-tiered omnibus** *(old)* bus with seating at two levels
23 **spectroscopic** *here:* trying to determine a colour with a spectroscope
30 **peroxide** chemical used to make hair blond
33 **to rear** *here:* to rise up

Exploring the text

1 Describe the incident in the poem in your own words.
2 Characterize the landlady based on evidence in the poem.
3 Describe how the African caller's feelings change during the conversation.

Close-up: structure and language

What elements make "Telephone conversation" a poem rather than a prose text? Refer to its structure and language in your answer.

A step further

- Rewrite the poem from the point of view of the landlady.
- Present the poem in class as a short dramatic scene.

PREJUDICES

Working either in pairs or small groups, do **one** of the following tasks:
– Describe what happens in each picture and compare with the situation in Wole Soyinka's poem.
– Write a sketch based on the situation and act it out in class.

Before you read

- a) In a few lines write down what you understand by the term 'ghetto'. What factors cause ghettos to come into existence?
  b) What historical examples come to mind? Give as much detail as possible.

Ghettos in the north

Many heads will be banging together drawing up the terms of reference for the new home secretary's review of last month's riots in Oldham. It is crucial that they get it right.

Oldham is a snapshot of other post-industrial northern towns. Nearby Rochdale, Burnley (where there was violence at the weekend), Bury and Bradford, as well as cities further afield like Birmingham, share similar economic depression and ethnic tension.

The recent report warning of the dangers of segregation in Bradford is timely. Ethnic separation is the key to understanding inner-city strife. In 1990 an Oldham council report into housing allocation revealed disturbing discrimination against Asians. The document was leaked to the commission for racial equality which in 1993 declared a verdict of "unlawful discrimination".

It found Asians did indeed spend longer on waiting lists, were more likely to be offered lower-quality housing, and were segregated on specific estates around the town centre.

What has changed? Not a lot that anybody can show. The CRE did complete a five-year plan of reforms with the council, one of which was the institution of ethnic monitoring. But the council still cannot, or is too embarrassed to, provide an accurate picture of how its "Asian" tenants are spread. Worse still, the comically inept CRE "cannot find" the final status report on its work in Oldham.

Oldham's estate agents did their bit for segregation too. In 1990 a separate CRE investigation found two firms guilty of "redlining", or setting limits to where Asians could buy. It is in such discrimination that the roots of Oldhams "no-go areas" lie, not the bombast of teenage gangs.

Economic decline has been another cause. When the cotton mills flourished 30 years ago, the Asian areas were ethnically mixed. Older residents in riot-hit Glodwick recall with some fondness when white and Asian men lived and worked side by side. With the collapse of manufacturing, the working-class areas fell into decline. Whites moved out in search of greener pastures, followed by the Afro-Caribbeans.

The Asians, mainly Pakistanis and Bangladeshis, stayed behind. Mostly from rural Punjab, Kashmir or Sylhet, unskilled and uneducated, those who didn't work in the factories set up small retail or catering businesses, usually to service their own communities. Their relatives arrived, mainly through marriage, and took up the slack left by the departing whites. As their areas became racially particular and the economic depression deepened, house prices hit the floor attracting even more Asian buyers. And so the ghetto has consolidated and grown. Grange school in Glodwick now has a 98 % Bangladeshi roll. This is the reality of modern multicultural Britain: a whole generation growing up deprived of any contact with people unlike themselves, their horizons bounded by the invisible but very real walls of the ghetto.

4 **snapshot** *here:* summary
10 **allocation** official distribution
14 **estate** *(BE) here:* area of land developed for houses
17 **institution** *here:* introduction
24 **bombast** important-sounding yet meaningless talk about s.th.
31 **Sylhet** city in eastern Bangladesh
34 **slack** *here:* space
37 **roll** *here:* list of pupils registered at a school
38 **to be deprived** [dɪ'praɪvd] **of s.th.** not to have s.th. one should have

The same applies to the white working-class estates in Oldham where an entrenched underclass has inherited, and will pass on, poverty, crime and unemployment. Segregation also explains the resentment caused by urban regeneration grants. Because whole neighbourhoods are now racially distinctive, a grant for one area is perceived as an award to an ethnic group. If people live apart they grow apart.

The breach, as the town's election results show, is an open invitation for the xenophobes of the British National Party. Letting ethnic groups develop distinctive identities has failed because it has not been balanced by a corresponding emphasis on integration. We need to encourage communities to engage with the wider world, not reward them for becoming reclusive and defensive.

Forget Asian versus white. Before they joined forces to battle the police, Pakistani and Bangladeshi youths in Glodwick were usually fighting each other. Tension can be traced back 3,000 miles and 30 years to the separation of east and west Pakistan. To the ire of local Pakistanis, a new housing development in Westwood is the preserve of Bangladeshi families. They may all be Muslims, but the groups even have their own mosques.

Intermarriage is still a matter of some scandal. However, not all is gloom. A local multi-denominational group is about to launch "Connect" with the aim of bringing together young people of different backgrounds. The Al-Aqsa housing association has adopted a multi-ethnic approach to accommodating Muslims.

It hasn't taken rocket scientists to develop these solutions, just people with a sense of duty, sincerity and some will. Getting people to live, work and play together is not asking too much, is it?

By Faisal Bodi, The Guardian, *June 25, 2001.*

41 **entrenched** firmly established
46 **breach** *here:* a breakdown in relations
49 **to engage with s.th.** *here:* to make contact with s.th. to understand it better
55 **preserve** [-'-] s.th. that is used by one group only

Exploring the text

1 According to the text, what causes ethnic tension in towns like Oldham?
2 Describe the development of ghettos in northern England as outlined in the text.
3 Why would it be incorrect to say that tensions only exist between whites and Asians?
4 What ways of easing racial tension does the writer mention?
5 What features characterize the text as a comment? (Cf. skills file, page 188.)

A step further

- One way of preventing segregation and ethnic tensions is to promote 'social cohesion' (= links between members of a community). Referring to the key words below, how could social cohesion be improved in a multicultural society?

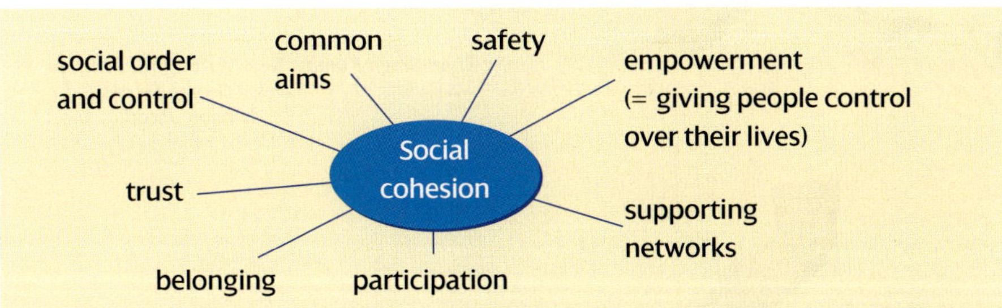

Before you read

- What things make someone feel as if they belong to a group? In pairs write down a list of at least five things and rank them in order of importance. Compare your list with another pair's list.

The Indian who thought he was English

1 **to be in with** *(informal)* to be friendly with
2 **thick with** *(informal)* close to
4 **local** *(BE, informal)* pub near one's home
6 **sojourner** ['sɒdʒɜːnər] *(formal)* s.o. who lives in a place for a time
7 **bud-bud** = buddy-buddy *(informal here)* friends
12 **to sup** to drink
13 **to take s.o. on** *here:* to challenge another team
17 **to tuck into s.th.** *(here fig.)* to adjust one's voice so it is not obvious
19 **estrangeness** = estrangement (= loss of friendship) + strangeness (= feeling like an outsider)
25 **frame** *(film term)* scene
27 **shrubby** *(dialect)* drunk

Just for a minute I was in with the English,
thick with their skin
or thick with just their words
and no one asked in the local:
where is it you really come from
you sojourner from a strange land
from a childhood of bud-bud
who has forgotten his own pubs
and tries to be part of the picture?

I was one of us, at ease,
welcoming late-comers when all my mates
were there supping for the great game
on an ends-of-the-earth nostalgia.
We were taking on foreigners,
shouting at the screen
as though our nation would live or die by it.

I tucked my voice into theirs
without splitting to a guilt-word from a turban'd ghost
or shame or feeling of estrangeness to a single voice.
I wasn't black or latin or half anything,
I was unconscious of a home
living its Indian life in my name,
or the need to keep that secret-self
from my friends, to still this smiling face
as I went back to the frame
of my tear-filled wife to hear:
Those shrubby people ...
where you go ...?
They colouring our wall ...
Why still we here ...?

By Khan Singh Kumar, New Writing 10, *Penelope Lively / George Szirtes (ed.), London: Picador, 2001.*

Exploring the text

1 In what way(s) does the speaker feel at one with the English?
2 What is his wife's attitude towards the English and England?
3 What conflict(s) does the poem present?

Close-up: language

1 Which lines in the poem do you find difficult to understand? Try to interpret them with a partner.
2 What distinguishes the last four lines from the rest of the poem?
3 Examine the diction, structure and imagery of the poem. Point out and explain the features which you find particularly striking.

A step further

- Rewrite the speaker's experience in the form of a letter to his best friend back home in India.
- Imagine the discussion between the Indian and his wife following ll. 27–30. What decision may the couple make about their future?
- Read the fact file below and sum up the information about each of the ethnic communities mentioned in your own words.

Multicultural Britain

Of a population of 59,755,700 (mid-2000) 'non-white' ethnic minorities account for 7.1 % of the British population: Indians are the largest group (24 %), then Pakistanis (17 %) and Afro-Caribbeans (13 %).

Age

Ethnic minority groups tend to be younger: the median age of whites is 37, Afro-Caribbeans is 33, Indians is 31 and Bangladeshis is 18.

Distribution

- The clustering of 'ethnic communities' in England's towns and cities has made multiculturalism an urban question.
- Almost half of all ethnic minority Britons live in London.
- Inner London is the only part of the country where black Britons outnumber British Asians, by almost two to one. British Indians are in the majority in outer London suburbs.
- Pakistanis form the largest ethnic group in the Northwest, Yorkshire and Scotland, while British Indians are the largest ethnic group in the West and East Midlands, as well as in most of the mainly white regions of England.
- Racial tensions in 2001 were greatest not in the areas with the largest ethnic populations but in towns in northwest England such as Oldham, Burnley, Rochdale and Blackburn. These towns have high levels of ethnic segregation. In Rochdale, 96 per cent of the Pakistani community and 89 per cent of Bangladeshis live in the five inner wards (= electoral districts), which are among the most deprived areas in the Northwest.

Economic status

- The Afro-Caribbean community is the most 'integrated', with the highest levels of interracial marriages (eight times higher than those for blacks in the US). Afro-Caribbean women are doing well in terms of employment and income.
- British Indians are, on average, slightly better off than white Britons, but there is high inequality within the group, particularly among women.
- Worst-off are people of Pakistani and Bangladeshi origin who are the most likely to be unemployed and living in poverty or overcrowded housing. They have lower levels of fluency in English than other ethnic groups, especially among women.

Education

- Children of black African origin – like those of Indian origin – achieve above-average school results.
- Approximately 300 languages are spoken in the capital's schools.

Before you read

- In the extract from the novel *White Teeth* one of the characters says "Do you think anybody is English? Really English? It's a fairy-tale." What do you think they mean?
- a) Study the statements below and make a note of any references to culture.
  b) Which statements would you agree / disagree with?

Talking about culture

- "Race and culture are not at all the same thing. Race is on the outside, culture on the inside. Which is why I don't underestimate the gravity behind the thinking when a white Brit, with a sorrowful shake of the head, attempts to explain to me how my kind can never be really British: 'It's not 'cos you're black but it's just that you don't have the culture, mate. In your bones, you know.'" *Diran Adebayo, black writer of Nigerian origin.*
- "I was brought up in Dudley and Birmingham and loved all that – Indian sweets, beautiful Asian women, wonderful clothes from another culture, the sense that a decaying white culture might be enriched by immigration." *Stuart Jeffries, white journalist*
- "While cherishing cultural diversity, Britain must remain a cohesive society with a shared national culture." *Bhikhu Parekh, "A Britain we all belong to",* The Guardian, *Oct. 11, 2000.*

Do you think anybody is English? Really English?

Teenager Millat Iqbal, a second-generation Anglo-Bengali and his friends are on a train to Bradford to take part in a demonstration against Salman Rushdie's novel The Satanic Verses. *At home, his parents Samad and Alsana watch a news report on the demonstration.*

"You read it?" asked Ranil, as they whizzed past Finsbury Park.

There was a general pause.

Millat said, "I haven't exackly read it exackly – but I know all about that shit, yeah?

To be more precise, Millat hadn't read it. Millat knew nothing about the writer, nothing about the book; could not identify the book if it lay in a pile of other books; could not pick out the writer in a line-up of other writers (irresistible, this line-up of offending writers: Socrates, Protagoras, Ovid and Juvenal, Radclyffe Hall, Boris Pasternak, D. H. Lawrence, Solzhenitsyn, Nabokov, all holding up their numbers for the mug shot, squinting in the flashbulb). But he knew other things. He knew that he, Millat, was a Paki no matter where he came from; that he smelt of curry; had no sexual identity; took other people's jobs; or had no job and bummed off the state; or gave all the jobs to his relatives; that he could be a dentist or a shop-owner or a curry-shifter, but not a footballer or a film-maker; that he should go back to his own country; or stay here and earn his bloody keep; that he worshipped elephants and wore turbans; that no one who looked like Millat, or spoke like Millat, or felt like Millat, was ever on the news unless they had recently been murdered. In short, he knew he had no face in this country, no voice in the country, until the week before last when suddenly people like Millat were on every channel and every radio and every newspaper and they were angry, and Millat recognized the anger, thought it recognized him, and grabbed it with both hands.

"So … you ain't read it?" asked Ranil nervously.

"Look: you best believe I ain't buying that shit, man. No way, star."

"Me neither," said Hifan.

"True star," said Rajik.

"Fucking nastiness," said Ranil.

7 **line-up** i.e. of people from which a police witness may identify a potential criminal
11 **Paki** *(BE, negative)* word used for s.o. born in Pakistan or whose parents come from there
14 **curry-shifter** *(informal, negative)* s.o. who has an Indian restaurant

"Twelve ninety-five, you know!" said Dipesh.

"Besides," said Millat, with a tone of finality despite his high-rising terminals, "you don't have to read shit to know that it's blasphemous, you get me?"

Back in Willesden, Samad Iqbal was expressing the very same sentiment loudly over the evening news.

"I don't *need* to read it. The relevant passages have been photocopied for me."

"Will someone remind my husband," said Alsana, speaking to the newsreader, "that he does not even know what the bloody book is about because the last thing he read was the bloody A-Z."

"I'm going to ask you one more time to shut up so I can watch the news."

"I can hear screaming but it does not appear to be my voice."

"Can't you understand, woman? This is the most important thing to happen to us in this country, ever. It's crisis point. It's the tickle in the sneeze. It's big time." Samad hit the volume button a few times with his thumb. "This woman – Moira whatever-hernameis – she mumbles. Why is she reading news if she can't speak properly?"

Moira, turned up suddenly in mid-sentence, said, "… the writer denies blasphemy, and argues that the book concerns the struggle between secular and religious views of life."

Samad snorted. "What struggle! I don't see any struggle. I get on perfectly OK. All grey cells in good condition. No emotional difficulties."

Alsana laughed bitterly. "My husband fights the Third World War every single bloody day in his head, so does everybody –"

"No, no, no. No struggle. What's he on about, eh? He can't wangle out of it by being rational. Rationality! Most overrated Western virtue! Oh no. Fact is, he is simply offensive – he has offended –"

"Look," Alsana cut in. "When my little group get together, if we disagree about something, we can sort it out. Example: Mohona Hossain hates Divargiit Singh. Hates all his movies. Hates him with a passion. She likes that other fool with the eyelashes like a lady! But we compromise. Never once have I burned a single video of hers."

"Hardly the same thing, Mrs Iqbal, hardly the same kettle with fish in it."

"Oh, passions are running high at the Womens' Committee – shows how much Samad Iqbal knows. But I am not like Samad Iqbal. I restrain myself. I live. I let live."

"It is not a matter of letting others live. It is a matter of protecting one's culture, shielding one's religion from abuse. Not that you'd know anything about that, naturally. Always too busy with this Hindi brain popcorn to pay any attention to your own culture!"

"My *own* culture? And what is that please?"

"You're a Bengali. Act like one."

"And what is a Bengali, husband, please?"

"Get out of the way of the television and look it up."

Alsana took BALTIC-BRAIN, number three of their 24-set *Reader's Digest Encyclopedia*, and read from the relevant section:

The vast majority of Bangladesh's inhabitants are Bengalis, who are largely descended from Indo-Aryans

28 **high-rising terminal** when the voice rises at the end of a sentence; a feature of Indian and Pakistani English

29 **you get me?** *(informal)* do you understand me?

39 **the tickle in the sneeze** *(fig.)* s.th. that has serious consequences

49 **to wangle out of s.th.** to get out of a difficult situation

Part of a protest by several thousand Muslims in Hyde Park against Salman Rusdie's novel, *The Satanic Verses*, January 28, 1989.

who began to migrate into the country from the west thousands of years ago and who mixed within Bengal with indigenous groups of various racial stocks. Ethnic minorities include the Chakma and Mogh, Mongoloid peoples who live in the Chittagong Hill Tracts District; the Santal, mainly descended from migrants from present-day India; and the Biharis, non-Bengali Muslims who migrated from India after the partition.

"Oi, mister! Indo-*Aryans* ... it looks like I am Western after all! Maybe I should listen to Tina Turner, wear the itsy-bitsy leather skirts. Pah. It just goes to show," said Alsana, revealing her English tongue, "you go back and back and back and it's still easier to find the correct Hoover bag than to find one pure person, one pure faith, on the globe. Do you think anybody is English? Really English? It's a fairy-tale!"

"You don't know what you're talking about. You're out of your depth."

Alsana held up the encyclopedia. "Oh, *Samad Miah*. You want to burn this too?"

"Look: I've no time to play right now. I am trying to listen to a very important news story. Serious goings on in Bradford. So, if you don't mind –"

"Oh dear God!" screamed Alsana, the smile leaving her face, falling to her knees in front of the television, tracing her finger past the burning book to the face she recognized, smiling up at her through light tubes, her pixilated second-son beneath her picture-framed first. "What is he doing? Is he crazy? Who does he think he is? What on earth is he doing there? He's meant to be in school! Has the day come when the babies are burning the books, *has it*? I don't believe it!"

"Nothing to do with me. Tickle in the sneeze, Mrs Iqbal," said Samad coolly, sitting back in his armchair. "Tickle in the sneeze."

When Millat came home that evening, a great bonfire was raging in the back garden. All his secular stuff – four years' worth of cool, pre- and post-Raggastani, every album, every poster, special edition t-shirts, club fliers collected and preserved over two years, beautiful Air Max trainers, copies 20–75 of *2000 AD Magazine*, signed photo of Chuck D., impossibly rare copy of Slick Rick's *Hey Young World*, *Catcher in the Rye*, his guitar, *Godfather I* and *II*, *Mean Streets*, *Rumblefish*, *Dog Day Afternoon* and *Shaft in Africa* – all had been placed on the funeral pyre, now a smouldering mound of ashes that was giving off fumes of plastic and paper, stinging the boy's eyes that were already filled with tears.

"Everyone has to be taught a lesson," Alsana had said, lighting the match with heavy heart some hours earlier. "Either everything is sacred or nothing is. And if he starts burning other people's things, then he loses something sacred also. Everyone gets what's coming, sooner or later."

By Zadie Smith, White Teeth, *London: Penguin, 2001, pp. 233–237.*

77 **the partition** *here:* the division of India into India and Pakistan
79 **it goes to show** it proves
83 **out of one's depth** talking about s.th. one does not understand
89 **pixilated** confused

Exploring the text

1 a) Why are the teenagers going to take part in the demonstration?
b) What seems to have caused their anger at the book?

2 a) Describe the relationship between Samad Iqbal and his wife Alsana.
b) How do their attitudes to the book, culture and tolerance differ?

3 How is the scene with Millat and his friends linked to the scene with his parents? What parallels do you notice?

4 Comment on the function of humour in the text.

Close-up: language
How does the writer use language as a means of *characterization*?

A step further
- Which aspects of the novel extract did you like / dislike? Would you be interested in reading the rest of the novel? If you are, look at the section below for ideas.
- In groups of three, imagine and act out the scene between Millat and his parents on his return from the demonstration.

Characterization
is the method by which the persons in a novel are presented directly, i.e. the narrator says what a character is like, or indirectly i.e. the reader judges a character from his / her actions, feelings and thoughts.

Using your skills

Reading a novel: White Teeth

After reading the extracts from the novel White Teeth *on pp. 44–46, you may decide to read the book in a group with a view to writing a book review, or a class paper about a particular aspect. Here are some ideas to get you started.*

Before you read
- Look at the front cover, the blurb on the back, quote(s) given at the beginning of the novel and the table of contents to find some useful clues about what to expect from the novel. You could also read the first few pages for an introduction to characters, setting, style, etc. Write down any questions which occur to you.
- Check reviews on the Web (www.guardian.co.uk or www.amazon.com) for information about plot and characters, and readers' opinions about the book.

While reading: groupwork
- The important elements of a novel are shown in the diagram below. Each member of the group should record details about one element. (Cf. glosssary on pp. 190–191 for definitions of some of the terms.)

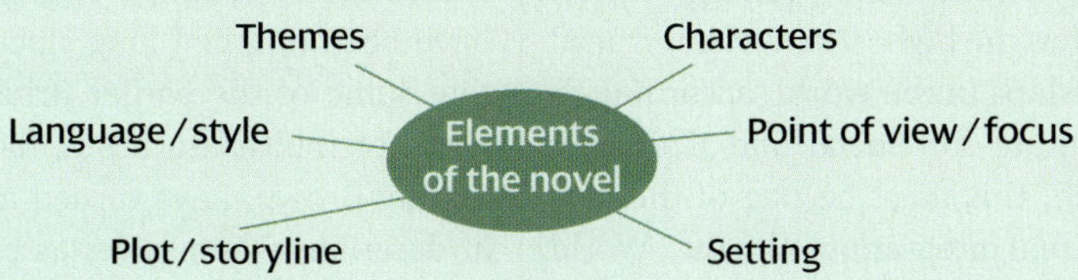

- Make a note of questions that occur to you while reading and discuss them later in the group. Record the conclusions that the group comes to.

A step further
- Write your own review of the novel.
- In a group, present the novel in class. Each member presents his / her special topic.
- Write a class paper. You could choose a topic such as "The experience of second-generation immigrants in Britain as reflected in the novel *White Teeth*", "What effect does Britain's colonial past have on its present?"

Talking about novels

The atmosphere
- is gloomy / depressing …
- stirs up … emotions

The writer
- adopts a … attitude
- points out … in detail …
- presents aspects of … ,
- comes to the conclusion that …
- draws several conclusions

A character
- plays a role
- undergoes a development
- is a main or a minor c.
- is the hero / heroine
- is depicted / portrayed as honest / generous …
- is driven by …

The dialogue
- is authentic / realistic / artificial / credible / lively …
- presents a conflict
- depicts a character
- advances the plot

The narrative structure
- is simple / complex
- leads to a surprise / open ending

The narrative rhythm
- is fast / slow(-moving)
- accelerates / slows down
- builds up tension / to a climax

The reader
- is introduced to the world of …
- is led to believe / feel …
- is constantly aware of …

A new understanding of Britishness

The recording "A new understanding of Britishness" is an extract from a speech given by former British foreign secretary Robin Cook on April 19, 2001.

Before you read

- a) Explain the differences between the following terms: assimilation – integration – multiculturalism.
  b) Which process is most likely to lead to racial harmony? Give reasons for your answer.
- What things would you associate with the term 'Englishness? Brainstorm your ideas in small groups.
- In the following text the writer claims that "multiculturalism is a recipe for division". Do you agree or disagree with this claim? Give reasons for your answer.

Multiculturalism – a recipe for racism

Anyone who saw policemen in flames on television, or who watched interviews with angry young Asian and white men, cannot help wondering about race relations in this country.

Most would probably agree that race relations here are, mostly speaking, relatively good and getting better. Britain has the highest rate of interracial relationships in the world, according to the Institute for Social and Economic Research; this must be one of the best signs of real integration. At a BBC World Service broadcast I took part in, a largely black audience agreed London was without a doubt the best city in the world to live in for a person from an ethnic minority.

It is premature to say we are a multiracial society. That is true only in certain cities and so far only about 6 % of the population belongs to an ethnic minority. But we are becoming multiracial, and may well do so very successfully. However, such a major transition, in only a few decades, cannot but be difficult. I strongly believe that one of the greatest obstacles in the way of good race relations here is multiculturalism.

Multiculturalism actually promotes racism. It engenders confusion, resentment and bullying; it encourages division and prevents people developing a shared British identity. This idea should have been dumped long since. I notice that some of the earlier British proponents of multiculturalism, like Yasmin Alibhai-Brown, have turned away from it, describing themselves as post-multiculturalists, and looking for the "ties that bind". Not a moment too soon. But unfortunately this subversive notion is now entrenched in the public mind.

Multiculturalism is the idea that all cultures are of equal value, and deserve equal respect – an understandable response to the confusions of mass mobility. Unfortunately it has become overloaded with anxieties about race; in fact to say you are against multiculturalism is pretty much to confess to racism.

31 **to engender** *(formal)* to cause

Exploring the text

1 Outline the writer's view of multiculturalism.

2 a) According to the writer, what attitude do people often have towards a "host culture" (l. 62)?
b) What would your own attitude be towards an "over-arching common culture" (l. 60)?

3 a) What events have led the writer to assume that Englishness is being excluded from the ethnic diversity in the UK?
b) Why does she criticize this tendency?

A step further

- What could you do to reduce racism? Summarize your ideas in the form of slogans and collect them on a poster.
- Listen to the recording of "A new understanding of Britishness" (cf. page 48). Do you think that Minette Marrin is justified in criticizing Robin Cook in ll. 75–78, or not? Write a short paragraph in which you explain your view.
- Debate the following issue: This House believes that the positive effects of immigration outweigh the negative ones.

This is absurd. Race has nothing to do with it; the time when race and culture were coextensive is long since past. It's history. If I truly value the beliefs of my culture, I cannot equally value the beliefs of another when they are opposed to mine. And in any case, what we must have to live together in harmony is a tolerant, over-arching common culture. We already have one, in what one might call our host culture, but the very idea of a host culture is denounced by multiculturalists as supremacist and racist; people have begun to feel confused by the fear of being thought racist into being ashamed of their own culture.

Multiculturalism is always celebrating difference. Of course it is right that everyone should be free to remember their traditions and practise their faith, within the limits of the laws and traditions of this country. Of course all these differences can enrich the common culture; to pontificate, like Robin Cook, about chicken tikka massala is to trivialise and to patronise all these contributions. But what we've seen too often is a vociferous insistence on ethnic differences, which constantly remind people of their otherness.

Worse still, this celebration of ethnic diversity has tended, pointedly, to exclude only one ethnic tradition – Englishness (or sometimes, more loosely, Britishness). There have been minor signs of this here and there – the abolition of Christmas festivities in schools, the substitution of a municipal 'Winterval' somewhere in the Midlands, the non-appearance of the word English in an academic book I have which purports to celebrate Britain's various cultures. English ungood. [...]

The American ideal of the melting pot may have gone too far in the direction of cultural homogenisation. The problem with multiculturalism is the opposite – it is a recipe for permanent division.

By Minette Marrin, The Guardian, *May 29, 2001.*

54 **coextensive** having the same extent
54 **long since** for a long time
60 **over-arching** *here:* which includes everyone
64 **supremacist** [suːˈpreməsɪst] s.o. who believes that their own race is better than others
92 **to purport** *(formal)* to claim
94 **ungood** bad

First peoples

Images of Aborigines

Looking and listening

- What aspects of Aboriginal life are shown in the photos below and are suggested by the music?
- As you work through this section of the chapter collect key words relating to Aborigines and organize them in a mind map.

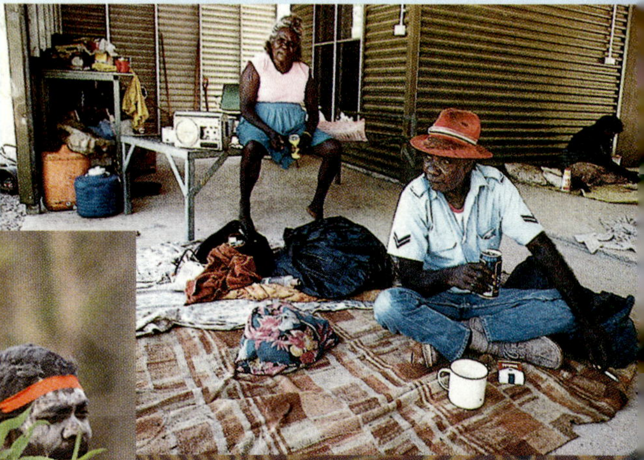

Aboriginal couple in their home

The mosquito dance

"Tingari Dreaming at Walawala" by Donkeyman Lee Tjupurrula, 1989

Aboriginal beliefs

An Aboriginal artist explains his paintings to some children.

According to the Australian Aborigine belief the world was created by Spirit Ancestors, who could take on various shapes, such as that of an animal. The ancestors' actions formed the stars, the earth, animals, plants and humans, e.g. where the Rainbow Serpent laid its eggs we now see some rocks. Having finished creation, the Spirit Ancestors "went back" into the earth to sleep. To the Aborigines, the landscape around them is visible evidence of the legends that explain creation. Activities which damage or change the land, such as the building of roads or railways, or mining for minerals, are sacrilegious, as they destroy the Aborigines' heritage and disturb the sleeping Spirit Ancestors.
The Spirit Ancestors were also the founders of the clans. For example, an ancestor in the shape of a wallaby (a small kangaroo) founded the clan of the "wallaby people" who live in northern Australia. The form the ancestor took determines whether the clan's totem is a sacred animal, plant or landscape feature. The clan's totem is taboo for its members: they may not approach, name or represent their totem in art, so, e.g. the wallaby people are forbidden to kill or eat wallabies. The Spirit Ancestors also laid down the laws of the clans and determined which ceremonies must be carried out at different times of the year.
The 'Dreamtime' is the mythological time when the earth was created by the Spirit Ancestors. The stories and songs which describe events during the creation and explain the meaning of ceremonies and laws are the 'Dreamings'. These are central to the existence of Aboriginal people and are handed down orally from generation to generation. When Aboriginal families or clans walk across the land belonging to their Dreamtime, they follow so-called 'Songlines' which may be compared to mental maps. Songlines still guide Aborigines to food and water, shelter and sacred sites today. By singing the songs the Aborigines take care of the land and thus guarantee its existence and their own survival.

The Songlines

In the following extract from the novel The Songlines *the narrator (probably the writer Bruce Chatwin) relates an incident he witnesses in Alice Springs. Mrs Lacey, the white Australian owner of the Desert Bookstore and Art Gallery, and Old Stan Tjakamarra present a dot-painting to an American couple interested in Aboriginal art.*

The painting was about four foot by three and had a background of pointillist dots in varying shades of ochre. In the centre there was a big blue circle with several smaller circles scattered around it. Each circle had a scarlet rim around the perimeter and, connecting them, was a maze of wiggly, flamingo-pink lines that looked a bit like intestines.

Mrs Lacey switched to her second pair of glasses and said, "What you got here, Stan?"

"Honey-ant," he whispered in a hoarse voice.

"The honey-ant," she turned to the Americans, "is one of the totems at Popanji. This painting's a honey-ant Dreaming."

"I think it's beautiful," said the American woman, thoughtfully.

"Like it's an ordinary ant?" asked the American man. "Like a termite ant?"

"No, no," said Mrs Lacey. "A honey-ant's something very special. Honey-ants feed on mulga sap. Mulga, that's a tree we have here in the desert. The ants grow honey-sacks on their rear ends. They look like clear plastic bubbles."

2 **ochre** ['əʊkər] yellowish-brown
9 **totem** cf. box above, ll. 16–19
9 **Popanji** an Aboriginal community

Aboriginal woman painted with a totem

"Is that so?" the man said.

"I've eaten them," said Mrs Lacey. "Delicious!"

"Yes," sighed the American woman. She had fixed her gaze on the painting. "In its own way, it is truly beautiful!"

"But I can't see any ants in this painting," the man said. "You mean it's like … like it's a painting of an ants' nest? Like those pink tubes are passages?"

"No," Mrs Lacey looked a little discouraged. "The painting shows the journey of the Honey-ant Ancestor."

"Like it's a route-map?" he grinned. "Yeah, I thought it looked like a route-map."

"Exactly," said Mrs Lacey.

The American wife, meanwhile, was opening and closing her eyes to see what impression the painting would make on her when, finally, she kept them open.

"Beautiful," she repeated.

"Now, sir!" the man addressed himself to Stan. "Do you eat these honey-ants yourself?"

Stan nodded.

"No! No!" the wife shrilled. "I told you this morning. You do *not* eat your own totem! You could be killed for eating your Ancestor!"

"Dearest, this gentleman says he does eat honey-ants. Is that correct, sir?"

Stan continued to nod.

"I'm confused," said the woman in an exasperated tone. "You mean that Honey-ant is not your Dreaming?"

Stan shook his head.

"Then what *is* your Dreaming?"

The old man quivered like a schoolboy forced to betray a secret, and managed to wheeze the word "Emu".

"Oh, I am *so* confused," the woman bit her lip in disappointment.

She liked this soft-mouthed old man in his yellow shirt. She liked to think of the honey-ants dreaming their way across the desert with the bright sun shining on their honey-sacks. She had loved the painting. She wanted to own it, to have him sign it, and now she'd have to think again.

"Do you think," she mouthed her words slowly and carefully, "that if we deposited the money with Mrs –?"

"Lacey," said Mrs Lacey.

"… that you could paint us an Emu Dreaming and send it … have Mrs Lacey send it to us in the United States?"

"No," Mrs Lacey interrupted. "He could not. No artist paints his own Dreaming. It's too powerful. It might kill him."

"Now I am *totally* confused," the woman wrung her hands. "You mean he can't paint his own Dreaming but he can paint somebody else's?"

"I get it," said the husband, brightening. "Like he can't eat emus but he can eat honey-ants?"

"You've got it," Mrs Lacey said. "Mr Tjakamarra cannot paint an Emu Dreaming because an emu is his paternal totem and it would be sacrilege to do so. He can paint honey-ant because that is the totem of his mother's brother's son. That's right, isn't it, Stan? Gideon's Dreaming is honey-ant?"

Stan blinked and said, "Right!"

40 **to quiver** to shake
54 **to wring one's hands** to twist one's hands; a sign that one is worried
62 **to blink** ▽ to open and shut your eyes quickly

"Gideon," she continued, "is Stan's ritual manager. They both tell each other what they can and cannot paint."

"I think I understand," said the American woman, doubtfully. But she still looked quite bewildered and took time to compose her next thought.

"You said that this Mr Gideon is an artist too?"

"He is," Mrs Lacey agreed.

"And he paints Emu Dreamings?"

"He does."

"Goodee!" the woman laughed, unexpectedly, and clapped her hands. "We could buy one of each and hang them as a pair."

"Now, dearest," said the husband in an effort to calm her. "First, we have to ascertain if this honey-ant painting is for sale. And if so, how much?"

Mrs Lacey fluttered her eyelashes and said, archly, "I couldn't say. You'll have to ask the artist."

Stan rolled the whites of his eyes to the ceiling and rustled his lips. Obviously, he was thinking of a price – the price he'd get from Mrs Lacey – and doubling it. Obviously he and Mrs Lacey had been through this rigmarole before. He then lowered his head and said, "Four hundred fifty."

"Australian dollars," Mrs Lacey chipped in. "Of course, I'll have to charge my commission. Ten per cent! That's only fair. And I'll have to add twenty for the paint and canvas."

"Per cent?"

"Dollars."

"Fair enough," said the man, looking rather relieved.

"It *is* beautiful," the woman said.

"Are you happy now?" he asked her in a soothing voice.

"I am," she said. "I am *so* happy."

"Can I pay American Express?" he asked.

"Surely," said Mrs Lacey. "As long as you don't mind paying *their* commission."

"Fair enough," the man gulped. "But now I want to know what's going on. In the painting, I mean."

Arkady and I crept up behind the Americans and watched Old Stan point his bony finger at the large blue circle on the canvas.

It was the Eternal Home, he explained, of the Honey-ant Ancestor at Tátátá. And suddenly it was as though we could see the row on row of honey-ants, their bodies striped and gleaming, bursting with nectar in their cells beneath the roots of the mulga tree. We saw the ring of flame-red earth around the entrance to their nest, and the routes of their migration as they spread to other places.

"The circles," Mrs Lacey added helpfully, "are honey-ant ceremonial centres. The 'tubes', as you call them, are Dreaming-tracks."

The American man was captivated. "And can we go and look for these Dreaming-tracks? Out there, I mean? Like at Ayer's Rock? Some place like that?"

"They can," she said. "*You* can't."

"You mean they're invisible?"

"To you. Not to them."

"Then where are they?"

71 **Goodee** *(exclam.)* showing that one is pleased
75 **archly** in a teasing way
77 **to rustle his lips** to rub his dry lips together
79 **rigmarole** *here:* a show put on for the tourists
83 **canvas** material on which oil paintings are done
94 **Arkady** the narrator's friend, son of Russian immigrants
96 **the Eternal Home** place in the earth the Honey-ant ancestor went back to after the Dreamtime (cf. box, page 51)

What the Aborigines see ...

What the Americans see ...

118 **to dab** *here:* to dry a tear
126 **some nerve** *(exclam.) here:* how impolite of her!

"Everywhere," she said. "For all I know there's a Dreaming-track running right through the middle of my shop."

"Spooky," the wife giggled.

"And only *they* can see it?"

"Or sing it," Mrs Lacey said. "You can't have a track without a song."

"And these tracks run every place?" the man asked. "All over Australia?"

"Yes," said Mrs Lacey, sighing with satisfaction at having found a catchy phrase. "The song and the land are one."

"Amazing!" he said.

The American woman had pulled out her handkerchief and was dabbing the corners of her eyes. I thought for one moment she was going to kiss old Stan. She knew the painting was a thing done for white men, but he had given her a glimpse of something rare and strange, and for that she was very grateful.

Mrs Lacey readjusted her spectacles to fill out the American Express form. Arkady waved goodbye to Stan and we heard the triumphant *rrumpff* of the machine as we went out on to the street.

"What a woman!" I said.

"Some nerve," said Arkady. "Come on. Let's go and get a drink."

From The Songlines *by Bruce Chatwin, London: Picador, 1988, pp. 27–31.*

Exploring the text

1 a) What do you learn about Aboriginal dot-paintings in the extract?
b) Compare your answer in a) with your impressions of the photos on pp. 50–51.

2 Which aspects of traditional Aboriginal life does the novel extract illustrate?

3 a) What is your impression of the American couple? Consider both their behaviour and the way they talk.
b) Analyse the relationship between the Aboriginal and white characters in the scene.

4 a) How would you characterize the overall *tone* the narrator uses?
b) To what extent does the *mode of narration* used help to create this tone?

Mode of narration
refers to the point of view from which a story is told. Cf. 'narrator', glossary pp. 190–191.

A step further

- Letter
  Imagine the American couple wants to order another dot-painting. Write a letter to Mrs Lacey for them. Refer to your first purchase and state the size, colours, theme and delivery terms that you require. Cf. p. 111 for ideas on how to write a letter.
- Conversation
  What impression may the scene in the gallery have made on the narrator and Arkady? Imagine they talk about it later in the pub. In pairs act out their conversation as you imagine it to have been.
- Aboriginal culture
  If you would like to find out more about:
  - forms and meanings of Aboriginal art, type the key words "Aboriginal Art" into a search engine such as google.com or try www.aboriginalaustralia.com .
  - Dreamtime stories, check under 'stories' at www.dreamtime.net.au/main.cfm .
  - the past and present situation of Aboriginal people in Australia, you could check:
    - www.hartford-hwp.com/archives (a portal of links and resources)
    - http://didjshop.com.au/didjlinks/links_AbOz.html (links to Aboriginal Australia).

Before you read

- Look at the photo and the extract from a poem by Bill Neidjie on this page. What do you imagine the significance of Uluru to be for the Aboriginal Anangu people in the "Red Heart" of Australia?

Land

Our story is in the land.
It is written in those sacred places.
My children will look after those places,
that's the law.
No-one can walk close to those sacred places.
No difference for Aborigine or white European,
that's the law.
We can't break law.

From "Land" by Bill Neidjie, Gagudju Man, *Marleston S.A.: J B Books, 2002, p. 32.*

Uluru, also known by the colonial name Ayers Rock.

Please don't climb our rock

The traditional owners of the world's largest monolith hope that the debut appearance of the Olympic torch here this week will help get the message out that their most sacred of sites should not be climbed on.

The steep ascent of the 348-metres high Ayers Rock is on most tourists' itineraries, despite the death of at least one climber a year, but the indigenous Anangu want it to stop.

Cassidy Uluru, the youngest of three brothers named after the rock and who was involved in the lighting of the torch on Thursday, said the debate about whether to climb was a matter of manners.

"If I go to another man's land, I would ask that man how I should act on his land," he said through an interpreter. "If I go to Melbourne or Sydney, I would ask someone who lives there what is right to do."

The Anangu are also lobbying for the colonial name, Ayers Rock, given by early explorers to commemorate a long-forgotten state governor, to be dropped in favour of its ancient title, Uluru.

It is estimated that fewer than half of the 400,000 people who venture deep into the red centre of this continent each year try to climb the rock, but to many white Australians it is almost a rite of passage.

The traditional owners of the surrounding world heritage site, Uluru-Kata Tjuta National Park, which is jointly managed with the federal government, have not banned the rock's ascent but discourage it for spiritual and safety reasons.

The ascent is closed when winds are high or temperatures exceed 36 C (97 F) but some locals are concerned that closing the climb altogether will damage business. One tour operator said the debate was driven by politics as much as beliefs. "There are two things people come for and that's to climb the rock and see the Aborigines," he said. "They won't take the climb away as they'd lose too much money."

By Christopher Zinn, The Guardian, *June 10, 2000.*

1 **world's largest monolith** this is actually Mt. Augustus, Western Australia, which is twice the size of Uluru
5 **indigenous** native
18 **rite of passage** ceremony marking the move to a new stage of development
19 **world heritage site** place that must be protected because of its beauty or uniqueness; UNESCO has put togther a list of sites
19 **Kata Tjuta** red rock formations west of Uluru, forming part of the National Park

Mourning closes Ayers Rock

6 **adverse** damaging
15 **to jeopardise** to endanger
17 **Northern Territory** Australia is divided into six states and two territories (Australian Capital Territory and Northern Territory)
22 **ancestral** of family members who lived long ago
22 **dreamtime** cf. box, p. 51

Uluru, the red sandstone rock which lures thousands of tourists to the arid centre of Australia every year, is to close for three weeks after the death of one of its Aboriginal owners.

Politicians and tour operators yesterday appealed to the Australian prime minister to stop the shutdown of the Aboriginal sacred site, formerly known as Ayers Rock, fearing adverse effects on tourism.

Uluru-Kata Tjuta national park officers announced a ban on climbing the largest monolith in the world, 280 miles south-west of Alice Springs, out of respect for the family of Tony Tjamiwa, who died last weekend. Tjamiwa was a key figure in negotiating the return of the rock to his Anangu people in 1985.

The 348-metre climb of Uluru is one of the highlights for its 400,000 annual visitors, although the rock is periodically closed because of high winds or excessive heat. Aborigines would prefer people not to clamber over their sacred site at all.

Although the national park and a six-mile walk around Uluru's base remain open, tour operators condemned the ban, saying it could jeopardise the multimillion-dollar tourist industry focused on the region.

The Northern Territory's chief minister, Denis Burke, called for the immediate reopening of the rock, saying a suitable compromise would be to close the monolith for the day of the funeral.

Tjamiwa was one of the owners of his people's creation story, which explains the role of Uluru. Anangu elders say the route over the rock is sacred as part of the route taken by ancestral wallaby men during their "dreamtime".

By Patrick Barkham, The Guardian, *May 16, 2001.*

Websites

Find out about *Ayers Rock* and the *dreamtime* stories at: www.crystalinks.com/ayersrock.html, or type the words in italics above into www.google.com. Check out the New South Wales Aboriginal Land Council website: www.alc.org.au/ for information about Aboriginal land claims.

Exploring the texts

1 Collect all of the facts about Uluru in the two newspaper articles.
2 Why is climbing Uluru so controversial? Refer to the two articles from the *Guardian* and also to Bill Neidjie's poem on page 55 in your answer.
3 Would you consider the articles to be neutral and objective, or biased towards a particular group? Analyse both the content and the way information is presented.

A step further

- Imagine you book a trip to Uluru only to be informed later that you may walk or drive around the rock, but not climb it. Depending on your reaction, write a letter to **one** of the following:
  - Denis Burke to protest against the ban;
  - Cassidy Uluru to support the Aborigines' plea not to climb the sacred site.
- How would a popular / tabloid newspaper report on the planned three-week closure of Uluru? Rewrite the above article for a tabloid, taking the following points into consideration:
  - What kind of headline would be suitable?
  - Which aspects would you emphasize?
  - Who would you quote to support your arguments?
  - How would you structure your text?
  - What kind of language and register would you use?

  For further ideas on how to write newspaper texts cf. skills file, page 188.

Before you read

- Read the information in the box below. Then try to imagine the effect the assimilation policy has had on children who were taken away from their families. How may they have felt at the time? How may they feel today?

The stolen generation

Between 1910 and 1971 thousands of light-skinned Aboriginal children were taken from their homes and families and placed in white homes or boarding schools, often hundreds of miles away from their Aboriginal families. The aim of this policy was to assimilate Aborigines into white Australian society. Many of the children never saw their Aboriginal families again. Problems that have arisen from the policy include difficulties holding down a job, severe psychological damage, alcoholism, drug abuse and a high rate of suicide. Since the official end of this policy, civil rights groups have been fighting to make the Australian government acknowledge its responsibility, apologize to victims and pay compensation.

Child of the stolen generation

John was removed from his family as an infant in the 1940s. He spent his first years in Bomaderry Children's Home at Nowra. At 10 he was transferred to Kinchela.

We didn't have a clue where we came from. We thought the Sisters were our parents. They didn't tell anybody – any of the kids – where they came from. Babies were coming in nearly every day. Some kids came in at two, three, four days old – not months – but days. They were just placed in the home and it was run by Christian women and all the kids thought it was one big family. We didn't know what it meant by 'parents' 'cause we didn't have parents and we thought those women were our mothers.

What does the photo tell you about relationships within traditional Aboriginal families?

It was drummed into our heads that we were white.

I was definitely not told that I was Aboriginal. What the Sisters told us was that we had to be white. It was drummed into our heads that we were white. It didn't matter what shade you were. We thought we were white. They said you can't talk to any of them coloured people because you're white.

I can't remember anyone from the welfare coming there. If they did, I can't remember. We hardly saw any visitors whatsoever. None of the other kids had visits from their parents. No visits from family. The worst part is, we didn't know we had a family.

When you got to a certain age – like I got to 10 years old, they just told us we were going on a train trip. We all lined up with our little ports [school cases] with a bible inside. That's all that was in the ports, see. We really treasured that – we thought it was a good thing that we had something. The old man from La Perouse took us from Sydney – well actually from Bomaderry to Kinchela Boys' Home. That's when our problems really started – you know!

This is where we learned that we weren't white.

This is where we learned that we weren't white. First of all they took you in through these iron gates and took our little ports off us. Stick it in the fire with your little

3 **the Sisters** nuns working at a mission station
15 **any of them** *(non-Standard)* any of those
17 **the welfare** *here:* government department for health, education and living conditions or its representatives

34 **to answer s.o. back** to argue with s.o.
35 **to knuckle** *(informal)* to beat violently
39 **bloke** *(informal) here:* boy
40 **cat-o'-nine-tails** a whip with nine strings

bible inside. They took us around to a room and shaved our hair off. They gave you your clothes and stamped a number on them. They never called you by your name; they called you by your number. That number was stamped on everything.

If we answered an attendant back, we were 'sent up the line'. Now I don't know if you can imagine, 79 boys punching the hell out of you – just knuckling you. Even your brother, your cousin.

They had to – if they didn't do it, they were sent up the line. When the boys who had broken ribs or broken noses – they'd have to pick you up and carry you right through to the last bloke. Now that didn't happen once – that happened every day.

Before I went to Kinchela, they used to use the cat-o'nine-tails on the boys instead of being sent up the line. This was in the 30s and early 40s.

Kinchela Boys' Home

Over a period of 47 years an estimated 400 Aborigines grew up in Kinchela Boys' Home after being taken from their families. The home was finally closed in 1971.

They thought you were animals.

Kinchela was a place where they thought you were animals. You know it was like a place where they go around and kick us like a dog. It was just like a prison. [...]

We never went into town. The school was in the home. All we did was work, work, work. Every six months you were dressed up. Oh mate! You were done up beautiful – white shirt. The welfare used to come up from Bridge St, the main bloke, the superintendent to check the home out – every six months.

We were prisoners from when we were born. The girls who went to Cootamundra and the boys who went to Kinchela – we were all prisoners. Even today they have our file number so we're still prisoners you know. And we'll always be prisoners while our files are in archives.

Confidential evidence 436, New South Wales, Human Rights and Equal Opportunity Commission, Reconciliation and Social Justice Library.

Exploring the text

1 What experiences does John recall from his time at the mission station and the boys' home?
2 How was he made to feel that being an Aborigine was something inferior?
3 What makes John's testimony so moving? You should consider both what he talks about and how he puts his experiences into words.

Websites

Australian Human Rights and Equal Opportunity Commission: www.hreoc.gov.au/social_justice/stolen_children/

Information about the Aborigines today is available from the Australian Board of Statistics at www.abs.gov.au .

A step further

- Put yourself in the shoes of an Aborigine who was taken from his / her family and placed in a children's home. Write a letter to the Australian government asking for an apology and compensation. Check out the websites on the left and refer to page 111 for ideas about writing letters.
- Write the script for a short play or scene for **one** of the following situations:
  - Aboriginal men and women talk about their experiences as stolen children;
  - a supervisor at the boys' home who wants to help the Aboriginal children talks to a welfare officer who is in favour of the assimilation policy. What arguments might the two characters put forward?
- Imagine John's story is turned into a film. Write an outline of the plot including the years after John leaves the boys' home.

Before you read

- What hopes and demands are reflected in the extracts from the declaration drafted by Aboriginal and Torres Strait Islander leaders?

Australian Declaration Towards Reconciliation, 2000

"We, the peoples of Australia, of many origins as we are, make a commitment to go on together in a spirit of reconciliation. We value the unique status of Aboriginal and Torres Strait Islander peoples as the original owners and custodians of lands and waters. [...] Reaffirming the human rights of all Australians, we respect and recognize continuing customary laws, beliefs and traditions. [...] Our nation must have the courage to own the truth, to heal the wounds of its past so that we can move on together at peace with ourselves. [...] As we walk the journey of healing, one part of the nation apologises and expresses its sorrow and sincere regret for the injustices of the past, so the other part accepts the apologies and forgives. [...] Our hope is for a united Australia that respects this land of ours; values the Aboriginal and Torres Strait Islander heritage; and provides justice and equity for all."

www.law.mq.edu.au/Units/law309/reconciliation.htm#adtrcar

4 **customary laws** *here:* laws accepted by everybody
5 **to own the truth** *here:* to say s.th. is true

Over to you!

- Now that you have dealt with a number of texts on the history, traditions and situation of Aboriginal people in Australia today, you can decide which points in the following article interest you in particular and how you want to analyse them. You could, for example:
  - share your point of view with the writer in the form of an e-mail;
  - prepare and give a short talk about the need for apology and reconciliation. You will find information at the websites on the left. Cf. also skills file, pp. 182–183.

Over to you

Websites

www.reconciliation.org.au
www.racismnoway.com.au
www.apology.com.au

Australian reconciliation off the cards

The year 2000 was supposed to have been the year that white and indigenous Australians were reconciled.

But last week, the government body given the task of determining what "reconciliation" should be was disbanded, with its final recommendations rejected by Australian prime minister John Howard.

"Reconciliation is and should be an unstoppable force," said Mr Howard in an upbeat address at the Council for Aboriginal Reconciliation's closing conference last Thursday, where the council delivered its final recommendations.

Both Mr Howard and the council were keen to emphasise the progress towards reconciliation. In the years since parliament voted to create the Council for Aboriginal Reconciliation in 1991, there has emerged a clear acknowledgement of the existence of the "stolen generation" – those Aboriginal children forcibly detached from their parents and their culture to be brought up in white children's homes and foster homes.

Mr Howard's position on reconciliation has also softened, from hostility to acceptance, in recognition that he was out of step with the majority of Australians. One million people joined reconciliation marches this year, a greater proportion of the population than those whose protests mobilised the black civil rights movement in America in the 1960s.

Mr Howard and the council agreed that reconciliation – reducing the inequalities between white and black Australians as well as healing the wounds from 212 years of white settlement – is not something that could or should be definitely completed.

Aboriginal flag

Torres Strait Islander flag

Look at the two flags and try to interpret them.

4 **to disband** *opp. of* to form a group
7 **upbeat** optimistic
15 **hostility** strong opposition

31 **steadfastly** continually
34 **flatly** completely
35 **to vilify s.o.** to criticize s.o. harshly
47 **tertiary** ['tɜːʃərɪ] **education** refers to college or university
49 **with his hand on the tiller** as the person responsible
59 **to bolster** to encourage
67 **to confer** to give

A private organisation, Reconciliation Australia, is to be established with A $ 5.5 m (£ 2.07 m) of government money to continue the process next year. A reconciliation "mall" will also be built in Canberra, containing a memorial to the stolen generation.

But Aden Ridgeway, Australia's only Aboriginal senator, criticised the decision to shift reconciliation to a private body. "The government is the one responsible for showing leadership, it's the one that's got to provide the backup and the resources and it's also got to give the legislative guarantees," he said.

Legislative guarantees, and a formal apology, are two things Mr Howard's government steadfastly refuses to give.

Reconciliation began in 1991 with calls for a treaty between the government and its indigenous citizens, and ended again on Thursday with another call for a treaty, which Mr Howard flatly rejected.

Admired by some for his pragmatism and vilified by others for his lack of imagination, the Australian prime minister preaches "practical" reconciliation, improving Aborigines' health and employment prospects.

He is suspicious of treaties, fearing they are divisive. "You make treaties with other countries, you don't make treaties with each other," he once said.

Statistics suggest that Aborigines already live in another country. They can expect to live 20 years less than white Australians, while Aboriginal men are 15 times more likely to spend time in jail than their white counterparts.

Years of practical multibillion dollar welfare programmes have yet to solve these problems. In areas such as Cape York, Aborigines' health is getting worse, according to every available measure, bar infant mortality.

The government points to an 18 % increase in the number of Aborigines undertaking tertiary education since 1996, but levels of indigenous unemployment remain as bad as ever: 26 % compared to 8 % for the general Australian population.

With his hand on the tiller of a stalled reconciliation process, Mr Howard refuses to acknowledge the connection between symbolic and practical reconciliation. He says that an apology and a treaty won't solve practical problems. But his opponents argue it could only help.

A treaty, such as Canada has with its indigenous people, would provide "some formal settlement of the issues created by our shared history, where Aboriginal and Torres Strait Islander peoples were dispossessed of their lands without treaty or consent," said Evelyn Scott, chairwoman of the Council for Aboriginal Reconciliation.

Even some of Mr Howard's allies suggest that a treaty, by providing a framework of rights and obligations for the government and Aborigines, could bolster practical reconciliation and make government welfare a more positive, rights-driven process.

Noel Pearson, an influential Aboriginal lawyer from Cape York, has stimulated much debate – and approving glances from Mr Howard's government – on how to reduce welfare dependency among Aborigines.

As he says: "The Cape York people and communities are traumatised. The social conditions and problems which they face are directly related to the history of their removal from land and the treatment that they and the land have received."

But the argument that a treaty could be an education in itself, conferring respect, rights and status which could help banish a passive acceptance of welfare or ill-health, appears to be one that Mr Howard does not want to hear.

By Patrick Barkham, The Guardian, *December 11, 2000.*

Angela: Growing up in Australia

Using your skills

Would you like to learn more about how young Aborigines try to bridge the gap between their traditions and history on the one hand, and the demands and opportunities of modern society on the other? In 1998, James Moloney published the novel Angela *about the friendship between Angela, a white Australian girl, and her Aboriginal friend Gracey. The book is the last in a trilogy.*

Have you become curious to know what happens? You may want to read Angela *on your own, either out of personal interest, or for discussion and analysis in class, or as the subject of a talk or term paper. Here are some ideas to make reading the novel easier.*

Before you start

- What do you expect from the book? To help you answer this question you could:
  - look at the cover of the novel and speculate as to what happens.
  - read the blurb on the back cover and the table of contents. What central themes are dealt with in the novel? What questions are raised that you would like to have answered?

  Make a note of your expectations and questions.
- Do a web search to find out more about the setting of the novel, Brisbane and Queensland. You could check out www.queenslandholidays.com.au.

While reading: Reading log

- Read the first chapter of *Angela*, "Schoolies" and record your impressions and findings in a reading log.

After reading the first chapter

- Look at the list of expectations you made to see whether you were right.
- a) What have you learned so far about Angela and Gracey, and their families and friends? Describe how you think they live.

  b) What kind of atmosphere is created in the first chapter?

  Note down your first impressions.
- Can you answer the five "w-questions": **who** are the main characters in the novel? **what** is the first chapter about? **where** and **when** does the story take place? **why** do the characters behave, talk and think as they do?
- As you read, you may want to focus on one or two aspects of the novel (especially if you want to talk or write about them later). Can you choose one aspect based on your understanding of the first chapter? If not, here are some suggestions:
  - Growing up: What does it mean to Angela? What does it mean to Gracey?
  - Friendship: What will become of Angela's and Gracey's friendship?
  - Australian society: What does Gracey (and the reader) learn about the relationship between white Australians and Aborigines, especially about the "Stolen Generation"? How is the topic of "racism" dealt with in the novel? What forms does it take?
  - Language: List examples of Australian English and their equivalents in British English, and / or examples of special Aboriginal expressions and their meanings.

  While reading take notes about your findings, ideas and questions.

Reading log: Angela
Chapter one: Schoolies

Characters:
Angela graduating high school student, white Australian, good friend to Gracey, talkative, optimistic
Gracey Aboriginal girl, first Aboriginal student to graduate, excellent athlete, orphan who has also lost a brother, determined, proud, able to stand up for herself
Cheryl Angela's mother, sympathetic, understanding character

Setting:
Hamilton College on graduation day, November (Australian summer), much of the action takes place in a bathroom ...

Using your skills

After reading the book

- a) Did you enjoy the novel, or not? Give reasons for your answer.
  b) What was the most interesting – or disappointing – aspect?
  c) What made the book easy or difficult to read?
- Look back at your initial expectations and questions: To what extent have they been fulfilled or answered?
- Would you like to have more information about the author and the other books in the trilogy? Then type "James Moloney Angela" into a search engine and go to James Moloney's homepage.

A step further

- Talk / term paper

In order to prepare a talk or a term paper, revise the notes you made while reading the novel:

- Do you feel confident that your notes will help you to develop a coherent talk or piece of writing about your special reading focus? If not, you may want to re-read some passages in the book in order to collect more relevant information.
- Order your findings and ideas in a logical, convincing way. Do not forget to include a short introduction and a conclusion.
- Check your references to the text: have you chosen the best passages to support your ideas?
- Do not forget to check your paper for grammar and spelling mistakes.

"He's right, you know, there should be an apostrophe."

- Creative ideas

Maybe you would prefer a more personal or creative response to what you have read. Here are some ideas:

- Book review: Write a review in which you outline why you liked or disliked the book, point out its merits and weaknesses, and finish by giving your personal recommendation.
- Changing the point of view: As you will have noticed, the novel is written from Angela's perspective. It might be interesting to put yourself in Gracey's shoes and re-write a passage from her point of view, to reveal her thoughts, attitudes and feelings.
- Diary entry: You may, of course, do the same by writing a diary entry for Gracey. Be sure to choose an important moment in her development.
- Personal letter: When the novel ends, nobody – not even the reader – knows if Angela and Gracey will be able to continue their friendship in the future, or even if they are interested in doing so.
  Imagine Angela or Gracey picks up the courage to write to her former close friend some years later. What might have happened since the events in the novel and what – consequently – might she write? Will the other girl write back, and if so, what? What might the tone of the letter(s) be like?

Being Maori

Looking and thinking

a) What do the texts and pictures on this page tell you about traditional Maori life?
b) What do you know about the Maoris of New Zealand?
c) Collect your ideas from a) and b) in a mind map which you can add to as you work through this section of the chapter.

Being Maori is
... respecting your elders because they have earned it.
... having 250,000 brothers and sisters.
... buying your son new shoes because he gave his to his cousin.
... talking tough.
... believing that your canoe is most certainly better than the Queen Mary.
... having your friends and relatives accuse you of being a traitor if you earn more than $7000, wear a tie and drive a new car.
Being Maori is hard, being Maori is sad, being Maori is to laugh, being Maori is to cry, being Maori is forever.

From The Listener Bedside Book I, *originally* The Listener, *January 14, 1978.*

0 **Maori** ['maʊrɪ] native population of New Zealand (*literally*) fresh, normal, native
6 **Queen Mary** British transatlantic passenger ship

hongi (traditional Maori greeting where noses and foreheads touch)

waka (Maori canoe). Carving, as seen on the boat, is an important art form among Maoris.

haka (traditional Maori dance which expresses the feelings of the dancers)

4 **sealer** s.o. who hunts seals (= *Robben*)
5 **sovereignty** ['sɒvrəntɪ] power to make and enforce laws

Before you read

- From what you have already learnt about Aborigines in this chapter and Maoris on page 63, do you think that it was as easy to colonize New Zealand as it was Australia, or not?
- Read the fact file below and answer these questions:
  a) Why was a treaty with the Maori important for the British?
  b) What reasons did Maori chiefs have to sign such a treaty?

Maori land rights and the Treaty of Waitangi

1779	Captain James Cook arrives in what is now New Zealand. Despite attacks by Maoris, he and his crew explore and chart the islands and claim them for the British Crown. Cook's accounts attract many settlers.
1800s	European missionaries, sealers and whalers are well established in New Zealand.
1835	Declaration of Maori Independence: The British Crown recognizes the sovereignty of Maori chiefs in New Zealand.
1837	E.G. Wakefield (1796–1862) puts forward plans to make the country a British colony. These are rejected by the British Parliament, but Wakefield's company starts operating anyway. It disregards Maori land rights and sells off more and more land to British settlers. Britain competes with France for colonies in the South Pacific Ocean. Land exploitation, lawlessness among settlers and a growth in "white supremacy" worry the Maori as well as the British missionaries.
Feb. 6, 1840	The **Treaty of Waitangi** (see extracts below) is signed by more than 500 Maori chiefs and the newly-installed British Governor of New Zealand.
1840s	Supporters of the New Zealand Company oppose the treaty because it interferes with their land trading operations. They finally gain support from the Colonial Office in England.
1860s	New Zealand Wars between Maori and British take place, mainly about land rights.

2 **to cede** *(formal)* to give up
4 **sole** only
10 **to retain** to keep
11 **to yield** *here:* to give up
11 **preemption** right to buy s.th. in preference to others
12 **proprietor** owner *here:* Maori chief
12 **disposed** prepared
12 **to alienate** *here:* to sell
17 **to impart** to give

The Treaty of Waitangi

Article the first

The Chiefs [...] cede to Her Majesty the Queen of England, absolutely and without reservation, all the rights and powers of Sovereignty [...] over their respective Territories as the sole Sovereigns thereof.

Article the second

Her Majesty the Queen of England confirms and guarantees to the Chiefs and Tribes of New Zealand, and to the respective families and individuals thereof, the full, exclusive and undisturbed possession of their Lands and Estates, Forests, Fisheries, and other properties which they may collectively or individually possess, so long as it is their wish and desire to retain the same in their possession; but the Chiefs [...] yield to Her Majesty the exclusive right of Preemption over such lands as the proprietors thereof may be disposed to alienate, at such prices as may be agreed upon between the respective Proprietors and persons appointed by her Majesty to treat with them in that behalf.

Article the third

[...] Her Majesty the Queen of England extends to the Natives of New Zealand Her royal protection and imparts to them all the Rights and Privileges of British Subjects.[...]

Exploring the text

1 Working in groups, explain the main ideas in articles 1 to 3 of the Treaty of Waitangi on page 64. You can record the key points in a grid like the one below.

The Maori		The British Crown	
get	give	gets	grants

2 Examine lines 10–14 of the treaty. What problems do you anticipate?

3 What exactly does "Article the third" on page 64 imply? What benefits did the Maoris probably expect to have:
a) from the protection of the Queen of England?
b) as holders of the rights and privileges of British citizens?

A step further

- Evaluating statements

Look at the statements below which were posted in an internet forum over 160 years after the signing of the Treaty of Waitangi. What light do they throw on the Treaty?

"The fact that the British Crown recognized Maori sovereignty did not mean that the settlers were going to follow suit. The lawlessness continued. [...] Maori chiefs around Northland had had enough. The Treaty of Waitangi was signed in an attempt to give the British Crown authority over settlers in Aotearoa." *www.arena.org.nz*

"The Treaty is a contract between the Crown and Maori. The Crown has never honoured its side of the contract. The Treaty of Waitangi was an agreement to share power in New Zealand."
http://aotearoa.wellington.net.nz/he/wai2000.htm

"Signing the Treaty was the best thing that Maori could ever have done for themselves. I mean look at the Aborigines, they were classed as flora and fauna right up to the 1970s. We as Maori could be a lot worse off."
New Zealand.com Discussion Forum
www.NewZealand.com/forums/index.php3, posted by Cam_NZ, February 12, 2002.

2 **to follow suit** to do the same as others have done
4 **Aotearoa** *(Maori)* New Zealand
11 **to be badly off** to be in a bad situation

- Role play / discussion

Not all of the Maori chiefs signed the Treaty, and there will have been serious disagreements before the first chiefs did. There will also have been some differences of opinion among the British leaders.

- Divide the class into four groups: Maori chiefs who plan to sign the Treaty, Maori chiefs who are sceptical about it, representatives of the British Crown, and members of the New Zealand Company (cf. fact file, page 64).
- Prepare questions which you wish to ask and / or arguments you want to put forward either for or against the Treaty. Then act out a meeting in class.

- Discussion

a) How could the Treaty have been improved in 1840 to protect the Maoris' rights more effectively?
b) In your opinion, would these improvements have been possible at the time it was signed, or not?

Before you read

- **Being Maori is** owning land and not being able to use it.
  Compare the above statement with the information in the fact file on page 64 and then say what you think happened in the years after the land wars in the 1860s.
- On the basis of the fact file below, discuss whether the Waitangi Tribunal can compensate the Maori for losses resulting from the colonization of New Zealand.

The fight for Maori land rights

1960	Maori land protests; Maori demonstrate to force the Pakeha government to fulfil their part of the Treaty of Waitangi.
1967	The government introduces measures to improve Maori land.
1970s	Demonstrations for the recognition of Maori cultural identity and land rights intensify; the public starts coming to terms with Maori issues.
1975	Treaty of Waitangi Act: A permanent commission makes recommendations to the government on how to settle Maori land claims.
1977	The Waitangi Tribunal is established.
1995	Ngai Tahu tribe receive land, NZ$170 million in compensation for confiscated land and some fishery rights.
1996	15 Maori MPs enter the 120 member Parliament.
1998	Waitangi Tribunal order: the government is to return confiscated Maori land to its owners.

1 **Pakeha** ['pɑ:keɑ:] *(Maori)* New Zealander of European descent
9 **confiscated** taken away officially

The following text is taken from a short story by Maori writer Patricia Grace and refers to events in New Zealand in the 1960s and 1970s. The main character in the story, Billy, has been made redundant. His wife Makere wants him to find a new job but he spends his time reading about thc colonization of New Zealand.

- Based on the information above, what do you expect the short story extract to be about, and what do you expect the tone to be like?

Ngati Kangaru

"The Wakefields' plan was based on the assumption that vast areas – if possible, every acre – of New Zealand would be bought for a trifle, the real payment to the people of the land being their 'civilising' ..." Hee hee, that's crafty. They called it 'high and holy work'."

And here. There was this 'exceptional Law' written about in one of EG's anonymous publications, where chiefs sold a heap of land for a few bob and received a section 'in the midst of emigrants' in return. But har, har, the chiefs weren't allowed to live on this land until they had 'learned to estimate its value'. [...] Then there was this 'adopt-a-chief scheme'. [...] They gave out coats of arms, lessons in manners and how to mind your p's and q's, that sort of stuff. I like it. You could do anything as long as you had a 'worthy cause'." [...]

[Billy finds his "worthy cause" when he learns that his cousin Hiko, who lives in Australia, is preparing a mass return of Maori to their homeland. The main problem is to find somewhere for the returning Maori to settle.]

"So all we need," said Billy to Makere, later in the evening, is a vast area of land 'as far as the eye can see'."

"Is that all?" said Makere.

0 **Ngati Kangaru** The Kangaroo Clan
1 **Wakefields** E.G. Wakefield (cf. fact file, page 64) was helped in his colonization plans by his brothers William and Arthur
2 **trifle** *here:* small amount of money, usu. s.th. of small value
3 **crafty** cleverly dishonest
6 **bob** *(informal, old)* shilling; coin worth about five pence

"Of 'delightful climate' and 'rich soil' that is 'well watered and coastal'. Of course it'll need houses on it too, the best sort of houses, luxury style."

"Like at Claire Vista," said Makere. Billy jumped out of his chair and his eyes jumped out, "Brilliant, Ma, brilliant." He planted a kiss on her unimpressed cheek and went scrabbling in a drawer for pen and paper so that he could write to Hiko:

"… the obvious place for the first settlement of Ngati Kangaru, it being 'commodious and attractive'. But more importantly, as you know, Claire Vista is the old stamping ground of our iwi that was confiscated at the end of last century, and is now a luxury holiday resort. Couldn't be apter. We must time the arrival of our people for late autumn when the holidaymakers have all left. I'll take a trip up there on Saturday and get a few snaps, which I'll send. Then I'll draw up a plan and we can do our purchases. Between us we should be able to see everyone home and housed by June next year. Timing your arrival will be vital. I suggest you book flights well in advance so that you all arrive at once." […]

"You'll have a hundred families all living in one house, I suppose," said Makere, "because that's all you'll get with four thousand dollars a family."

"Possess yourselves of the homes," said Billy.

"What's that supposed to mean?"

"It's a 'wasteland'. They're waste homes. They're all unoccupied. Why have houses unoccupied when there are people wanting to occupy them?"

"Bullshit. Hana and Gav didn't say the houses were unoccupied."

"That's because it's summertime. End of March everyone's gone and there are good homes going to waste. 'Reclaiming and cultivating a moral wilderness', that's what we're doing, 'serving to the highest degree', that's what we're on about, 'according to a deliberate and methodical plan'."

"Doesn't mean you can just walk in and take over."

"Not unless we get all the locks changed."

By the end of summer the money was coming in and Billy had all the deeds of sale printed, ready for signing. Makere thought he was loopy thinking that all these rich wallahs would sign their holiday homes away.

"Not *them*," Billy said. "You don't get *them* to sign. You get other people. That's how it was done before. Give out pressies – tobacco, biscuits, pipes, that sort of things, so that they, whoever they are, will mark the parchments."

Makere was starting to get the hang of it, but she huffed all the same.

"Now I'm going out to get us a van," Billy said. "Then we'll buy the trifles. After that, tomorrow and the next day, we'll go and round up some derros to do the signing."

It took a week to get the signatures, and during that time Billy and the kids handed out – to park benchers in ten different parts of the city – one hundred bottles of whisky, one hundred packets of hot pies and one hundred old overcoats.

"What do you want our signatures for?" they asked.

"Deeds of sale for a hundred properties up in Claire Vista," Billy said.

"The only Claire Vista we've got is where our bums hit the benches."

"Well, look here." Billy showed them the maps with the allotments marked out on them and they were interested and pleased. "Waste homes," Billy explained. "All these fellas have got plenty of other houses all over the place, but they're simple

25 **iwi** *(Maori)* tribe
30 **vital** extremely important
45 **deed** legal document
46 **loopy** *(informal)* crazy
47 **wallah** ['wɒlə] *(Anglo-Indian)* s.o. who has power
49 **pressie** ['prezɪ] *(informal)* present
50 **parchment** *here:* document
51 **to get the hang of s.th.** *here:* to understand how s.th. works
51 **to huff** [ʌ] to be annoyed
53 **derro** *short for* **derelict** homeless person
61 **allotment** piece of land; *here:* enough for a house and garden
63 **fella** *(informal)* fellow; *here:* person

65 **aptitude** ability
68 **Te Whare Ngahau o …** Meeting House of …
71 **dell** small valley
71 **glen** valley
75 **to roll one's eyes round** cf. photo of haka, page 63
78 **Ara Hakena** Hakena Road
80 **lilo** ['laɪləʊ] airbed
84 **tee** *(informal)* T-shirt
84 **zinked** covered with protective lotion
90 **spanking** *here:* completely
91 **sea urchin** *Seeigel*
91 **prow** front part of a ship
94 **in unison** at the same time and in the same way
101 **singlet** shirt without sleeves (= *Ärmel*)
102 **baggies** loose-fitting swimming trunks
102 **jandals** rubber sandals
104 **dinghy** ['dɪŋgɪ] small rubber boat

people who know nothing about how to fully utilise their properties and they can 'scarcely cultivate the earth'. But who knows they might have a 'peculiar aptitude for being improved'. It's 'high and holy work', this." […]

On the fifth of November there was a big welcome-home ceremony, with speeches and food and fireworks at the Claire Vista hall, which had been renamed Te Whare Ngahau o Ngati Kangaru. At the same time Claire Vista was given back its former name of Ikanui and discussions took place regarding the renaming of streets, parks, boulevards, avenues, courts, dells and glens after its reclaimers.

By the time the former occupants began arriving in mid-December, all the signs in the old Claire Vista had been changed and the new families were established in their new homes. It was a lovely, soft and green life at that time of the year. One in which you could stand barefooted on grass or sand in your shorts and shirt and roll your eyes round. You could slide your boat down the ramp, cruise about, toss the anchor over and put your feet up, fish, pull your hat down. Whatever.

On the day that the first of the holidaymakers arrived at 6 Ara Hakena, with their bags of holiday outfits, Christmas presents, CDs, six-packs, cartons of groceries, snorkels, lilos and things, the man and woman and two sub-teenagers were met by Mere and Jim Hakena, their three children, Jim's parents and a quickly gathering crowd of neighbours.

At first, Ruby and Gregory in their cotton co-ordinates, and Alister with his school friend in their stonewash jeans, apricot and applegreen tees, and noses zinked pink and orange, thought they could've come to the wrong house, especially since its address seemed to have changed and the neighbours were different.

But how could it be the wrong house? It was the same windowy place in stained weatherboard, designed to suit its tree environment and its rocky outlook. There was the new skylit extension and glazed brick barbecue. Peach tree with a few green ones. In the drive in front of the underhouse garage they could see the spanking blue boat with *Sea Urchin* in cursive along its prow. The only difference was that the boat was hitched to a green Landcruiser instead of to a red Range Rover.

"That's our boat," said Ruby.

"I doubt it," said Mere and Ken together, folding their arms in unison.

"He paid good money for that," a similarly folded-armed neighbour said. "It wasn't much but it was good."

Ruby and Alister didn't spend too much more time arguing. They went back to Auckland to put the matter in the pink hands of their lawyers.

It was two days later that the next holidaymakers arrived, this time at 13 Tiritiroa. After a long discussion out on the front lawn, Mai and Poto with their Dobermen and a contingent of neighbours felt a little sorry for their visitors in their singlets, baggies and jandals, and invited them in.

"You can still have your holiday, why not?" said Mai. "There's the little flat at the back and we could let you have the dinghy. It's no trouble."

The visitors were quick to decline the offer. They went away and came back two hours later with a policeman, who felt the heat but did the best he could, peering at the papers that Mai and Poto had produced, saying little.

"Perhaps you should come along with me and lay a formal complaint," he suggested to the holidayers. Mai, Poto and a few of the neighbours went fishing after they'd gone.

From "Ngati Kangaru" by Patricia Grace, The Sky People, *Penguin Books (NZ), 1994, quoted from the edition of The Women's Press Ltd., London, 1995, pp. 27–43.*

Exploring the text

1 Describe how Billy plans to secure a place for the returning Maori to settle.

2 How does he use historical events and documents to justify his actions?

3 a) In groups, think of three to five adjectives each to characterize the Maori and non-Maori characters in the extract.
b) What do you think Patricia Grace was trying to achieve by characterizing the two groups in such a way?

4 Which of the following words would you use to describe the tone of the text, and why?
humorous – absurd – realistic – *satirical* – wishful – bitter – ironic

Satire ['sætaɪə]
combines humour and criticism in order to expose and ridicule evil and stupidity. It attempts to correct and reform.

A step further

- Target group
In your opinion, who is the main target group of the short story – the Maori or the non-Maori New Zealanders, or both? Argue your point. You could refer to your answer in "Exploring the text, 3" above for ideas.
- Language
a) Patricia Grace often mixes English and Maori in her writings, usually to a greater extent than in the text printed here. Try to think of reasons why she does so.
b) Would you have preferred a 'straight' English text, or not?
- Possible ending
a) The short story does not end here, but a few months later. Discuss whether the ending is most likely to be: surprising – serious – one in which the non-Maori get their property back – one in which the Maori triumph – happy for both parties.
b) Develop your ideas in small groups and then write your own ending.
- Creative tasks
Imagine how the media cover the resettling of Claire Vista by the returning Maori. Form groups and do **one** of the following tasks:
  - Write a *news report* for a serious national newspaper. Refer to the skills file on page 188 for ideas.
  - Write a *news story* for a tabloid / popular newspaper. Decide whether your story is going to be pro- or anti-Maori. Refer to the skills file on page 188.
  - Record a radio interview with Billy.
  - Plan a one-minute television newscast.

News report
deals objectively with events of general importance. It concentrates on the five 'w's': who, what when, where, why. These questions are usually answered in the first paragraph, and extra information is given in the remaining paragraphs.
News stories
may include the reporter's impressions and opinions and / or quotations from eye witnesses or experts.

Before you read

- **Being Maori is**

  ... punching a Pakeha in the mouth for saying you are dumb.

  ... to listen to all-white administrators telling you that we are all New Zealanders and not know what that is.

  a) What do the above statements reveal about relations between the Maori and non-Maori New Zealanders?

  b) Try to imagine situations in which each of these statements might apply.

- a) Why would someone hang a pair of antlers on a wall?

  b) What do you expect a short story entitled "The Pakeha judge's antlers on the wall" to be about?

The Pakeha judge's antlers on the wall

In the following short story extract, Simeon, the only Maori in a group of non-Maori students, is going to watch a court in session. He has already got into trouble with his teacher, Miss Dalrymple, for speaking Maori and is extremely ill at ease.

Clerk Simpson guided us to Judge Forbes' schedule. One by one we filed past and oohed and aahed at the number of cases on his plate.

JUDGE FORBES, Presiding Judge

9 a.m.	White v. Hakopa
10.30 a.m.	Crown v. Wharepapa
1 p.m.	Crown v. Karaitiana
2 p.m.	Williamson v. Heke

On and on and on. Page after page of cases involving being drunk and disorderly, murder, intent to obstruct justice, manslaughter, casting offensive matter in public, grievous assault, car stealing, domestic dispute, indecent behaviour, theft, petty larceny, land dispute, attempt to defraud, and so on.

"Simeon?" Miss Dalrymple interrupted. "Don't take up all the time. Let someone else look."

I stepped to one side. The rest of the class had their turn. When we had become suitably impressed Clerk Simpson said, "Well then, let's go into the public gallery, shall we?"

We filed into Courtroom No. 1.

This was the place of judgement. Here in this large room panelled with polished wood and hushed with the weight of legal process, people were put on display, like deer's antlers, their futures determined with a stroke of the gavel. Over there, higher than anybody else, was where the judge sat. In front of him sat the lawyer for the defence. At right a small corridor led to the room where the defendant waited to be called for trial. In front were the seats for the public.

"Not a word," Miss Dalrymple hissed.

The public gallery was packed. I knew just about all the people there. All of them stared straight ahead, down a narrow funnel of vision, as if afraid to see who was sitting left and right. That suited me fine. I hunched down, hoping I wouldn't be seen either. I felt as if I was on the wrong side.

The session that morning seemed to be one where the defendants had already pleaded guilty and were being processed for sentencing.

2 **on s.o.'s plate** having s.th. to deal with
9 **to obstruct justice** to prevent the law from working properly
10 **petty larceny** theft of items of small value
11 **to defraud** to be dishonest in order to make money
20 **gavel** judge's hammer

42 **heinous** ['heɪnəs] wicked
48 ***te rori*** *(Maori)* stupid
49 **implacability** being impossible to change

"How do you plead?"

"The defendant pleads guilty, Your Honour."

"Fined £100."

The judge lifted his gavel, and bang. A pair of antlers on the wall.

"How do you plead?"

"The defendant pleads guilty, Your Honour."

Term of imprisonment, one year."

Bang, the gavel again. Another pair of antlers.

"How do you plead?"

"The defendant pleads guilty, Your Honour."

This time the judge paused and looked gravely down at the defendant. "Your crime is a particularly heinous one in our society, young man. Assault on another person with intention to commit grievous harm must carry with it the maximum penalty available to the law. Five years imprisonment."

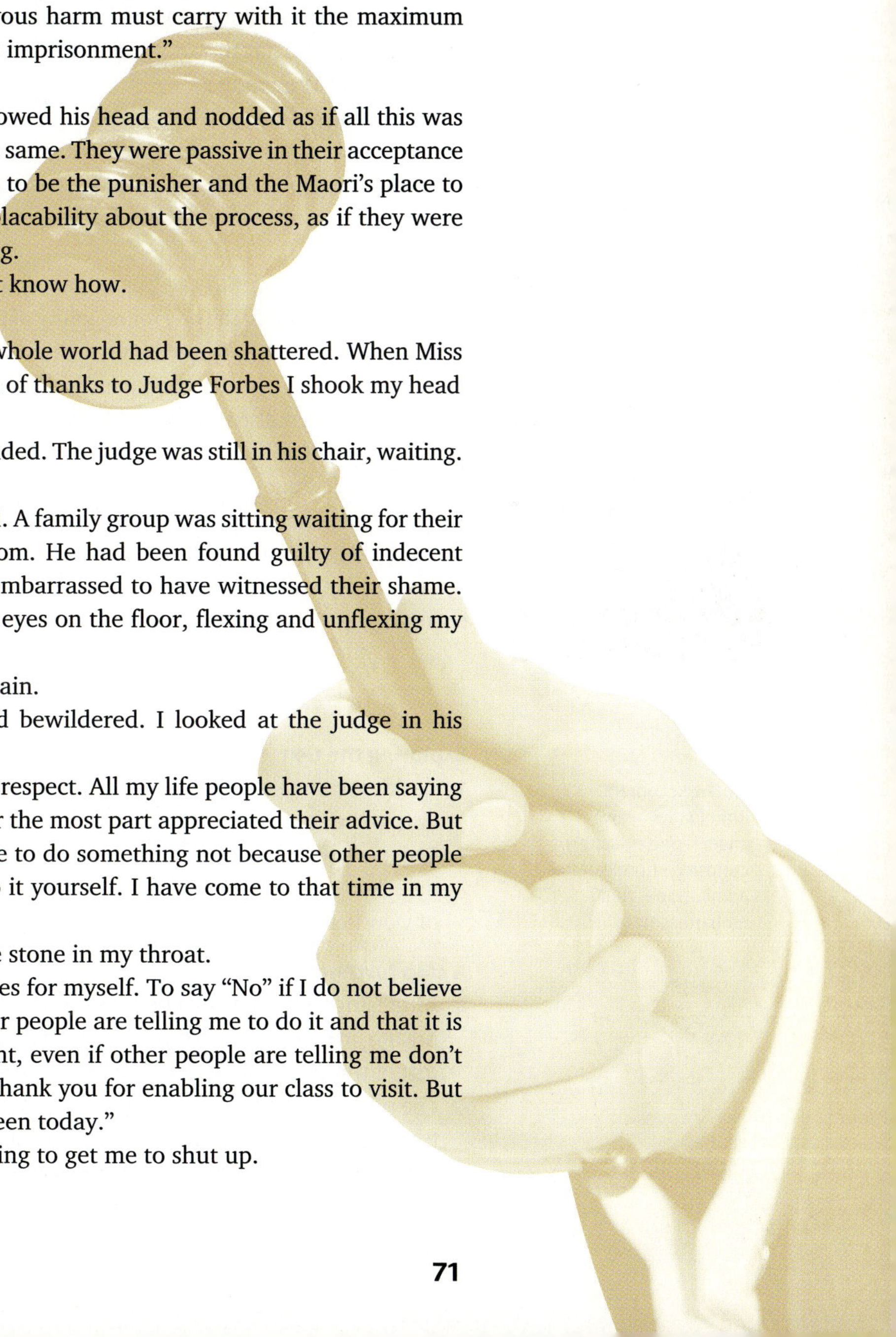

Bang. More antlers for the wall.

At each sentencing the defendant bowed his head and nodded as if all this was to be expected. His family group did the same. They were passive in their acceptance of the law and of *te rori* Pakeha's place to be the punisher and the Maori's place to be punished. There was a sense of implacability about the process, as if they were always right and we were always wrong.

Why didn't we fight back? We didn't know how.

Bang Bang Bang Bangbang ang ang

By the end of the court session my whole world had been shattered. When Miss Dalrymple asked me to give my speech of thanks to Judge Forbes I shook my head

"No."

"Just do it," Miss Dalrymple commanded. The judge was still in his chair, waiting.

Do it do it it ititit it.

The courtroom was not quite cleared. A family group was sitting waiting for their son to come out from the holding room. He had been found guilty of indecent exposure. I knew the family and was embarrassed to have witnessed their shame. For most of the proceedings I kept my eyes on the floor, flexing and unflexing my fists.

"Simeon!" Miss Dalrymple hissed again.

I wasn't angry, really. Just lost and bewildered. I looked at the judge in his ridiculous wig and –

"Sir, I am 15 years old. I mean no disrespect. All my life people have been saying to me, "Do this, do that," and I have for the most part appreciated their advice. But there must come a time when you have to do something not because other people tell you to but because you want to do it yourself. I have come to that time in my life."

I tried to swallow. There was a huge stone in my throat.

"Your Honour, I want to make choices for myself. To say "No" if I do not believe what is happening is right, even if other people are telling me to do it and that it is right. To say "Yes", if I believe it is right, even if other people are telling me don't do it. I have to start listening to me. I thank you for enabling our class to visit. But I cannot thank you for what we have seen today."

By this time Miss Dalrymple was trying to get me to shut up.

96 **to commend** to praise
103 **Ka pai …** *(Maori, literally)* Very good, that speech. Stay strong, boy / son.
107 **hongi** *(literally)* to smell; Maori greeting, cf. photo on p. 63
108 **Mahana** Simeon's clan

"There is something wrong, Your Honour, with a place like this, if the majority of the cases which come before you are Maori and are placed by Pakeha against Maori. I cannot thank you for being part of a court which enables this to happen. I cannot."

Someone in the family group began to sob.

"How can I thank you for all the Maori people you have jailed or sentenced for one crime or another? All those names in your book, do you know that I am related to all of them? Or that I know them? Sir, what is more, I know them as good people, not as names that you bang your hammer at or put in prison or make pay huge fines. That boy we met when we were just coming in, he was my cousin's boyfriend, your Honour. And what was his crime? That he swore at his employer! You call that assault? Are you telling me he should be sent to jail for that? If I thank you, what am I saying to my relations? My aunts, uncles and cousins who have appeared before you this month? That they deserved it? They didn't … " It was a cry from the depths of my heart. "They didn't."

I was almost done.

"Therefore, Your Honour, I will not thank you."

Miss Dalrymple was grim-faced as she apologised to Judge Forbes. He was thoughtful and answered – "No, the boy is entitled to his opinion. I commend him for that."

I was told to go out to the bus at once and wait there.

The family group of the boy found guilty of indecent exposure was waiting beside the kerb, hoping to see him before he was taken away. The boy's mother nodded at me, and as I passed she laid a hand to stop me. She kissed me and I felt her tears against my cheek.

Then somebody else was there. I knew who it was.

"Ka pai tena korero," he said. "Ka pai. Kia kaha, e tama. You spoke very well, young one. Very well. Your grandmother would have been pleased. Continue to be strong." He shook my hand and motioned that we should hongi. Then Saul Poata came out, and his mother, Agnes Poata, began to call to him.

I touched my nose and forehead in hongi with Saul's grandfather – Rupeni Poata, arch enemy of the Mahana clan.

From Bulibasha, King of the Gypsies *by Witi Ihimaera, http://hammer.prohosting.com/~penz/aotearoa/bulibasa.htm, originally* Te Ao Marama: Contemporary Maori Writing #5, *Witi Ihimaera (ed.), 1988.*

Does the judge in the photo below correspond to your picture of Judge Forbes, or not?

Talking about emotions

fear – excitement – intimidation – awe – anger – pride – spite – curiosity – humiliation – admiration – guilt – embarrassment

Exploring the text

1 Decide which of the emotions in the box on the left Simeon experiences during his visit to the courthouse. Use quotes from the text to support your answer.
2 Simeon is the narrator of the story as well as being an active main character and a detached observer. Find examples of each role and describe the effect each point of view has on you the reader.

A step further

- After Simeon has left the courthouse, Mrs Dalrymple apologises to Judge Forbes in private. In pairs, write down your version of the scene and act it out in class. The rest of the class should decide which version is the most convincing.
- The next day Mrs Dalrymple reports the incident at a staff meeting. The teachers – two of them Maori – discuss whether to cancel further visits to the court. Collect arguments and then act out the meeting.

Before you read

a) In 1930, February 6 was declared a national holiday in New Zealand, called Waitangi Day. In 1974 it was renamed New Zealand Day. What significance does this date have, and what does the renaming of the day suggest to you?
b) The two photos below were taken on Waitangi Day in New Zealand. Characterize the attitudes of the people in the photos.

Waitangi Day with gritted teeth

It's the one day of the year when the past refuses to be another country. For a few hours we confront our tenuous hold on nationhood as Maori and Pakeha eyeball each other over the cultural, political and social divide.

The majority of people I spoke to on the day said they'd prefer a New Zealand Day on which we could all celebrate as one. It's been tried before.

I turned to the excellent website (www.nzhistory.net.nz/Gallery/treaty/index.htm) which reminded me of Norman Kirk's inaugural New Zealand Day in 1974.

February 6 had finally been declared a public holiday. To celebrate, there was what sounded like a gruelling musical extravaganza. If I ever saw it, I have wiped it from my memory. The high point was, apparently, an enormous moa laying a giant egg on the spot where the treaty was signed.

I'll stick with Waitangi Day, thanks, for all its tension, bizarre symbolic acts and power struggles. And there were signs this year that Waitangi Day could yet become the New Zealand Day many yearn for.

Maori protesters demonstrate against the Treaty of Waitangi on Waitangi Day.

A couple watch a pipe band perform at celebrations to commemorate the signing of the Treaty of Waitangi.

And Helen Clark came back. I've changed my mind about how she's handled Waitangi since Titewhai Harawira made her cry in 1998. [...]

It was a brilliant, if chilly, display of Clark doing what she does best – keeping things, including her own feelings, firmly under control. This time, she took interruptions and insults on the chin, which any leader of a free society has to be able to do.

A joyous celebration it was not. But the efforts made by almost everyone to literally save the day were heartening. It spoke, if through slighty gritted teeth, of underlying good will.

As national days go, Waitangi is still young, wracked by the tears and tantrums of adolescence. But this year it felt like a step forward rather than the usual two steps back.

Adolescents do grow up, eventually.

By Diane Wichtel, www.nzherald.co.nz,
The New Zealand Herald – New Zealand, *February 9, 2002.*

0 **with gritted teeth** *(literally)* pressed together; *here:* being determined in a difficult situation
2 **tenuous** weak
3 **to eyeball s.o.** to look at s.o. in a threatening way (cf. haka, p. 63)
10 **Norman Kirk** Prime Minister of New Zealand (1972 – 1974)
12 **gruelling** tiring
15 **moa** huge native bird of New Zealand
21 **Helen Clark** Prime Minister since 1999
22 **Titewhai Harawira** Maori activist; she interrupted Helen Clark's speech because she had disregarded Maori protocol
26 **to take s.th. on the chin** to remain calm in a difficult situation
33 **wracked** pained
34 **tantrum** sudden expression of anger
36 **eventually** ⚠ in the end

After all, we're one people, aren't we? from Waitangi Day to New Zealand Day

3 **waka** cf. photo p. 63
5 **pohutukawa** indigenous tree with red flowers
16 **punt** *here:* risky undertaking
22 **core** central part
27 **to transcend** to go beyond

Our parents or grandparents, Pakeha and Maori, sailed here, to the "last, loveliest" place on Earth on a boat or a waka. There were no photographs of palm trees or pohutukawa to lure them, no prospectus, no promises.

And our ancestors, pushed by a thirst for adventure and a hunger to find a better life, hitched up their grass skirts and crinolines and stepped into the unknown.

We were the self-selected bravest people around. Even for those great waves of migrants who came later – the Asians who now inject life into our cities, families craving light and space – New Zealand was a punt. So it is no wonder that our children still have that restless spirit that drives them to search the world for fresh and better opportunities. The fact that most of them eventually come home simply means they love it here.

That common core that is New Zealand culture may now be surrounded by conflict and controversy but it is still solid.

At the very centre of what it means to be a New Zealander are things like love of the land – which transcend both Maori and Pakeha.

By Carroll du Chateau, www.nzherald.co.nz,
The New Zealand Herald – New Zealand,
April 25, 2001.

Exploring the text

1. What reasons does Carroll du Chateau give to justify celebrating New Zealand Day?
2. What problems does Diane Wichtel have with the national holiday?
3. How does the tone of the two articles differ?

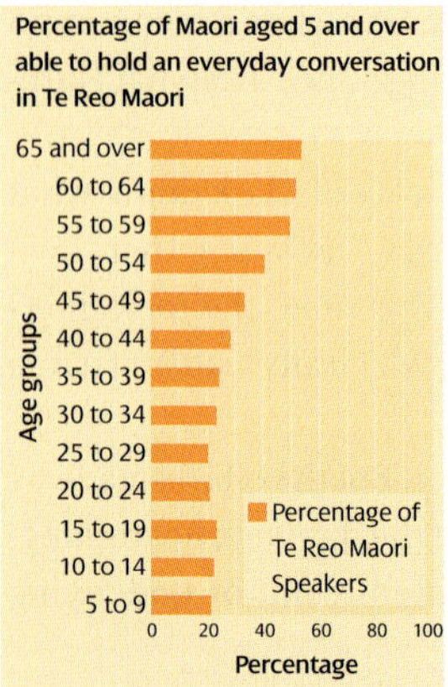

A step further

- Imagine and act out a discussion between the two journalists in which they talk about each other's article and criticize the tone and point of view.
- **Being Maori is** to welcome a Pakeha at a marae (= sacred courtyard in front of a *whare* or Maori meeting house) meeting with the height of Maori poetic art and to receive a cup-of-tea conversation in reply.
  a) What insight does this statement give into Maori / non-Maori relations?
  b) Based on the statement, what might a Maori activist say about the two *New Zealand Herald* articles? Write a letter to the editor from this point of view.
- Look at the statistics on the left and read the information in the box below. How might a) a Maori activist and b) a government representative view the state of Maori education?

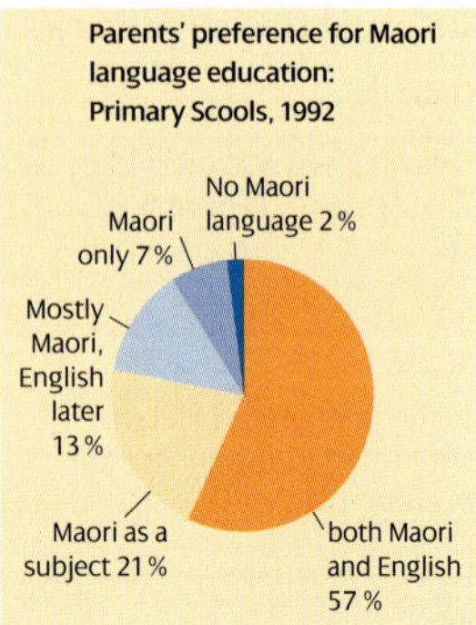

Source: AGB, McNair, 1982

Reviving Maoritanga

1847	Mission schools for Maori only receive state subsidies if they teach in English.
1858	Native Schools Act: missionary schools for Maori education are subsidised to support assimilation.
1865	Mission schools are abandoned due to the New Zealand Wars.
1867	Native Schools Act: The government provides Maori communities with education facilities; Maori language is discouraged to assimilate the Maori into European culture.
1905	Maori language is banned in schools.
1928	Both Maori and non-Maori children have the same national school syllabus.
1960s	Training programmes for Maori are instituted on a large scale. The education system promotes Maori customs, history and language in all schools.
1976	Some universities and training colleges offer courses in the Maori language.
1994	More than 800 schools teaching in Maori have been established.

Native American past and present

Looking and thinking

1 a) Describe the photos below of the Native American reality, past and present.
b) What other images / photos would you include in a collage on Native Americans? What images are suggested by the lyrics of "My country 'tis of thy people you're dying" (below right)?

2 In your opinion, why did Native-American singer Buffy Sainte-Marie use a line from the American classic "My country, 'tis of thee" in her own song?

3 Collect key words about the situation of Native Americans, both past and present, in a mind map as you work through this section of the chapter.

Capture of Seminole Indian chiefs (1816)

My country 'tis of thy people you're dying

Now that your big eyes have finally opened,
Now that you're wondering how must they feel,
Meaning them that you've chased across
America's movie screens.
Now that you're wondering how can it be real
That the ones you've called colorful, noble and
proud
In your school propaganda
They starve in their splendor?
You've asked for my comment I simply will
render:

Chorus: My country 'tis of thy people you're
dying.

Buffy Sainte-Marie, My country 'tis of thy people you're dying

My country, 'tis of thee
My country, 'tis of thee,
Sweet land of liberty,
Of thee I sing;
Land where my fathers died,
Land of the pilgrim's pride,
From every mountainside
Let freedom ring.

Words: Samuel F. Smith, 1832,
Music: America

Before you read

- a) What memories do you have of primary school?
  b) How important are a child's experiences at primary school for his / her later development?
- How can schools help to integrate the children of non-nationals in society?

Indian education

First grade

My hair was too short and my U.S. Government glasses were horn-rimmed, ugly, and all that first winter in school, the other Indian boys chased me from one corner of the playground to the other. They pushed me down, buried me in the snow until I couldn't breathe, thought I'd never breathe again.

They stole my glasses and threw them over my head, around my outstretched hands, just beyond my reach, until someone tripped me and sent me falling again, facedown in the snow.

I was always falling down; my Indian name was Junior Falls Down. Sometimes it was Bloody Nose or Steal-His-Lunch. Once, it was Cries-Like-a-White-Boy, even though none of us had seen a white boy cry. […]

Second grade

Betty Towle, missionary teacher, redheaded and so ugly that no one ever had a puppy crush on her, made me stay in for recess fourteen days straight.

"Tell me you're sorry," she said.

"Sorry for what?" I asked.

"Everything," she said and made me stand straight for fifteen minutes, eagle-armed with books in each hand.

One was a math book; the other was English. But all I learned was that gravity can be painful.

For Halloween I drew a picture of her riding a broom with a scrawny cat on the back. She said that her God would never forgive me for that.

Once, she gave the class a spelling test but set me aside and gave me a test designed for junior high students. When I spelled all the words right, she crumpled up the paper and made me eat it.

"You'll learn respect," she said.

She sent a letter home with me that told my parents to either cut my braids or keep me home from class. My parents came in the next day and dragged their braids across Betty Towle's desk.

"Indians, indians, indians." She said it without capitalization. She called me "indian, indian, indian."

And I said, Yes, I am. I am Indian, Indian, I am. […]

Seventh grade

I leaned through the basement window of the HUD house and kissed the white girl who would later be raped by her foster-parent father, who was also white. They both lived on the reservation, though, and when the headlines and stories filled the papers later, not one word was made of their color.

14 **puppy crush** a child's love
14 **recess** [-'-] *(AE)* lunch break
14 **straight** *here:* in a row
21 **scrawny** very thin
34 **HUD** *(US)* refers to the Department of Housing and Urban Development; government agency which provides housing for the poor

Just Indians being Indians, someone must have said somewhere and they were wrong.

But on the day I leaned through the basement window of the HUD house and kissed the white girl, I felt the good-byes I was saying to my entire tribe. I held my lips tight against her lips, a dry, clumsy, and ultimately stupid kiss.

But I was saying good-bye to my tribe, to all the Indian girls and women I might have loved, to all the Indian men who might have called me cousin, even brother.

I kissed that white girl and when I opened my eyes, she was gone from the reservation, and when I opened my eyes, I was gone from the reservation, living in a farm town. […]

Ninth grade

At the farm town high school dance, after a basketball game in an overheated gym where I had scored twenty-seven points and pulled down thirteen rebounds, I passed out during a slow song.

As my white friends revived me and prepared to take me to the emergency room where doctors would later diagnose my diabetes, the Chicano teacher ran up to us.

"Hey," he said. "What's that boy been drinking? I know all about these Indian kids. They start drinking real young."

Sharing dark skin doesn't necessarily make two men brothers. […]

Eleventh grade

Last night I missed two free throws which would have won the game against the best team in the state. The farm town high school I play for is nicknamed the "Indians", and I'm probably the only actual Indian ever to play for a team with such a mascot.

This morning I pick up the sports page and read the headline: INDIANS LOSE AGAIN.

Go ahead and tell me none of this is supposed to hurt me very much.

Twelfth grade

I walk down the aisle, valedictorian of this farm town high school, and my cap doesn't fit because I've grown my hair longer than it's ever been. Later, I stand as the school board chairman recites my awards, accomplishments, and scholarships.

I try to remain stoic for the photographers as I look toward the future.

Back home on the reservation, my former classmates graduate: a few can't read, one or two are just given attendance diplomas, most look forward to the parties. The bright students are shaken, frightened, because they don't know what comes next.

They smile for the photographer as they look back toward tradition.

The tribal newspaper runs my photograph and the photograph of my former classmates side by side.

From The Lone Ranger and Tonto Fistfight in Heaven *by Sherman Alexie, London: Vintage, 1993, pp. 171–180.*

50 **to pull down rebounds** to catch the ball when it does not go into the basket
53 **Chicano** Mexican-American
69 **valedictorian** *(AE)* best student of a graduation class

How might the Native American boy in the cartoon respond to the question?

Exploring the text

1 Have a close look at Junior's school years and record his positive and negative experiences in a grid like the one below.

reservation school experiences		state high school experiences	
positive	negative	positive	negative
…	…		

2 What makes Junior's school years different from those of his classmates?

3 What stereotype views of Native Americans does the writer include in the story?

4 How does the point of view used in the short story affect the tone?

A step further

- Sherman Alexie is popular with both Native American and non-Native American readers. Try to account for his popularity based on the text you have read.
- Letter of application / CV
  Imagine that Junior trains as a teacher and decides to apply for a job at a reservation school.
  - Write his letter of application to the reservation school board, explaining his wish to teach at a reservation school.
  - Write the part of his CV that deals with his education (cf. p. 112 for ideas).

Storyboard
Key scenes are visualized in drawings by the director and illustrators before the scenes are shot. The drawings are collected on a board.

- Storyboard
  Imagine a film is made about Junior's life. Working in groups, choose and prepare one scene in the short story for filming. Make drawings for the *storyboard* and write the dialogue.

Meet the media: *Dances with Wolves* and *Smoke Signals*

- E-mails
  When *Dances with Wolves* was released in 1990, it was praised as the first feature film to have real Sioux actors speaking real language, thus helping to compensate for all the Westerns which depict Native Americans as blood-thirsty savages. But *Chicago-Sun Times* film critic Robert Ebert called it "a sentimental fantasy".
  Depending on how you feel about the film, do **one** of the following:
  - find evidence that proves Roger Ebert right and write a critical e-mail to the director of the film, Kevin Costner;
  - write an e-mail to Roger Ebert disagreeing with his point of view.
- Web search
  The film, *Smoke Signals* (1999), is based on a short story by Sherman Alexie. In a review Roger Ebert describes the film as being "free of the oppressive weight of victim culture; these characters don't live in the past and define themselves by the crimes committed against their people. They are the next generation".
  a) Do a web search for other reviews of *Smoke Signals.*
  b) What do you find out about the plot and characters?
  c) What evidence supports / contradicts Roger Ebert's claim?

Voices of the Navajo

Before you watch

- The woman in the photo on the right, Nellie Martin, and the girl in the photo on page 75, Shayna Lynn, both live on reservations. What do you think they would say about their lives?
- a) Imagine you were to make a documentary about "life on the reservation". (Cf. skills files, "Documentaries" on page 185 for ideas.)
  - What aspects of life there would you focus on?
  - How could you include Nellie and Shayna's stories?

  b) In groups, choose one aspect of life on the reservation which you would like to deal with more closely. How would you cover this topic, e.g. by means of interviews, (historical) footage and a voiceover, a journalist's report?

  c) Report your ideas back to the class and decide on a logical order for the different aspects of your documentary.

Sequence 1: Growing up on the reservation

1 What does the documentary sequence tell you about the situation of children and young people on reservations?

2 a) Watch the sequence again with the sound turned down. What specific information does the film material convey?

b) Play this sequence again and this time concentrate on the voiceover. What function does it have?

Sequence 2: Navajo land rights

1 Make notes about how the following people in the documentary sequence feel about Navajo land: Maxine – Teddy – Leroy.

2 What do you learn about land rights from the sequence?

A step further

- Discussion in role play

  Although gambling is illegal in most US states, it is allowed on the reservations occupied by Native Americans. An increasing number – the so-called 'casino tribes' – rely on gambling as their main source of income.

  Imagine there are plans to build a casino on the reservation you have seen in the documentary "Voices of the Navajo". The tribe's elders discuss the pros and cons of the plans. Collect arguments in a grid relating to the headings below and add any other headings and arguments you can think of.

	pros	cons
relationship with non-natives		
employment opportunities		
effect on the land		
social consequences		
traditional way of life		
...		

Describe the atmosphere in the photo below of a reservation casino in New Mexico.

Getting rich with the casino tribes

One of the most successful of the "gambling" reservations is the Pojoaque pueblo, 26 miles north of Santa Fe, which has just opened the first Indian-owned luxury hotel in the state. The hotel, with 140 rooms, a shop and a restaurant, is the latest addition to the Cities of Gold complex, which also has a shopping mall, a museum and cultural centre and, of course – the fount of all subsequent development – a casino. [...]

At weekends, the casino operates round the clock, and at 9 pm on a Friday night, cars were circling the mammoth carpark in search of a space. The bingo hall is packed to capacity. Inside, you would have been hard put to find a slot machine that was not occupied. From white-haired grannies in Crimplene to bulky lads in blue jeans, everyone was concentrating on the task in hand: men and women, whites, blacks, browns and Indians side by side, making up one of the most racially integrated scenes I have witnessed anywhere in the States.

Cities of Gold is understandably cagey about exactly how much the tribe earns from its gambling palace, but the figure runs into tens of millions of dollars. And from this money flows more money. Having cash allows the reservation to take out bank loans that were never available to Indians before. [...]

Running the commercial and planning side of the reservation is James Rivera, a clean-cut forty-something who grew up on the reservation. [...]

Rivera is proud of Pojoaque's achievements, and of its priorities. An unemployment rate in the 80 per cent range has been reduced to near zero, thanks to the casino and shopping mall. There is a new nursery, youth club and basketball court, and a new senior citizen's centre. Construction of a clinic has begun. There is an emphasis on education, with grants and scholarships available for those who want to study off the reservation, and the new cultural centre teaches the tribal language and trains young people in traditional Indian crafts – for which there are now nationally recognised credits. The pueblo employs its own police and now has nine squad cars.

If Rivera has his way, life on the reservation could in time offer a good deal more security for the Pojoaque Indians, and perhaps no less opportunity, than life outside it.

But nothing is quite so simple: money has brought its own problems. There is criticism (from inside and outside the Indian world) about how the gambling windfall is spent. Not from Pojoaque, but elsewhere, come tales of individual chiefs growing rich, building lavish personal palaces, buying expensive cars and even boats, rather than investing in the reservation.

That, says Rivera, is a MYTH – and he makes sure that I write this in my notebook in capital letters. Rivera himself drives a small BMW, but the new houses and cars at the Pojoaque pueblo seemed generally modest. He says that the biggest change to his tribe from jobs and money had been in personal dignity and expectations: "How shall I put it, people are looking after themselves better". In other words, the slovenliness that so often characterised Indians on the reservations is starting to disappear.

Perhaps more worrying for the tribes than others' resentment is whether the new income will continue to flow back on to their reservations at current rates – for the

5 **fount** source
5 **subsequent** following
9 **to be hard put to do s.th.** to find it difficult
10 **Crimplene** *(trademark)* synthetic material
14 **cagey** ['keɪdʒɪ] *(informal)* unwilling to give information
42 **slovenliness** ['slʌvənlɪnəs] being untidy and dirty

state is now eyeing their new money with more than casual interest. It was only last year that the New Mexican state legislature – after a struggle lasting nearly five years – legalised most forms of gambling. The price to the Indians, however, was a 16 percent tax on casino earnings. The tribes signed the deal under protest and are refusing to pay. That amount of tax, they object, would make gambling unprofitable and halt most of their development projects.

Negotiations have now opened, with the tribes insisting that anything more than three or four per cent would be unacceptable. But some feel strongly that they should not be liable to pay state tax at all: are not Indian tribes and their lands sovereign (and so exempt from state tax), according to the terms on which the land was ceded to them?

State officials pose essentially the same question from a different angle. If some Indian tribes are growing rich, how come they continue to enjoy big government subsidies, for their schools and social benefits? Should the handouts not be concentrated in the poorer, by and large traditionalist, tribes which have rejected gambling as a solution? And in this country of self-help, why shouldn't rich tribes be expected to help poor tribes – so relieving the state of a large burden? [...]

And while gambling may not be the most salubrious of businesses, the Indians have a point when they say that the neglect and prejudice they faced from mainstream America left them with few other avenues for self-improvement. Rivera's idea is that the Pojoaque tribe will eventually throw off the stigma by making the casino just one part of a top-notch resort.

But there is a downside. Even if social harmony prevails on the reservations for the time being, gambling money is potentially divisive. Already, it is dividing rich tribes from poor and complicating relations with the authorities. It is also fuelling breakneck development in some of the most spectacular landscape in north America, with scant regard for the environmental and aesthetic consequences.

That, though, is the rich man's view. If I were an Indian, I would be 100 per cent behind the Pojoaque and their casino. After centuries of indigence, what have they to lose?

By Mary Dejevsky, The Independent, *July 18, 1998.*

63 **salubrious** [sə'lu:brɪəs] pleasant
65 **avenue** *here:* opportunity
67 **top-notch** of the highest quality
69 **divisive** causing disagreement
72 **scant** little
74 **indigence** poverty

Exploring the text

1 What pros and cons of the casinos does the writer mention?
2 Which expressions or passages in the text reveal the writer's opinion?
3 a) What elements of a *feature* does the text have? Compare it with a newspaper article in this chapter, e.g. "Mourning closes Ayers Rock" (p. 56), as regards: composition / line of argument – inclusion of background information – degree of human interest – use of quotations – the possibility to form one's own opinion.
b) Do you think this is a good feature, or not?

Feature
piece of writing which goes deeper into a subject than a news article

A step further

- If Mary Dejevski had been asked to write a *comment* instead of a feature, what would she have written differently? Write this comment. (Cf. skills files, page 188.)
- Write a letter to the editor of the *Independent* from the point of view of **one** of the following people: a police officer – the chief of the Pojoaque – a non-native American hotel manager – James Rivera – the governor of New Mexico – a Native American living on a traditional reservation which does not have a casino.

Comment
piece of writing in which s.o. voices an opinion on a certain situation, event, etc.

Again you have the opportunity to decide how to deal with the text.

Over to you

Indians hear a high-tech drumbeat

Hundreds of butte-desert miles from any sizable town, a protest is building. A lone-Indian chant is punctuated by scuffling feet and shaking rattles, while demonstrators lift hand-held signs: "Low-level dump/High-level hazard" and "We can't pick up and move like others can."

The scene has played out in scores of settings across the West, ever since the United States government targeted Indian reservations in the late 1980s as favorable sites for nuclear and other waste disposal. But this protest, like many of the others, includes a new element that is tipping the balance in native Americans' favor: the spirit of collective empowerment nudged forward by modern technology.

"We are seeing the result of years of coalition-building coming together with the aid of new ways to communicate to very remote, rural populations," says Tom Goldtooth, founder of the Indigenous Environmental Network.

Leaning over the hood of a faded blue Chevy, Mr. Goldtooth works a bank of portable cell phones with the urgency of a lobby receptionist. He directs protesters at two base camps a mile away; he choreographs the arrival of tour-bus-size contingents of sympathizing tribes from Texas to Oregon. He fields questions from the press about the protest in front of him, as well as one he just left in New Mexico.

Using cell phones, fax machines, and the Internet, a national native American movement is coalescing, helping disparate tribes communicate, educate, mobilize, and stand up for themselves.

From New York to Washington State and from Florida to California, coalitions made up from 552 federally recognized tribes are demanding enforcement of existing laws and the creation of new ones. Via phone or e-mail, they are asking far-flung tribes to show up at protests, write to local and national lawmakers, send money, appear at hearings, and visit web sites to bone up on issues and strategy. "This is a sea change in the way tribes see themseles as activists on issues ... from environment to health care," says John Dossett of the National Congress of American Indians in Washington.

Native Americans' connections with one another – and with the rest of the world – have grown exponentially in the past 25 years. Back then, Alaskan tribes were not aware of major federal legislation affecting them until a year after Congress passed it, Mr. Dossett says. "Now they know what each other is doing and can lend support in dozens of ways," he says. [...]

Back at the grass roots, meanwhile, the fight over nuclear-waste disposal has been as much internal as external. Tribes have stood to gain hundreds of millions of dollars if they would agree to allow the US to bury nuclear waste on their land. But so far, all have resisted.

"Due to networking, among the more than 500 Indian nations that were approached, only a handful even considered the proposal," says Bryan Angel, executive director of Green Action, an environmental activist group. "Most who considered it voted it down after pressure from the coalitions that have been formed. Considering the lure of incredible sums of money for very poor tribes, that is amazing." [...]

By Daniel B. Wood, The Christian Science Monitor, *February 19, 1998.*

1 **butte** [bju:t] *(AE)* rock with steep sides and a flat top
9 **to nudge** *here:* to move gently
25 **to bone up on** *(informal)* to study hard for a special purpose
26 **sea change** complete change
32 **what each** *grammatically correct:* what the other is

First peoples

- "Indian education" (pp. 76 – 77), "The Pakeha judge's antlers on the wall" (pp. 70 – 72)
  Compare "Indian education" and "The Pakeha judge's ..." taking the following points into consideration:
  - Which of Junior's experiences are most similar to Simeon's?
  - What characteristics do they have in common? How do they differ?
  - Which common aims may Sherman Alexie and Witi Ihimaera have had when they wrote the short stories?

- "Indian education" (pp. 76 – 77), "The Pakeha judge's ..." (pp. 70 – 72) and "Child of the stolen generation" (pp. 57 – 58)
  Discuss which text made the greatest impression on you – one of the two short stories or John's experiences in "Child of the stolen generation".

- Theme: Modern vs. traditional lifestyles
  Study the photo on the right carefully. Then, divide the class into two groups. One group prepares arguments in favour of the photo, the other criticizing it. One student from each group takes part in a discussion as to whether the photo should be included in a reader for Australian primary school children.

- Indigenous people and their lifestyles
  a) In Western industrialised nations there has been increased interest in indigenous people's beliefs and lifestyles. Can you think of any examples of this interest, e.g. in adverts, fashion trends, films, music?
  b) Make a mind map, like the one below, in which you collect reasons for this interest.

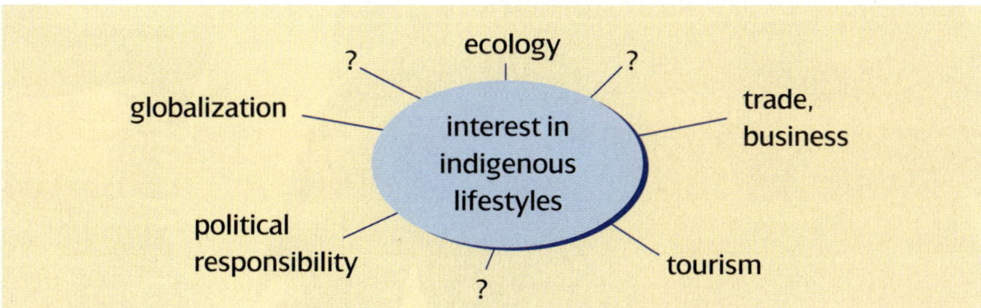

  c) Collect the classes' results on the board in one large mind map. You may add to things other students have written and you do not need to give an explanation at this stage. When the group has finished, look at the results and discuss entries that are not clear.
  d) Write a short essay **or** prepare a one-minute talk on one of the topics which evolved in the mind map. (Cf. skills files, "Essays", page 187 or "Presentations", pp. 182–183.)

Focus on the Matrix

First impressions

Looking and thinking

a) Look at the photo from the *The Matrix* film poster. What impression does it convey of the film?
b) Which film genre(s) would you apply to the film based on the photo? Cf. the box on the right for ideas.
c) In your opinion, what appeal does the film have for film goers?

Talking about film genres

a science-fiction movie / a sci-fi – a thriller – a love story – an action film – a fantasy film – a horror film – an adventure film – a Western

Understanding the plot

Looking and thinking

1 Put the pieces of the plot of *The Matrix* in the correct order.

1. The outcome of this war was that the sun went dark. The machines now hold people in special pods and use them as an energy source. The humans are fed a virtual world so that they do not realise that they are slaves.

2. Unfortunately, one of Morpheus's team members, Cypher, betrays them and Neo is killed by one of the Matrix's agents.

3. Trinity brings Neo to see Morpheus, who confronts Neo with the truth about his existence: Neo's life and in fact the whole world do not exist in reality. The world is an illusion created by a computer simulation called The Matrix. It came into being because intelligent machines generated it following a war between humans and the machines.

4. Trinity succeeds in bringing the dead Neo back to life.

5. Thomas Anderson is a young computer expert who leads a double life – during the day he works for a large software company, at night he is a computer hacker who goes under the name of Neo.

6. Neo finally defeats the computer-controlled agents and continues the fight against the all-powerful Matrix.

7. Morpheus, Trinity and some others have escaped from the machines. They live an underground existence and try to liberate humans from their enslavement. Morpheus is looking for a saviour to defeat the computer-controlled agents. He believes that Neo is that person.

8. Neo is contacted by two mysterious characters, Trinity and Morpheus. He is later interrogated by agents who seem to know about these people and want his help in catching Morpheus.

9. Neo undergoes special training and initially manages well in confrontations with the agents.

2 a) The word 'matrix' has a number of meanings. Check your dictionary and make a list of the meanings you find.
b) Based on what you know about the plot, which meaning might be the most appropriate for the film?

3 Watch the introduction to the film two or three times. What overall impression is created by the fast sequence of *shots*?

4 At the end of the preview Morpheus says: "Welcome to the real world". What kind of world is he referring to?

Shot
A continuous block of film from a single point of view

Film analysis

- The following activities are linked to themes in the film. Choose one of the themes and become an expert on it. Take notes while you watch the film. The excerpts from the shooting script will help you to complete the tasks.

The future world

Watching and thinking

1 *The Matrix* is set in the year 2197. Collect references in the film that make us aware that the story happens in a future world. Record your findings in a grid like this:

Physical features	Human aspects	Machines
ruined cities, wasteland...	slaves ...	rulers ...

Dystopia
an unpleasant, imaginary society

2 Describe the structure of the future world in your own words.

3 What elements of a *dystopia* does the future world have?

The following scene from the shooting script takes place when Neo first meets Morpheus.

1 **to click on** to turn on
7 **Baudrillard, Jean** French social theorist who wrote about simulations in society
14 **inebriation of hubris** inability to think as one is under a strong influence

[Morpheus] picks up a remote control and clicks on the television. On the television we see images of the twentieth-century city where Neo lived.
Morpheus This is the world you know. The world as it was at the end of the twentieth century. It exists now only as a part of a neural-interactive simulation that we call the Matrix.
He changes the channel and we see a very different city as we enter the televison.
Morpheus You have been living inside a dreamworld, Neo. As in Baudrillard's vision, your whole life has been spent inside the map, not the territory. This is the world as it exists today.
In the distance, we see the ruins of a future city protruding from the wasteland like the blackened ribs of a long-dead corpse. […]
Morpheus We have only bits and pieces of information. What we know for certain is that, at some point in the early twenty-first century, all of mankind was united in celebration. Through the blinding inebriation of hubris, we marveled at our magnificence as we gave birth to A.I.
Neo A.I.? You mean artificial intelligence?
Morpheus Yes. A singular consciousness that spawned an entire race of machines. […] We don't know who struck first. Us or them. But we do know it was us that scorched the sky. At the time, they were dependent on solar power. It was believed they would be unable to survive without an energy source as abundant as the sun. […] The Machines discovered a new form of fusion. All they needed was a small electrical charge to initiate the reaction. […] The Matrix is a computer-generated dreamworld built to keep us under control in order to change a human being into this.
He holds up a coppertop battery.

Exploring the text

1 List the images Morpheus uses in the above scene to explain the world to Neo.

2 What information can he **not** give in the explanation?

How real is reality?

Watching and thinking

a) The film operates on different levels of reality. Identify and characterize these levels.

b) How does the viewer know which level is being presented? Which *special effects* does the director use to characterize a particular level? Refer to the box on the right for ideas.
Record your ideas for a) and b) in a grid like the one below.

Level of reality	Characteristics	Special effects

Special effects
artificial effects used to create an illusion. Examples of effects include computer-generated imaging (3D images are created by computer and integrated into films, cf. photo, p. 31), slow motion and voice-over narration.

The following key scene from the shooting script occurs when Morpheus takes Neo into a computer programme in order to explain the Matrix.

Neo is standing in an empty, blank-white space.
Morpheus This is the construct. […] It is our loading program. We can load anything from clothes, to weapons, to training simulations. Anything we need. […]
Neo stands at the back of the chair as Morpheus sits.
Neo Right now, we're inside a computer program?
Morpheus smiles.
Morpheus Is it so hard to believe? Your clothes are different, the plugs in your arms and head are gone. Look at your hair, you were bald a moment ago. […] It's what we call residual self image. The mental projection of your electronic self. Wild isn't it?
Neo's hands run over the cracked leather.
Neo This-This isn't real?
Morpheus What is real? How do you define real? If you're talking about what you feel, taste, smell, or see, then real is simply electrical signals interpreted by your brain.

10 **residual self image** what one looks like in the Matrix compared to the real world

Exploring the text

a) Study the above excerpt carefully. How does Morpheus describe the nature of reality?

b) Which level of reality in the film is he referring to?

c) What is the function of this particular level in the film?

Characterization: Who am I?

Watching and thinking

1 a) Closely study scenes in the film which feature the character of Cypher. How is he characterized by what he says and by his actions?
b) Check a dictionary to find out the meaning of his name. How fitting is the name for the role he plays on the ship?

2 Compare the characters of Neo and Cypher. What self-image do they have? What do they know about reality and the Matrix? How do they each answer the question: Who am I? Record your ideas in a grid like the one below.

	Cypher	Neo
characterization		
self-image		
attitude to reality / Matrix		
Who am I?		

The following key scene from the shooting script takes place after Neo starts his training.

1 **int.** *short for* interior, indoors
2 **to soak** *(fig. here)* to fill every corner
3 **serrated** having sharp V-shaped points
3 **to saw, sawed, sawn** to cut with backward and forward movements
10 **bliss** perfect happiness

Int. Restaurant – Night

Chamber music and the ambiance of wealth soak the restaurant around us as we watch a serrated knife saw through a thick, gorgeous steak. The meat is so perfect, charred on the outside, oozing red juice on the inside, that it could be a dream.

We hear a voice that we recognise immediately.

Agent Smith Do we have a deal, Mr. Reagan?

A fork stabs the cube of meat and we follow it up to the face of Cypher.

Cypher You know I know that this steak doesn't exist. I know that when I put it in my mouth, the Matrix is telling my brain that it is juicy and delicious. After nine years, do you know what I've realised? […] Ignorance is bliss […]

Agent Smith Then we have a deal?

Cypher I don't want to remember nothing. Nothing! You understand? And I want to be rich. Someone important. Like an actor. You can do that, right?

Agent Smith Whatever you want, Mr. Reagan.

Cypher takes a deep drink of wine.

Cypher All right. You get my body back into a Power Plant, reinsert me into the Matrix, and I'll get you what you want.

Exploring the text

1 Examine the scene in detail. What makes Cypher do what he does in the end?

2 How important are Cypher's actions in the development of the plot?

Neo – a second Christ?

Watching and thinking

1 Work out parallels between Neo's life and the life of Jesus and record your findings in a grid like the one below.

	Christ	Neo
Birth		
Role		
Disciples		
John the Baptist		
Predicted coming		
Death and resurrection		

2 Look at the scenes in which Neo is killed and comes back to life again. What actually brings him back to life?

The following key scene from the shooting script takes place after Neo finally defeats the agents.

Int. Computer Screen

Close on a computer screen as in the opening. The cursor beating steadily, waiting. A phone begins to ring.

It is answered and the screen fills instantly with the trace program. After a long beat we recognise Neo's voice.

Neo *(V.O.)* Hi. It's me. I know you're out there. I can feel you now. I imagine you can also feel me.

You won't have to search for me anymore. I'm done running. Done hiding. Whether I'm done fighting, I suppose is up to you.

I believe deep down, we both want this world to change. I believe that the Matrix can remain our cage or it can become our chrysalis, that's what you helped me to understand. That to be free, truly free, you cannot change your cage. You have to change yourself. [...] Now I see another world. A different world where all things are possible. A world of hope. Of peace.

From The Art of the Matrix, *New York: Newmarket Press, 2000, pp. 310–313, 309–310, 330–331, 393.*
Original screenplay: Larry & Andy Wachowksi

4 **trace program** search to find out where the phone call is coming from
4 **beat** *here:* moment
6 **V.O.** *short for* **voiceover**; commentary by s.o. offscreen
8 **I'm done** *(informal)* I have finished
11 **chrysalis** ['krɪsəlɪs] resting state before one begins to grow

Exploring the text

1 How would you interpret the end of the film? How did the director change the script for the final scene? How significant are these changes?
2 Examine and explain the images Neo uses in the above excerpt to describe the Matrix.
3 How has the character of Neo developed in the course of the film?

Cinematic devices

Watching and thinking

As you do the following tasks, record your results in a grid like the one below.

1 a) How is the scene with Trinity and the policemen filmed at the beginning of the film (cf. photo on the right)? Which camera operations make the scene more tense?
b) What special effects are used in the scene? What effect does the use of *fast motion* have on the scene?
2 Study the use of camera angles and positions in the scene where Agent Smith interrogates Neo. What effect do they have on the scene? Cf. p. 184 for ideas.
3 At the end of the film, when Neo comes back to life, how do the sound effects, and the music in particular, contribute to the atmosphere of the scene?
E.g. for question 1:

scene	location	characters	cinematic devices	effect
Trinity fights the police	*inside a hotel*	*Trinity, policemen*	...	...

A step further

- The scenes in which Trinity and Neo rescue Morpheus from the high-rise building contain much violence. How is violence presented in these scenes and what is its function?

Fast motion
A shot in which time appears to move more quickly than normal.

Before you read

- Think of a catchy title for a review that you would write about *The Matrix*. If possible, it should reflect your opinion of the film.
- Make a list of words and phrases which you would apply to *The Matrix* and which you would expect to find in a review of the film.

We love you, Keanu!

The Matrix is a wonderfully enjoyable pulp classic – an unalloyed pleasure from first to last, crammed with hi-tech, high-camp action sequences and spiffy effects. And it achieves what I never dreamt was possible – it makes us fall in love with Keanu Reeves all over again. […]

Keanu plays a computer hacker called Neo. (A name which deserves an Academy Award itself.) By day, he has a straight job in a software company, but by night he gets down with the alternative online community, busting into secure systems, pirating ultra-cool games and gossiping about the electrifying rumour concerning something called "The Matrix", an occult alternative reality or higher-consciousness system accessible only to those enlightened in the way of artificial intelligence.

Neo is contacted from the other side by a devastatingly sexy cyber-warrior called Trinity (Carrie-Anne Moss), dressed in liquefying black leather, who leads him to the one man who can tell him the sinister truth about The Matrix: Morpheus (these names!), who is big, bald, powerful and played by Laurence Fishburne. It is Morpheus who reveals the terrifying reality about The Matrix: namely, that our waking lives are a gigantic, baroque dream implanted in our minds by a race of machine-monsters to whom we humans came second in a nuclear war, that our bodies are now being bred in darkness on gigantic intergalactic factory farms to provide "bio-energy" for the conqueror, and that we are kept docile with a virtual reality illusion of a rich, busy existence.

How can I describe the expression on Keanu's face on hearing this terrifying news? It is the same as the expression on anyone else's face on opening a higher than expected gas bill. But it is precisely this impassivity, this tough, stoic alertness which inspires extravagant adoration not merely from all of us in the auditorium, but also from Morpheus, Trinity and the rest of the resistance, who think of him as the "Chosen One" who will lead the insurrection against The Matrix.

The fight scenes in this film are a complete joy. Keanu gains expertise in various Oriental techniques via implanted software – a mini-disc is clunked into the back of his neck, he turns around and breathes wonderingly: "I know Kung Fu..." I say, Keanu, do you really? Yes indeed, and pale, wussy Keanu gets fight scenes that are stylish, exhilarating and beautifully designed.

Movies about virtual reality, or those ostentatiously sporting virtual reality effects, usually tend to be bad; they rely on a lot of sub-William Gibson babble, no-brainer stuff – artificial intelligence for the naturally unintelligent. Moreover, they fail to understand that a good movie should itself be a form of virtual reality, and that a second level of techno-fantasy added in this medium looks tinny, tacky and surplus to requirements.

But *The Matrix* winningly surmounts these obstacles; it unselfconsciously creates its own weird, deadpan universe, its visual effects are worn lightly, and Andy and

1 **pulp classic** a success in popular culture
1 **unalloyed** pure, complete
2 **high-camp** *here:* exaggerated
2 **spiffy** *(informal)* fashionable, tidy
7 **to get down** *(AE)* to relax and enjoy o.s.
30 **wussy** *(slang)* stupid
32 **to sport** to present s.th. in a proud way
33 **William Gibson** (b. 1948) writer of cyberpunk fiction
36 **tacky** *(informal)* cheap, badly made

Larry Wachowski, who wrote and directed it, appreciate that there has to be a lot of sweaty action on the level of actual reality. [...]

This is a fantastically enjoyable summer movie which should easily see off some other dinosaur contenders I could mention. Check it out this weekend. *The Matrix* rocks!

From "Carry on up the cyber" by Peter Bradshaw, The Guardian, *June 11, 1999.*

42 **to see off** to defeat
44 **to rock** *(informal)* to be full of action

Exploring the text

1 a) What information about the plot of *The Matrix* does the writer include in the review?
b) Outline the structure of the review by using key words to summarize the function of each paragraph.

2 a) How does the writer characterize the main protagonists?
b) Choose three other characters in the film and characterize them using a minimum of three adjectives each.

3 Describe the writer's attitude to the film. Which aspects of the film does he find convincing, which does he criticize?

A step further

- Do you agree or disagree with the writer's attitude in "Exploring", task 3? Write a letter to Peter Bradshaw in which you take up some of his ideas critically. Refer to the letter on page 111.
- Find further reviews of *The Matrix* on the internet. Which aspects of the film do the reviewers discuss? Put the information into categories such as plot, acting ability, camerawork, etc.
- a) The writer describes *The Matrix* as a "pulp classic" (l. 1). In groups, agree on five films produced in the last five years which would also earn this title. Try to agree on a list of factors which make these films "classics".
b) Form new groups. Think up a plot of a film which includes as many of the factors you collected as possible. You could even decide on a cast for your film.
- The photo shows Keanu Reeves in the film *Chain reaction* (1996), which was made before *The Matrix*. Imagine and act out a conversation between Keanu Reeves and the directors of *The Matrix*. They describe Neo and suggest ways in which the actor could achieve this image. Be as polite as possible!

Project

- a) Find two or three reviews of the sequels to *The Matrix*, *The Matrix Reloaded* and *The Matrix Revolutions* in the internet. Which aspects of the films do the critics praise, which ones do they find fault with?
b) Write a summary of developments in the plot. Consider in particular the roles of the keymaker and the architect in *The Matrix Reloaded.*
c) Watch the sequence "The Second Renaissance" from *The Animatrix* and report back to the class about how and why the machines have become the masters of this future world.

Again you have the opportunity to deal with a text as you wish. As the text is quite long you could divide it up among the members of a group. Each person summarizes his / her section before the group starts work on the text. Also try to answer the question below to prepare yourself for the work on the text.

Before you start

The following text was written by Kevin Warwick, Professor of Cybernetics at the University of Reading, UK. How do you think he, as a scientist, would react to the concept of the Matrix and machine-domination of the world?
On pp. 118–119 there is another text by Kevin Warwick, "Professor Cyborg", which you might like to read before you continue.

Over to you

The Matrix – our future

Is *The Matrix* merely a science fiction scenario, or is it, rather, a philosophical exercise? Alternatively, is it a realistic possible future world? The number of respected scientists predicting the advent of intelligent machines is growing exponentially. Steven Hawking, perhaps the most highly regarded theoretical scientist in the world and the holder of the Cambridge University chair that once belonged to Isaac Newton, said recently, "In contrast with our intellect, computers double their performance every 18 months. So the danger is real that they could develop intelligence and take over the world." [...]

In *The Matrix*, the story revolves around the battle between humans and intelligent robots. Yet Neo, and most of the other humans, each have their own brain port. When out of the Matrix, they are undoubtedly human; but while they are in the Matrix, there can be no question that they are no longer human, but rather are Cyborgs. The real battle then becomes not one of humans versus intelligent robots but of Cyborgs versus intelligent robots. [...]

What of the machine network, the Matrix, itself? With an intellect well above that of collective humanity, surely its creativity, its artistic sense, its value for aesthetics would be a treat to behold. But the film keeps this aspect from us – perhaps to be revealed in a sequel. Humans released from the Matrix grip, merely regard it as an evil, perhaps Cypher excluded here. Meanwhile the Agents are seen almost as faceless automatons, ruthless killers, strictly obeying the will of their Matrix overlord. Possibly humans would see both the Matrix and Agents as the enemy, just as the Matrix and Agents would so regard humans – but once inside the Matrix the picture is not so clear. As a Cyborg, who are your friends and who are your enemies? It is no longer black and white when you are part machine, part human. [...]

Morpheus tells Neo that the Matrix is control. This in itself is an important revelation. As humans, we are used to one powerful individual being the main instigator, the brains behind everything. It is almost as though we cannot even conceive of a group or collection running amuck, but believe, rather, that there is an individual behind it all. In the second world war, it was not the Germans or Germany who the allies were fighting but Adolf Hitler; meanwhile in Afghanistan, it is Bin-Laden who is behind it all. Yet in the Matrix we are faced with a much more realistic scenario, in that it is not some crazed individual up to no good, but the Matrix – a network.

5 **chair** *here:* position as a professor
11 **port** *here:* connection to a computer
13 **cyborg** part human, part machine
32 **up to no good** doing or planning s.th. bad

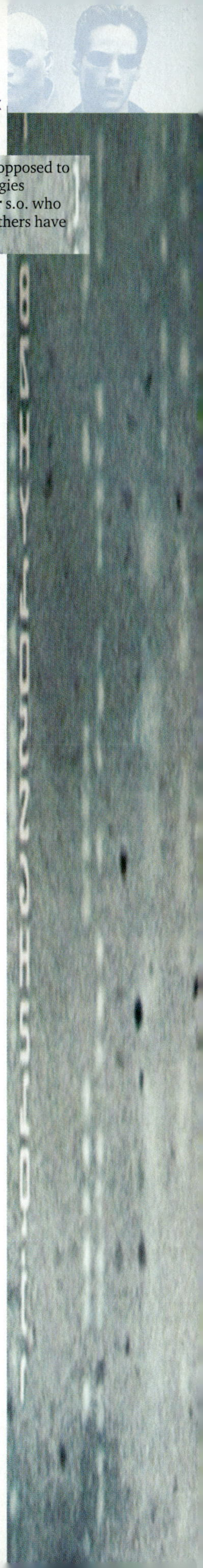

When I find myself in a discussion of the possibility of intelligent machines taking over things, nine times out of ten I am told – following a little chuckle to signify that I have overlooked a blindingly obvious point – that "If a machine causes a problem you can always switch it off." What a fool I was not to have thought of it!! How could I have missed that little snippet?

Of course it is not only the Matrix but even today's common Internet that gives us the answer, and cuts the chuckle short. Even now, how is it practically possible to switch off the Internet? We're not talking theory here, we're talking practice. Okay, it is of course possible to unplug one computer, or even a small subsection intranet, but to bring down the whole Internet? Of course we can't. Too many entities, both humans and machines, rely on its operation for their everyday existence. It is not a Matrix of the future that we will not be able to switch off, it is a Matrix of today that we cannot switch off, over which we cannot have ultimate control. […]

In a sense, *The Matrix* is nothing more than a modern day "Big Brother," taking on a machine form rather than the Orwellian vision of a powerful individual using machines to assist and bring about an all-powerful status. But *1984*, the novel in which the story of Big Brother was presented, was published in 1948. *The Matrix* comes fifty years later. In the meantime, we have witnessed the likes of radar, television for all, space travel, computers, mobile phones, and the Internet. What would Orwell's Big Brother have been like if he had had those technologies at his disposal – would Big Brother have been far from the Matrix?

With the first implant I received, in 1998, for which I had no medical reason (merely scientific curiosity), a computer network was able to monitor my movements. It knew what time I entered a room and when I left. In return it opened doors for me, switched on lights, and even gave me a welcoming "Hello" as I arrived. I experienced no negatives at all. In fact, I felt very positive about the whole thing. I gained something as a result of being monitored and tracked. I was happy with having Big Brother watching me because, although I gave up some of my individual humanity, I benefited from the system doing things for me. Would the same not be true of the Matrix? Why would anyone want to experience the relatively tough and dangerous life of being an individual human when he or she could be part of the Matrix? […]

In the Matrix, no human fuel cells are killed, not even the unborn – there is no abortion. Yet, naturally dying humans are allowed to die naturally and are used as food for the living. Importantly, they are not kept alive by chemicals merely for the sake of keeping them alive. The Matrix would appear to be more morally responsible to its human subjects than are human subjects to themselves. Who therefore wouldn't want to support and belong to the Matrix, especially when it is making life easier for its subjects?

Neo is kidnapped by Luddites, dinosaurs from the past when humans ruled the earth. It's not the future. We are in reality heading towards a world run by machines with an intelligence far superior to that of an individual human. But by linking into the network and becoming a Cyborg, life can appear to be even better than it is now. We really need to clamp down on the party-pooper Neos of this world and get into the future as soon as we can – a future in which we can be part of a Matrix system, which is morally far superior to our Neolithic morals of today.

By Kevin Warwick, http://whatisthematrix.warnerbros.com/

74 **Luddite** s.o. opposed to new technologies
78 **party-pooper** s.o. who does not let others have any fun

Barriers and bridges

Pictures in our heads

Before you look

- a) Choose 10 adjectives from the box below left which best describe the German and British national characters (if such a thing exists). Check any unknown words in a dictionary.
  b) Characterize a third nation of your choice.

Looking and thinking

1 What image of German and British people do the pictures on these pages convey?
2 In your opinion, to what extent do the pictures reflect German and British realities today?

friendly • confident
hard-working • efficient •
civilised • patriotic •
practical • communicative
easy-going
humorous • polite
religious • inventive
materialistic
insular • obedient
arrogant
imaginative
trustworthy
prosperous
democratic • violent
bureaucratic • organised
old-fashioned
superstitious • shy
talkative • modest
tolerant • sporty
fun-loving • generous
narrow-minded
money-minded
ambitious
peace-loving • hospitable
sociable • kind-hearted
superficial
straightforward • boastful
restless • mobile • flexible
creative • selfish

If only we all played cricket...

- a) Watch the extract from "If only we all played cricket ...", a documentary about attitudes the British and Germans have towards one another. How do the young people interviewed in the documentary perceive one another?
  b) In your opinion, what factors determine the image we have of other nationalities? Refer to the box below for useful vocabulary.

Talking about images

a controversial / vague / inaccurate image	a general idea / notion / assumption
a popular / (un)flattering / justified image	to view / label / perceive s.o. as being s.th.
a restricted / blurred / distorted perception of s.th.	s.o. is labelled / characterized as being ...
	to paint a picture

c) Do you accept that there is such a thing as a 'national character'? Say why, why not.

A step further

- The psychology of stereotypes
  a) Read the information below about stereotypes (= fixed, oversimplified images that many people know and repeat, usu. in a catchphrase, e.g. 'the efficient Germans'). Does the information come as a surprise to you? Why, why not?

Stereotypes ...
- are pictures in our heads and, as such, are 'easy explanations' which help us to order the world and orientate ourselves.
- may be either positive or negative.
- are not genetically determined but gradually learned.
- usually contain at least some truth.
- are survival tools in a complex world which puts many demands on our attention.
- give people a sense of belonging ('us' versus 'them').

b) Write an interview with a psychologist who explains how stereotypes work. Refer to the information above and the phrases in the box below.

Talking about stereotypes

national / racial / sexual stereotypes	to fit into a stereotype
prejudice (= fixed, negative attitude) / preconceived idea	to have a strong / deep-seated bias
	to be prejudiced / biased against s.o.
to create / perpetuate a stereotype	to make a sweeping statement / generalization
to debunk / break down a stereotype	

- Speeches at Speaker's Corner
  Every Sunday ordinary people go to Speaker's Corner in Hyde Park, London to make speeches about all kinds of issues.
  - Prepare and act out a speech about some aspect of German life or people, e.g. cars, football (hooliganism), typical holidays, being a tourist abroad.
  - Attract listeners by being provocative, humorous or one-sided.
  - The class takes on the role of passers-by who move around listening to the speakers. You are free to respond to the speeches any way you like.

- Postcard: stereotypes
  a) What stereotypes does the postcard below play on? Which ones are you already familiar with?
  b) In groups, try to think of one physical feature and three characteristics which are often applied to the citizens of at least six European countries. Collect your ideas in a grid. Then try to think of reasons for, or exceptions to, these expectations.

Using your skills

The ambassadors' game

How to play the game

Half the class are diplomats from the German Foreign Department and the other half are ambassadors from various countries, e.g. you could have 12 German diplomats and 12 ambassadors from 12 countries. You all meet at a diplomatic reception. The visiting ambassadors wish to put their respective country's case for more foreign aid to the Foreign Department representatives.

Before you play

a) Read through Steps 1 – 4. What skills do you need to play the game?
b) Allocate roles and decide how much time you wish to spend on each step.
c) What role could the teacher have in the simulation?
d) Refer to page 193 for useful discussion phrases.

Step 1 Preparation

- In groups of three or four, the **German diplomats** try to reach agreement on:
  - what is considered polite when welcoming guests;
  - what information you will give about Germany and yourselves.

  Each group makes a list of questions which can be put to the guests. Concentrate on themes which are relevant to the decision to give foreign aid.
  Note: Be careful not to offend your guests as the German government feels that it is essential to maintain good relations with your guests' countries.

- The **foreign ambassadors** study the role cards and memorise the name of your fictional country and its basic rule of politeness. You should also invent a name for yourself and note down basic facts and interesting information about your country on the role card.
  Note: Be prepared to make polite conversation and answer questions about your country.

Step 2 The diplomatic reception

- Bring in props such as glasses or plastic cups, and water or soft drinks as a substitute for wine. If you wish, you could even dress up.
- The foreign diplomats enter the room. The German diplomats welcome them and offer them a drink. One German diplomat talks to one guest at a time. After a suitable length of time, the host excuses him- or herself, e.g. to refill his / her glass, and moves on to another guest.

Step 3 After the reception

- The **German diplomats** share the information about the guests.
  - Based on the questions you made up before the reception, make a grid with the name of each ambassador's country and the themes you agreed on.
  - Record the answers you got from each ambassador.
  - Note down each country's main rule of politeness, if you have managed to identify it.
- The **foreign ambassadors** meet in small groups. You should still observe your country's rule of politeness. Share your experiences at the reception. (You still see each other as competitors for a limited foreign aid budget.)

Step 4 Reporting back

- The **German diplomats** write a report for the German foreign minister which includes insights gained at the reception.
- The **foreign ambassadors** write a report about the meeting for the country's head of state.

A step further

- The whole class evaluates the effectiveness of the simulation.
- How important is politeness in life? Give your opinion in a short speech.
- In the role of a German diplomat, write a letter to one of the ambassadors you met at the reception in which you do **one** of the following:
  - Explain your country's guidelines for granting foreign aid and give reasons as to why you will be unable to give his / her country any.
  - Grant foreign aid and outline the conditions for its use.

Phrases for a formal letter

Saying "thank you": I would like to express my gratitude for ... / I really appreciated ...
Introductory phrases: With respect / In the present circumstances ...
Useful adverbs: Hopefully, ... / Understandably, ... / Regrettably, ...
Making suggestions: Our interest would be to make sure that ... / It would (not) be advisable / useful / helpful to ... It might be more acceptable / beneficial / advantageous to ...

The Germans throw in the towel

Looking and laughing

In 1992, Britain's oldest travel firm, Thomas Cook, was bought by LTU, the German charter airline. The cartoon below shows the new standards in package tours.

"At least there's a guaranteed sunbed."

1 Where is the above cartoon set? What is the significance of the destinations on the sign?
2 What nationalities can you identify? Give reasons for your answer.
3 What do you think the caption of the cartoon is referring to?
4 Write a speech bubble for one of the characters in the cartoon.

Exploring the text on page 99

1 Explain the title of the article "The Germans throw in the towel".
2 What image of the Germans on holiday does the article present?
3 a) Explain the *images* used in the text.
b) What main area(s) are they taken from?
4 How does the journalist use language to create humour? Refer to specific examples in the text.

A step further

- Write a letter to the editor of *The Daily Mail* in response to the article from **one** of the viewpoints below. Refer to the sample letter on page 111 for ideas.
  - a British tourist who "struck back" (ll. 13 – 14);
  - Christa Konermann;
  - the manager of a hotel on Lanzarote;
  - a spokesperson for a major German tour operator.
- Turn the article into a short sketch or holiday *anecdote*.

Anecdote
a simple, short and usually amusing or thought-provoking story about a real person or event, usually passed on by word of mouth

The Germans throw in the towel

Victory to Britain's Wine Army in Battle of the Poolside sunbeds

It was indeed a victory to savour. For once, the Germans had suffered a humiliating defeat in the battle of the poolside loungers.

On countless sunshine holidays abroad, Britons are left fuming when they find that German tourists have got up early and left their towels out to claim the best seats.

This year, however, the British struck back.

They rose at the crack of dawn and roped together sets of sunbeds with their towels.

A metaphorical white flag was hoisted by the other side in a report in the Cologne newspaper *Express*. "We hardly had a chance against the Englanders," 60-year-old German holidaymaker Christa Konermann complained on her return from Lanzarote in the Canaries.

She said she had backache brought on by lying for hours on a towel on the ground beside the hotel pool because she and her husband failed to grab one of the 85 sunloungers serving 244 apartments.

"The English always bagged them first," she moaned. "We Germans didn't get a look-in. Sometimes the Englanders were up at 5.30 a.m. and tied as many as eight loungers together with towels."

Some German guests complained to the manager, who suggested they untied the towels. But, said Christa Konermann, they were afraid of the British, many of whom were "huge and tattooed" and appeared to spend a great deal of time drinking, possibly toasting their victory.

Express conceded: "Sadly, we have lost the first round."

But the paper predicted that the war would hot up in three weeks when the holiday season begins in earnest.

Germany is blamed for beginning hostilities on Majorca in the Eighties. There, despite his countrymen's victory in Lanzarote, one angry Briton was conceding defeat yesterday.

John Ivy, 40, from Camden, North London, a guest at the Belle Vue Hotel in the northern resort of Alcudia, said: "I thought sunbed-grabbing was a joke, but now I've seen it for myself. I'm sure the Germans are paying one of the staff to reserve the loungers for them."

"Our hotel is full of Germans and you'd think they owned the place. I can't get a quiet drink because they talk at the tops of their voices. The waiters are furious, too, because they click their fingers at them."

Mr Ivy also claimed that Germans grabbed front seats reserved for VIPs at a festival. "They had to be moved by police so the mayor and his guests could sit down."

Residents of Majorca are bracing themselves for another summer of international tension. One local said: "We are afraid of taunts from the Germans because the English are out of the World Cup."

By Roger Scott, The Daily Mail, *June 2, 1994.*

Col. 2: 3 **to bag s.th.** *(informal)* to take s.th. before s.o. else can get it – 5 **look-in** *(informal)* chance to do s.th.
Col. 3: 26 **to brace o.s.** to get ready to deal with s.th. difficult

Before you read

- Quote

  "Few countries, certainly in Europe, arouse as much antipathy (= dislike) among foreigners as Germany."

  a) Who might have made this statement, and in what kind of context?

  b) Would you agree with the statement? Why, why not?

Auf wiedersehen, with great respect

Robin Gedye, who is leaving after nearly 7 years as correspondent in Bonn, looks back on his time in Germany.

The man in an ankle-length black leather coat had crossed two fields to lean on our fence and inquire whether we had permission to light a bonfire on a Sunday or whether he ought to call the fire brigade.

He was not from the council, nor did he own the land, but he hung around for 10 minutes in intimidatory pose to make his point. As an introduction to Germany in November, 1989, the experience could hardly have better fulfilled our stereotyped preconceptions. Interfering strangers, a plethora of regulations, uncompromising bureaucrats and intolerance have long been popularly accepted hallmarks of the archetypal Teuton.

Few countries, certainly in Europe, arouse as much antipathy among foreigners as Germany. Whether brought out by its wartime past or out of envy over its present successes, foreign opinion of Germany tends to the pejorative.

Many of the national characteristics we mock them for are found to some degree in our own countries. Germany just seems to have them in higher concentration.

You never hear of foreigners speaking of their "love" for Germans as you might of French or Italians. But most of us leave with respect for their struggle to live down their past and for their enthusiasm in building a new country in a Europe of largely self-satisfied and resentful neighbours.

The cartoonists' German is rosy-cheeked and creased with laughter as he sits at the trestle table, beer mug in hand, Lederhosen stained to a professional sheen. Or sun-bed tanned, his white hair swept back, we glimpse him as he glides past us in his Mercedes coupe at 140 mph.

Sometimes he sports a swastika on his arm, a pelmet of greasy black hair covers an eyebrow and a pencil moustache his upper lip. The images carry an undertow of threat. The beer hall rabble, the once-blond Aryan master race now at the driving wheel of a ruthless economy. It is hard to go shopping without wondering what that man over 70 did in the war.

Baroness Thatcher and President Mitterand of France were [...] terrified by the thought of a united Germany [...] and convinced out of a sense of national self-preservation that only a divided Germany could be kept in bounds. The Germans themselves hardly make the job of forgetting their past any easier. Politics are formulated through the prism of their wartime guilt. They cannot move internationally without hesitating a hundred times to check for compromising nuances. [...]

9 **plethora** ['pleθərə] too much of s.th.
18 **to live s.th. down** to make people forget s.th.
25 **pelmet** *here:* covering
26 **pencil** *here:* thin
26 **to carry an undertow** to give an impression
30 **Baroness Thatcher** former British prime minister who opposed German reunification
33 **formulated through the prism** strongly influenced
35 **compromising** ['kɒmprəmaɪzɪŋ] embarrassing

Germany remains a mass of contradictions, tortured by its past, yet determined to treat itself as a normal country. One of the three wealthiest nations, its money floods abroad because entrepreneurs cannot afford its production costs. It has the world's longest holidays, highest rates of pay and shortest working hours. It prides itself on trade union co-determination in management areas while pleading for their iron grip on working practices to be loosened so that fundamental structural faults can be corrected.

It is a country trying to join two alien economic and political cultures, united only in language, while searching for a new identity. [...]

Is it to be feared? Germans have racked up some extraordinary achievements. They have bankrupted themselves, triumphed, destroyed, murdered and rebuilt. They have sworn allegiance to five regimes: the Emperor, Weimar, Hitler, East Germany and the Federal Republic.

In their present incarnation they have become one of the world's richest societies. Their welfare state is second to none and their wealth on permanent display.

Not for them the impoverishment of the British middle classes through school fees and mortgages. Their children are educated free in an excellent system and most people prefer to rent.

We may snipe at them for their intolerance, but they live in a highly structured society where householders sweep the pavements, people greet total strangers in lifts and where they call one another Mr and Mrs after working together for 20 years.

No yob culture here. Pubs in Germany do not spill their young clientele routinely on to pavements and streets in the hot summer months to intimidate passers-by.

Past excesses demand a tight social structure where exaggerated formality keeps emotions at bay. "Don't rock the boat" is the catch-phrase of modern Germany. [...]

German economic domination of Europe is inevitable. Self-discipline, driven by fear of repeating history, will ensure Germany enters the 21st century streamlined and fit. Whether it does so as part of a unified Europe or as a dominant entity is largely up to us.

By Robin Gedye, *Electronic Telegraph, issue 426, July 12, 1996.*

40 **trade union co-determination** workers' representatives influence how a company is managed
41 **practice** *here:* regulation
45 **to rack up** to collect
49 **incarnation** *here:* form
54 **to snipe** to criticize nastily
59 **to keep at bay** to control
62 **streamlined** *here:* well prepared
64 **to be up to s.o.** to be s.o.'s responsibility

Exploring the text

1 a) According to the writer, what image does Germany have in the world?
b) What factors have created this image?

2 How does the writer describe German reality in the 1990s?

3 Describe Robin Gedye's feelings about his host country.

4 Do you think that the *Daily Telegraph*, in which the article was first printed, is a popular or a quality newspaper? Examine the style, language and tone of the article for evidence to support your answer.

A step further

- Chat show
  Hold a TV chat show in class in which you talk about Germany's image and role in the world. First agree on the rules of the TV format, especially for the speakers. Define the role of the show's host and audience during the discussion.
- Speech
  The German chancellor is giving a speech in the European Parliament about Germany's image, history and future. Write the speech using ideas from the text.

Talking like a politician

Dealing with problems
to face a problem
to address an issue
to tackle a task
to overcome difficulties

Taking action
We have to make sure that ...

We should take care (not) to ...

We are prepared / determined to ...

Looking to the future
in (the near) future
in the short / long term

We are hopeful / confident that ...

Before you read

- Statistics

a) Read the statements in the box below. Which ones are supported by the figures in the bar chart on the left?

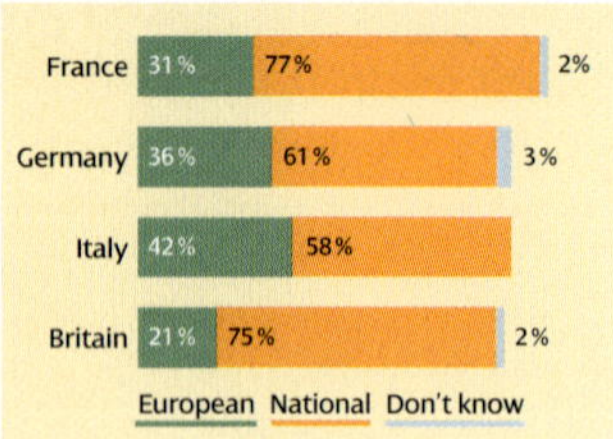

MORI, Feb. – March, 2001.

Who are we? To what extent do you see yourself as European?

- Most young Europeans consider themselves to be primarily British, French, German or Italian rather than European. Yet almost one-third now regard themselves more as Europeans than as nationals of their home country.
- The Italians see themselves as more European than the other nationalities surveyed, with two in five regarding themselves as more European than Italian. The Italians also have the greatest enthusiasm for integration.
- Over one-third of Germans view themselves as primarily European, while the British are least likely to feel any European identity. […]
- The British are the least enthusiastic about political union and would like to see a shift of power back to the British government.

From Time, *April 2, 2001.*

b) How would you answer the question: To what extent do you see yourself as a European?

Britain and Europe

The following text is an extract from a speech by former British foreign secretary Robin Cook on April 19, 2001.

To deny that Britain is European is to deny both our geography and our history. Our culture, our security, and our prosperity, are inseparable from the continent of Europe.

Underlying the anti-European case is the belief that there is an alternative future available to Britain. It used to be argued that the European Union is not Europe and that Britain could exist perfectly comfortably as one of a number of European countries maintaining a loose association with Brussels. But with the majority of non-EU states now clamouring for full membership, the changing geopolitics of Europe have consigned that argument to the past.

Some anti-Europeans now argue that Britain's destiny lies outside Europe, as part of "the English-speaking world" and a member of NAFTA.

Yet Britain trades three times more with the rest of the EU than we do with NAFTA. The reason why over four thousand US companies have located here is because they want to export to Europe. If they only wanted to sell to NAFTA, they would have stayed at home.

Europe is where our domestic quality of life is most directly at stake, whether the issue is environmental standards, the fight against organised crime, policy on asylum or stability on the continent.

But it is not simply a question of economic and political realism that ties Britain to Europe, compelling as those arguments are. Britain is also a European country in the more profound sense of sharing European assumptions about how society should be organised. The last international survey of social attitudes put Britain squarely within the European mainstream on our approach to social justice and public services, such as health.

There are strong ties of kinship between Britain and North America. These are an immense asset to us in the modern world. The US and the UK are each other's closest

11 **NAFTA** *short for* **North American Free Trade Agreement** between the USA, Canada and Mexico

allies. But our value as an ally to our friends in Washington is in direct proportion to our influence with our partners in Europe.

I do not accept that to acknowledge our European identity diminishes our Britishness. Nor do I accept that membership of the European Union is a threat to our national identity.

None of our European partners, with their own proud national traditions, seem afflicted by this self-doubt and insecurity. The idea that the French, the Germans or the Spanish are attempting to erase their national identities by constructing a "country called Europe" is the mother of all Euromyths. On the contrary, our partners see their membership of a successful European Union as underwriting, not undermining, their assertion of national identity.

For France, Germany and Italy, the European Community was central to the renewal of their nations and the regeneration of their economies in the post-War period. To Spain, Portugal and Greece, joining the European Community was an affirmation of their freedom from fascism and a guarantee of a democratic future. To Austria and Finland, joining the European Community was a celebration of the end of the Cold War, which enabled them to make a free choice in their national orientation.

Britain has everything to gain from being a leading partner in a strong Europe. All we have to lose is the timidity which prevents us from embracing our European destiny and from recognising that it is a source of confidence in our nation's future.

In the aftermath of Nice, it is clearer than ever that a strong Europe requires strong nations. With the accession of up to twelve new member states, the European Union is set to become even more diverse. In the next Inter-Governmental Conference, the challenge is to find the right balance between European and national decision-making and to enhance the EU's legitimacy by harnessing the democratic traditions of its member states.

This is a debate that Britain can play a pivotal role in shaping. But we can only do so if we reject insular nationalism and the politics of fear by engaging fully and confidently in Europe.

35 **Euromyth** untrue story about absurd laws introduced by the EU
36 **to underwrite** *here:* to support
48 **Nice** refers to the Treaty of Nice which laid down rules for the acceptance of new member states
52 **to harness** to control and use to achieve s.th.

Over to you!

Analysing the text in pairs

Step 1 Prepare the text at home. Write no more than 22 key words on a sheet of paper. Indicate the line of argument by connecting the words with lines, arrows, etc.

Step 2 In class, an equal number of students sits in two circles, one inside the other. Each student faces a partner in the other circle. Cf. diagram on the right.

Step 3 Using only the notes from step 1, the inner circle sums up Robin Cook's views (3 minutes). Then the outer circle adds missing points or corrections (1 minute). Each student notes down any open questions or points of disagreement.

Step 4 The outside circle moves three places to the left, the inner circle stays seated.

Step 5 This time the students in the outer circle summarise the text based on their notes (3 minutes) and the inner circle adds to or corrects the summary. Again, both students note down any open questions or points of disagreement.

Step 6 The outer circle moves around again three places to the left. The new pairs discuss, and try to find answers to, any open questions.

Step 7 The whole class discusses whether the method was effective or not.

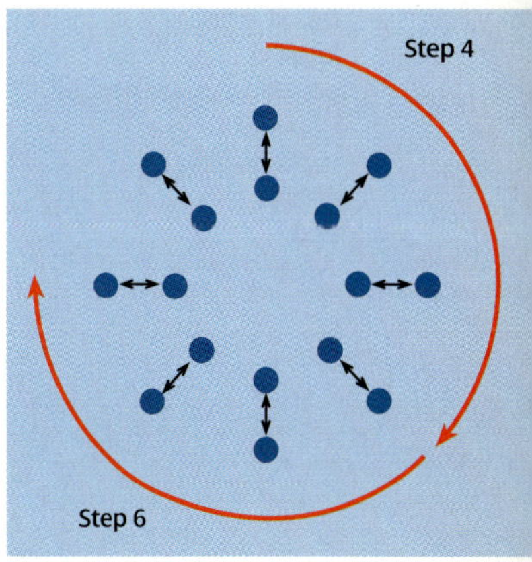

- Teach yourselves!
  A group of three or four students develops a 45-minute teaching plan dealing with the speech extract "Britain and Europe" (pp. 102 – 103).
  - Divide the lesson into three parts:
    1 an introductory activity involving as many students as possible;
    2 an analysis phase which ensures a good understanding of the topics and opinions presented in the text;
    3 a post-reading activity based on the ideas and new vocabulary in the text (cf. "A step further" below for ideas).
  - Scan your book for teaching ideas which can be applied to the text.
  - Give students enough opportunities to use the target language.
  - Try to use a variety of methods (teacher-guided discussion, pair work, group work) and media (the blackboard, overhead projector, posters).

A step further

- a) Write down questions which you would like to ask Robin Cook about 'Britain and Europe'.
  b) Practise an interview in pairs and then stage a 'live' TV interview in class.
- A political opponent of Robin Cook's also gives a speech. He / she has very different views on Britain's role in Europe. Exploit the text for ideas and add further arguments. Then write and give this speech. Refer to skills file, "Presentations", on pp. 182–183 for ideas.

Using your skills

Analysing an advert

brand image
positive characteristics
desired effect
target group
age, gender, income, interests
AIDA strategy
attracting **a**ttention
arousing **i**nterest
appealing to a **d**esire
taking **a**ction
layout
position and size of copy (= the text)
visual material
colours
text
slogan, copy

Advertising a German product abroad

a) How do advertisers appeal to a target group? Find print adverts and try to work out who the target audience is and how advertisers appeal to them. Refer to the box on the left and also to skills file, "Adverts" on page 187 for ideas.
b) Read the task below. Then form groups and decide how much time is available to work on the projects and make presentations in class. Define the teacher's role.

Task

Develop an advert for a German product, company or tourist attraction and then present it in class.
- Form groups of four 'ad designers'. Your group should include at least one 'graphic designer' who can translate your ideas into an advert.
- Choose a German product / company / tourist attraction which is of interest abroad. An already existing one-page print advert would be a good starting-point.
- Organize your work on your own. Decide which advertising format best suits your product and ideas, e.g. a transparency for a printed one-page advert, pre-recorded material for a radio advert, an outline for a TV commercial. Take into account what you can realistically include in a 20-minute presentation. Refer to skills file, "Presentations", on pp. 182 – 183 for ideas.

Evaluation

How successful was the project as a whole? Suggest possible improvements.

Before you read

- a) Think of examples of the following types of humour:
  situational humour – verbal humour – *black humour* – *slapstick*.
  b) What *sitcoms* do you know? Briefly describe the characters, the situations they usually find themselves in, the types of humour used and the target audience.

Situational humour
comedy which is created by a character's actions

Black humour
situations / jokes which make fun of unpleasant aspects of life

Slapstick
the use of exaggerated physical action to amuse the audience

Sitcom
short for situation comedy; a TV programme that shows the same set of characters in amusing situations

Making fun of it all

Fawlty Towers *is one of the funniest comedies ever shown on British TV. It features Basil Fawlty, a hotel owner, Sybil his wife, Manuel, a Spanish waiter and Polly, the hotel assistant. The following text is taken from an episode entitled "The Germans". In his wife's absence, Basil has proved incapable of running his hotel Fawlty Towers alone. Following a nervous breakdown he finds himself in hospital but he manages to escape and return to the hotel.*

What impression do you get of Basil Fawlty and Manuel? Describe each character's appearance and body language.

The hotel reception. Polly is finishing a phone call. As she puts the receiver down, a guest approaches the desk, clicks his heels, and bows.

First German Gnädiges Fräulein, können Sie mir sagen, wann das Mittagessen serviert wird, bitte?

Polly Um ein Uhr, fünf Minuten.

First German Vielen Dank.

Polly Bitte schön.

Polly goes into the kitchen. The German retires upstairs. Misses Tibbs and Gatsby come down the stairs as Basil enters through the main doors, dressed but still bandaged.

Basil *(masterfully)* Manuel!

Miss Tibbs Oh, Mr Fawlty!

Basil Ah, good evening.

Miss Tibbs Are you all right now?

Basil Perfectly, thank you. *(Handing Manuel, who has just come in, his case.)* Take this to the room please, dear.

(Manuel takes it, somewhat taken aback.)

Miss Gatsby Are you sure you're all right?

Basil Perfectly, thank you. Right as rain.

He makes his way a little unsteadily towards the desk, but misses. He reappears and takes up his position behind the desk.

2 **to click one's heels** *die Hacken zusammenschlagen*
8 **Misses Tibbs and Gatsby** guests at the hotel
16 **taken aback** surprised
18 **(as) right as rain** *(informal)* in good health

Manuel You OK?

Basil Fine, thank you, dear. You go and have a lie-down.

Manuel Qué?

Basil Ah, there you are. Would you take my case … how did you get that?

Manuel What?

Basil Oh never mind … take it … take it upstairs!

Manuel Qué?

Basil Take it … take it …

Manuel I go get Polly.

Basil I've already had one. Take it, take it now … *(Manuel hurries off.)* Tch! The people I have to deal with …

He looks up to see a couple approaching the desk. He beams at them.

Elderly German Sprechen Sie Deutsch?

Basil … Beg your pardon?

Elderly German Entschuldigen Sie, bitte, können Sie Deutsch sprechen?

Basil I'm sorry, could you say that again?

German Lady You speak German?

Basil Oh, German! I'm sorry. I thought there was something wrong with you. Of course, the Germans!

German Lady You speak German?

Basil Well … er … a little. I get by.

German Lady Ein bisschen.

Elderly German Ah – wir wollen ein Auto mieten.

Basil *(nodding helpfully)* Well, why not?

Elderly German Bitte.

Basil Yes, a little bit tricky … Would you mind saying it again?

German Lady Please?

Basil Could you repeat … amplify … you know, reiterate? Yes? Yes?

Elderly German Wir …

Basil Wir? … Yes, well we'll come back to that.

Elderly German … Wollen …

Basil *(to himself)* Vollen … Voluntary?

Elderly German Ein Auto mieten.

Basil Owtoe … out to … Oh, I see! You're volunteering to go out to get some meat. Not necessary! We have meat here! *(Pause; the couple are puzzled.)* We haf meat hier … in ze buildink!! *(He mimes a cow's horns.)* Moo! *(Polly comes in.)* Ah, Polly, just explaining about the meat.

Polly Oh! We weren't expecting you.

Basil Oh, weren't you? *(Hissing through his teeth.)* They're Germans. Don't mention the war.

Polly I see. Well, Mrs Fawlty said you were going to have a rest for a couple of days, you know, in the hospital.

Basil *(firmly)* Idle hands get in the way of the devil's work, Fawlty. Now …

Polly Right, well why don't you have a lie-down, and I can deal with this.

Basil Yes, yes, good idea, good idea, Elsie. Yes. Bit of a headache, actually …

Miss Tibbs We don't think you're well, Mr Fawlty.

Basil Well, perhaps not, but I'll live longer than you.

22 **lie-down** a short rest
30 **one** Basil has understood A-**polli**-naris (a mineral water) instead of **Polly**
32 **to beam** *here:* to smile broadly
48 **to amplify** *(formal) here:* to explain in more detail
48 **to reiterate** [rɪˈɪtəreɪt] *(formal)* to repeat
63 **Idle hands…** *(proverb)* The devil finds work for idle hands *(= Müßiggang ist aller Laster Anfang).*

Miss Gatsby You must have hurt yourself.
Basil My dear woman, a blow on the head like that … is worth two in the bush.
Miss Tibbs Oh, we know … but it was a nasty knock.
Basil Mmmmmmmm … would you like one? *(Hits the reception bell impressively.)* Next please.
Two men and two women come down the stairs.
Basil *(a hoarse whisper)* Polly! Polly! Are these Germans too?
Polly Oh yes, but I can deal …
Basil Right, right, here's the plan. I'll stand there and ask them if they want something to drink before the war … before their lunch … don't mention the war! *(He moves in front of the guests, bows, and mimes eating and drinking.)*
Second German Can we help you?
Basil *(gives a startled jump)* Ah … you speak English.
Second German Of course.
Basil Ah, wonderful. Wounderbar! Ah – please allow me to introduce myself – I am the owner of Fawlty Towers, and may I welcome your war, your wall, you wall, you all … and hope that your stay will be a happy one. Now would you like to eat first, or would you like a drink before the war…ning that, er, trespassers will be – er, er – tied up with piano wire. … Sorry! Sorry! *(Clutches his thigh.)* Bit of trouble with the old leg … got a touch of shrapnel in the war … Korean, Korean war, sorry, Korean.
Second German Thank you, we will eat now.
Basil bows gracefully and ushers them into the dining room.
Basil Oh good, please do allow me. May I say how pleased we are to have some Europeans here now that we are on the Continent…

From Fawlty Towers, Three Episodes *by John Cleese / Connie Booth, Hg. von R. Gratzka, Stuttgart: Reclam, 1997.*

69 **A blow … bush** *(proverb)* A bird in the hand is worth two in the bush.
85 **trespassers…** from the phrase "Trespassers will be prosecuted"; warning to stop people entering private property
92 **on the Continent** *here:* a part of Europe

Exploring the text

1 a) What impression of the three nationalities does the text convey?
b) Which parts of the dialogue would you expect to create humour? Find examples of different types of humour (cf. "Before you read" on page 105). You can use phrases from the box on the right in your answer.
2 Guess what will happen in the dining room. Think of further humorous effects.
3 If "The Germans" is available on video, watch the second part of the episode.
- Check your answers to questions 1 and 2.
- Assess whether the humour in the text has been transferred successfully to the screen.

A step further

- Add more stage directions which create humour. Then act out the scene in class.
- Imagine how Basil might deal with other nationalities. Write a script for a further scene in *Fawlty Towers*.
- Comment on the following statements:
  - John Cleese (Basil Fawlty) once said: "'The Germans' is much more about the fact that Basil is stuck in the past than it is trying to make fun of the Germans."
  - "The Germans" is regularly repeated on British television whereas German TV has never broadcast it at prime time (i.e. when viewing rates are highest).

Talking about humour

to amuse / entertain the audience
to be amused by s.th.
to find s.th. extremely / highly amusing
to make fun of / ridicule / laugh at s.o. / s.th.
to produce / create a humorous / comic effect
to provoke / induce laughter
to be a laughable / ridiculous / humorous figure
to roar with laughter
to chuckle = to laugh quietly
to titter = to laugh in a nervous way
to giggle = to laugh in a silly way

Before you read

- How would you prepare for a trip to a foreign country?
- a) Try to think of some important rules of behaviour in Germany, e.g. when you say "du" or "Sie", what you do / say when you are introduced to someone. Then, explain these rules to a partner.
  b) What serious mistakes would you warn a tourist **not** to make in Germany?
  c) In which countries / areas of the world would you expect to find the biggest cultural differences compared to Germany?
- Quickly scan the text for unknown words and list them on the blackboard. Then try to guess their meaning from the context.

Over to you

Culture shock Asia

On your best behaviour

However much you dislike the notion of being an ambassador for your country, that is how local people will see you. Similarly, your view of their country will almost certainly be coloured by how they treat you. So it pays for everyone to respect everyone else. No one expects you to traipse around Asia dressed in the local fashions, but it is polite – and in some places expedient – to adapt your Western behaviour to suit the local culture. Because social rules tend to be more rigid in Asia, it's relatively easy for tourists to do the wrong thing – nine times out of ten, you'll be forgiven for being ignorant of the niceties, but there are a few behaviour codes you should definitely follow.

- Asian men and women dress modestly and find exposed flesh an embarrassment anywhere but the beach (and even when swimming they plunge in fully clothed). [...] Shoes are never worn indoors (except in hotels and offices), so remember to take them off in religious buildings and when entering people's homes – this includes some small guest houses.
- Getting angry at anything is a very un-Asian thing to do. In fact, it's considered to be a loss of face and therefore an embarrassment both for the perpetrator and the recipient – a bit like being heard farting loudly in a posh restaurant.
- Canoodling in public is frowned upon in most parts of Asia (even Japan). It's quite common for friends of the same sex to wander about with their arms round each other, but passionate embraces with the opposite sex are considered rather gross, regardless of marital status.
- Throughout Asia, the head is considered the most sacred part of a person's body, and the feet the most profane. Try not to touch anyone on the head (even kids) or to point at anyone, or anything, with your feet.
- Avoid making eye contact with members of the opposite sex – in some Asian cultures it's seen as an unabashed come-on.
- Be sensitive when discussing religion and politics with local people. In most parts of Asia, a person's faith is inviolable and should not be questioned. Censorship is rife in some Asian countries and penalties can be severe for a resident who goes public with unfashionable views. This is very much the case in Indonesia at the moment, and in Burma, China and Tibet. Even in happy-go-lucky Thailand anyone who makes disrespectful remarks about the king is liable to be put in jail. In India, on the other hand, opinionated debate is standard fare on train journeys and in newspaper columns.

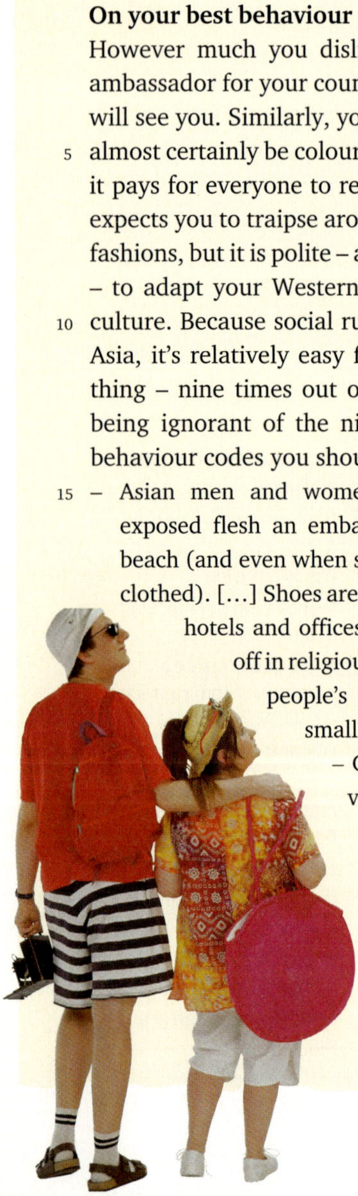

43 **unabashed come-on** *unverfrorene „Anmache"*

Being an alien

As an obvious outsider (or "alien", as foreigners are known in Japan), you will arouse a lot of interest, for your novelty value as well as your commercial potential.

In Asia it's just not rude to be nosy, so try not to get offended by the unflinching stares, or by women stroking your oddly coloured skin and feeling your strangely fine hair. And, if you're blond-haired or black-skinned, get ready for movie-star treatment!

Be prepared to answer endless questions about your marital status and also about your children (in most parts of Asia to be single is a calamitous state of affairs and to be childless a great misfortune). In fact, be prepared to answer questions about absolutely any private matter at all: how old you are, how much you earn and how much your air ticket cost are common conversational openers. People will read your letters over your shoulder, and eavesdrop quite blatantly too, even if they can't understand what's being said.

Being a wealthy tourist

All over Asia, people will express amazement at the price of your air ticket – it will seem an absolute fortune to them. Regardless of how impecunious you are, or feel, to an Indian factory worker on less than a dollar a day or a Thai waiter on the daily equivalent of $3, you are quite literally a millionaire. And your camera, watch and sun-glasses will do little to change his or her opinion. Small wonder that Asians can't understand why travellers dress in torn and dirty clothing – surely if they can afford an air ticket they can stretch to a new outfit?

From First-Time Asia: A Rough Guide Special, *Lucy Ridout, Lesley Reader, Rough Guides Ltd, 1998, pp. 190–192, 188, 195.*

Over to you!

- Use the three texts on these pages as a basis for the following activities:
  - Sketch: Turn the information in "Being an alien" and "Being a wealthy tourist" into a sketch with the title "Entering alien territory". Then act it out in class.
  - Diary: Write a diary of a trip to Asia. Include the traveller's feelings and thoughts.
  - Parallel texts: Write texts for Asian tourists entitled "Culture shock Germany", in which you try to explain how German society works.
  - Story: Write a boy-meets-girl love story which focuses on a culture-related misunderstanding. You can refer to "On your best behaviour" for ideas.

Meet the media

In the film *Dances with Wolves* army officer Lieutenant John Dunbar (Kevin Costner) meets Native Americans and gets to know their culture. In groups watch **one** of the following scenes which highlight the clash between the white man's and the Native American's customs and values. Compare your observations with another group's.

- Sioux medicine man Kicking Bird unexpectedly discovers that the deserted Fort Sedgewick has a new resident, John Dunbar.
- The Sioux council meets to discuss how to deal with the unexpected visitor. We are introduced to Chief Ten Bears and the powerful warrior Wind in his Hair.
- John Dunbar meets a group of Sioux warriors led by Wind in his Hair. They try – unsuccessfully – to steal his horse.

Using your skills

Working abroad

job / placement search

www.jobstar.org
www.careersonline.com.au/
content.monster.co.uk/job_hunting
www.jeunesse.gc.ca
www.rileyguide.com

Finding a job abroad takes a lot of planning, no matter whether you want to be an au-pair, find a holiday job, or do voluntary work or an internship with a company. In each case, you will have to write and send off an application.

A job application consists of:

- a **covering letter** in which you introduce yourself to the company / organisation you want to work for or in reply to an advert,
- a **résumé** ['rezju:meɪ] in which you give basic details about your life, education, skills and – if they are relevant – your hobbies.

If you wish to draw attention to qualifications you have acquired, include **copies** of diplomas, certificates or references in a folder with your application.

Preparation

The purpose of a job application is to advertise you as a potential employee! After all, you want to be chosen over all the other applicants. However, be truthful!

- Personal qualities
  - Write down qualities for each of your classmates on separate pieces of paper. Use a dictionary, if necessary. Then, collect what the others have written about you and compare it with what you think of yourself.
  - Decide which of the qualities might be useful when applying for a job.
- Analysing a job advert
  The following advert (and source) is fictitious, but you will find similar ones in newspapers or magazines and, of course, in the internet.
  - Examine the advert for information about the company. Even the style in which it is written will tell you something about it.
  - Define in detail what is expected of applicants.

The company describes itself.

The company defines the kind of employee it is looking for.

application details

Out of school – Ready to have FUN?

We are a leading tour operator with holiday resorts all over the world.
We offer ecologically-sound holidays for the whole family.
Are **you** 18 or over and speak at least one foreign language?
Are **you** enthusiastic, sport-loving, motivated, responsible and good with children?
Are **you** available to start work in July?
Then, **we** want to hear from **you**.
Send your application to:

Ms. Holly Day,
GlobalCamps,
15 Sunstreet,
Philadelphia, PA 29810

From: YouthMag, May 2003.

- Skills, interests
  When you apply for a job, do not just give exam results. Make a list of activities or courses done in or outside of school, work experience from part-time or holiday jobs, voluntary work, e.g. in the community or for a charity and achievements related to hobbies or past-times, e.g. captain of the football team.
  - Define why your experience makes you more suitable than other applicants.
  - In pairs, discuss which qualifications may be relevant for the job at GlobalCamps.
  - Make a note of the relevant qualifications and why they are useful.

Using your skills

Covering letter (*AE* cover letter) / letter of application

A covering letter should not be longer than one page.
It consists of: **1** contact details, **2** the employer's correct address, **3** a reference to the job you are applying for, **4** your qualifications and skills, **5** a conclusion and **6** a complimentary close.

1 Katja Müller
Hauptstraße 10
D-53101 Bonn
Phone: +49-228 93 82
E-mail: kmueller@internet.de
27 May 2003

> AE alternatives are:
> May 27, 2003 or
> 05 / 27 / 2003
> The date may also go here.

> you do not know the addressee's me, use: Dear Madam or Sir you are male) or Dear Sir or adam (if you are female).

Ms. Holly Day
GlobalCamps **2**
15 Sunstreet
Philadelphia, PA 29810

....

Summer job at GlobalCamp

Dear Ms. Day,

I have read your advertisement for ... **3, 4**

> Alternatives:
> – Your advert in ... indicated that you were looking for...
> – I would like to apply for the position of ... which you advertised in...
> – I am writing with regard to ...

References are available on request ...

Thank you for taking my application into consideration ... **5**

> Alternatives:
> – I look forward to hearing from you soon.
> – I would like to meet with you ...

Yours sincerely,

Katja Müller **6**

Enclosures

> *AE:* Sincerely yours
> If you do not know the name of your addressee use:
> *BE:* Yours faithfully, *AE:* Faithfully yours

- Work out the differences between the above letter and a German business letter.
- a) Write a covering letter in reply to the advert on page 110.
  b) In small groups, discuss the strong and weak points of your letters. Is the content and order of the paragraphs logical? Could you express passages more clearly and /or more concisely? Do you notice any spelling or grammar mistakes? On the basis of these corrections and suggestions, write a second draft.
  c) Check a partner's letter for mistakes. Look at the letter from a distance to see whether the layout is well-balanced. Write a new draft and check again.
- Which of the expressions below are formal / casual? Which ones could you use when applying to GlobalCamps? Make two lists with a partner. Then put the sentences in a logical order as they would appear in a covering letter.

Covering letter: useful phrases

Please, contact me by phone or e-mail. I will return your call / letter within 24 hours. / Naturally I would be prepared to come for an interview at your convenience. / My interest in ... started when I ... and developed when... / Please find enclosed my CV (résumé) showing .../ I hope that my application is of interest to you / I wish to broaden my horizons by ... / I am writing with regard to the ... in ... / I enclose my résumé for your consideration. / I was able to use my skills at ... when ... / I would like to apply for the position of ... advertised in ... / I came across the advert which you placed in ... / My experience as ... qualifies me as ... / I read your company's description in ... and would like to inquire about ... / I think my experience in ... would enable me to ... / I would welcome an interview to ... / I would like to use my skills in ...

Using your skills

Résumés and CVs

Strictly speaking, you only send in a CV (= a complete record of your qualifications without any 'gaps') when applying for a job in a profession, e.g. a doctor, lawyer. Everything else is usually called a résumé. This presents your education and work experience in chronological order, usually starting with the most recent information. Résumés (and CVs) should include:

- career / job objectives, i.e. what you want to achieve in the job you are applying for (usually with reference to what you have already achieved),
- a personal profile which sums up the skills and experiences which are relevant for the job you are seeking.

Résumés written for the US and UK do **not** usually include:
a photo – a date and place of birth (unless the job is in the UK) – information about parents (profession, marital status) – marital status – ethnic background – religious affiliation – references (may be offered on request, cf. covering letter) – a date or signature (as each résumé is written specially for one job application) – all schools attended (only include the highest school or university qualification).

"Oh, CV ... I thought you said bring a CD."

■ Based on this information, write your résumé to accompany your letter of application to GlobalCamps. See the following example for ideas:

Katja Müller
Hauptstraße 10
D-53101Bonn
Phone: +49-228 93 92
E-mail: kmueller@internet.de

Objective:	I hope to start studying social science in October and wish to work later with young people.
Personal profile:	patient, open-minded, adaptable, team worker
Qualifications:	School leaving certificate: Abitur (2003) Overall result: 1.8
Work experience:	6-week summer job as a lifeguard in a local pool (2002), Part-time job as a babysitter (since 1999)
Education:	1995 – 2003: *Stephangymnasium* (High school)
Additional skills:	Native speaker of German, fluent English, working knowledge of Spanish Clean driving licence
Further interests:	Coach for the under 12s volleyball, active member of a volleyball club

- Exchange your first draft with a partner and check for mistakes. Pay special attention to the layout. Keep it simple and clear!
- If you search for a job in the internet, you will find a great variety of electronic résumés. Download some of them for ideas which you can use in your résumé.

Using your skills

Electronic résumés

www.content.monster.co.uk/job_hunting
www.crossculturalsolutions.org
www.horizoncamps.com

Job interview: role play

- Choose one of the following role plays:
  Job A You are invited for a job interview by Holly Day of GlobalCamps.
  Job B You are a native speaker of English applying for a position as assistant teacher at your school.
- Divide the class into two groups:
  Group 1 has the potential interviewers. Prepare questions to ask the applicant.
  Group 2 has the potential applicants. Prepare a fictitious biography, including special qualifications which might be of interest for the job you chose.
- Draw lots in each group to decide the candidates for the role play.
- Those students who are not involved in the role play act as observers. You should discuss the interviewees' strong and weak points later.
- Afterwards, sum up what you have learnt from the role play, and go through the role play again.

"Perhaps I should warn you – he makes interviews hell."

Follow-up letter

In the follow-up letter, thank your interviewer for giving you an interview. The formal requirements of this type of letter are the same as those in a business letter. The text has three functions. You should:

- thank the addressee for the job interview.
  E.g. It was a pleasure to meet you at ... for... / Thank you again for taking the time to...
- refer to qualifications discussed during the job interview.
  E.g. As I mentioned during the interview, I think my experience in ... would be of benefit for ...
- express your interest in the job again.
  E.g. I am interested in working for GlobalCamps because... / I welcome the opportunity to ...

Facing a global future

Building a dream

Looking and thinking

1 Describe the photo below. Pay particular attention to details such as:
   - the size and position of the robot;
   - how it relates to the other figures;
   - the mood and atmosphere conveyed.

2 Write product information for the robot in the photo. What qualities and characteristics would you emphasize?

Exploring the text

1 Compare your text from "Looking and thinking" with the product information in the advert below.
2 What predictions does Honda make as regards the future of robot technology?
3 a) Look at the definitions in the box on the right and try to identify the *tagline* and the company *slogan*.
b) What message do they try to convey?

Tagline
short, catchy summary of the message of an advert

Slogan
concise phrase associated with a product

A step further

- Do you think that the use of robots in the home will have a positive or negative impact on our lives? Give reasons for your answer.
- Do **one** of the following:
  - A travelling salesperson tries to sell a robot to someone who is against household gadgets. In pairs, write down the dialogue and act it out in class.
  - Imagine your family owns the robot in the advert. Write a *mini-saga*. Try to have a surprise ending.

Mini-saga
a story of exactly 50 words (excluding the title)

We're building a dream, one robot at a time.

The dream was simple. Design a robot that, one day, could duplicate the complexities of human motion and actually help people.

An easy task? Hardly. But after more than 15 years of research and development, the result is ASIMO, an advanced robot with unprecedented human-like abilities.

ASIMO walks forward and backward, turns corners, and, amazingly, goes up and down stairs with ease. All with a remarkable sense of strength and balance.

The future of this exciting technology is even more promising. ASIMO has the potential to respond to simple voice commands, recognize faces, carry loads and even push wheeled objects. This means that, one day, ASIMO could be quite useful in some very important tasks. Like assisting the elderly, and even helping with household chores. In essence, ASIMO might serve as another set of eyes, ears and legs for all kinds of people in need.

All of this represents the steps we're taking to develop products that make our world a better place. And in ASIMO's case, it's a giant step in the right direction.

HONDA

The power of dreams

6 **unprecedented** that did not exist before
15 **chore** task, e.g. cleaning

Robots

Before you watch

- What is the difference between a machine and a robot?
- Design your own robot. What qualities and functions will it have? Will it have human characteristics such as reason and emotions? Present your ideas in class.

While you watch

You are going to watch an interview with Dr Nick Pears, a computer scientist and expert on robots at the University of York. While you watch the sequence make notes to help you to answer the following questions.

1. Describe the tasks which the robots perform in the sequence.
2. Dr Pears mentions that his robot is equipped with sensory systems. How do these systems help it to function?
3. a) Why are many of the robots in use not "really robots"?
   b) What is special about Sony's robot Ivo?
4. How will we benefit from household robots such as Arnold and other more sophisticated robots in the future?

A step further

- Think of machines and electronic gadgets you use every day. What would you miss about them most if you suddenly had to do without them?

Before you read

- Make predictions about future trends in science and technology. Will mankind be better or worse off?
- Which technological developments in the last centuries have changed people's lives the most? Consider in particular areas such as medicine, manufacturing and telecommunications.

Surefire predictions

People alive now are living in the midst of what may well be the most extraordinary three or four centuries in human history. The "industrial revolution" and its technical aftermath – even including the spectacular rise in living standards for most human beings from near subsistence to the level of today's modern nations – is only part of the upheaval. The process has already been completed for perhaps a third of humanity … and within a century or two (unless there is a holocaust) the rest of humanity is almost sure to attain the amenities of modern living standards; the worst holocaust imaginable could only delay the process by a century or two.

The most spectacular development, and by far the most meaningful in both human and economic terms, is the revolution in health that we are witnessing in the second part of the twentieth century. Barring catastrophic surprises in the first half

0 **surefire** certain
4 **subsistence** state in which one has just enough to live on
7 **amenity** s.th. that makes life more comfortable
11 **barring** *here:* unless there are

of the twenty-first century, most of humanity will come to share the long healthy life that is now enjoyed by the middle-class contemporary residents of the advanced countries.

The technical developments of the past two centuries certainly depended on earlier discoveries. But the knowledge that emerged before the last two centuries was only infrastructure. Until the most recent generations, most people could not observe the effects or gain the benefits of this progress in their own lives. Now we are reaping the full fruits of that earlier investment.

The spreading of a high level of living will be speeded by another phenomenon that can be predicted for sure: increased migration from poor to rich countries. The lure of a higher standard of living pushes migrants from their native countries and pulls them to richer places. And the felt need in the richer countries for youthful persons in the labor force to balance the ever greater concentrations in the older age cohorts fuels the demand for them. One can see the drama of this process in the youthful medical and custodial staffs in big-city hospitals who came from abroad to tend to the aged natives and the veterans of earlier migrations.

Might there not be even more and faster and more radical change in the future? In human terms, I doubt it. Life expectancy and child mortality cannot fall much faster unless we change genetically. Concorde-like supersonic speed of travel demonstrably does not matter very much (and the trip to and from airports will take a long time to speed up). Communications cannot become much faster, many being at the speed of light now. The distances one can travel – to the planets and beyond – will eventually increase greatly, and this will alter life significantly, though I cannot imagine how.

The only impending shortage is a shortage of economic shortages ... as to the non-material aspects of human existence – good luck to us.

From "Surefire Predictions" by Julian L. Simon, Visions of Technology, *ed. Richard Rhodes, New York: Touchstone, 2000, pp. 337–338.*

26 **custodial staff** personnel which cares for patients
36 **impending** that is about to happen

Exploring the text

1 According to the writer, how important was the industrial revolution as a milestone in recent human history?
2 Why is the revolution in health described as "the most spectacular development ... in the second part of the twentieth century" (ll. 9–11)?
3 What factors have led to an increase in migration from poorer to richer countries?
4 What restrictions on continued growth and change does the writer mention?
5 What "non-material aspects of human existence" might the author be referring to in l. 37? Why should he wish mankind luck?
6 a) Describe the tone of the article.
b) In your opinion, how does the writer feel about technological progress?

A step further

- Which of Julian Simon's predictions do you doubt will happen? Write a short criticism of the text in which you point out that his predictions may not be so "surefire" after all.
- Work in two groups. One group prepares questions for Julian Simon, the other group prepares possible answers. One student from the second group takes the hot chair and answers questions posed by the first group.

Professor Cyborg

The following text deals with Kevin Warwick, Professor of Cybernetics at the University of Reading in the UK, and his experiments with implants which are linked directly to a computer.

In August 1998, Warwick played the part of guinea pig in what was then touted as the first non-medical implant experiment. With a tiny glass capsule full of transponders under the skin of his arm, Warwick essentially became a human remote control: Every time he walked through the door of his building at the University of Reading, sensors in the doorways would immediately register the presence of the transponders in his implant. The lights would come on, his computer would boot up and connect to his website, doors would open, and his office would greet him with a "Hello, Professor Warwick!" In a very Big Brother touch, his computer could also track his comings and goings and his exact location within the building.

The experiment was simple, especially when compared with some of the more complex medical implants that neurosurgeons are now working on, but it was evocative nonetheless. Warwick admits that he has been contacted by government officials interested in potential use of implants in prisons or for tracking pedophiles – but Warwick himself breezily glosses over the Orwellian implications of widespread computer-implant use.

"I didn't feel like Big Brother was watching, probably because I benefited from the implant: The doors opened and lights came on, rather than doors closing and lights turning off," he says. "It does make me feel that Orwell was probably right about the Big Brother issue – we'll just go headlong into it; it won't be something we'll see as being a negative because there will be lots of positives in it for us."

Warwick only wore the implant for nine days – he says he was worried about the possibility that the glass capsule might explode or migrate around his body. But Warwick believes that was long enough to get a sense of what effect a mind-machine interface might have on our relationships with computers. "After a few days I started to feel quite a closeness to the computer, which was very strange," he muses. "When you are linking your brain up like that, you change who you are. You do become a 'borg. You are not just a human linked with technology; you are something different and your values and judgment will change."

His next implant experiment will engineer an even closer link between humans and computers. In 18 months, Warwick will again undergo surgery, this time receiving not just a transponder implant in his arm but a connection to his nervous core – a tiny collar that encircles the bundle of nerve fibers at the top of his arm, reading the signals from his nervous system and transmitting those to his computer. Of course, just how his nervous signals will translate into computer commands remains to be seen – much of the experiment will involve testing to see if he can turn on lights on his computer by waving his arm in certain ways.

Again, it's a simple experiment that has vast implications for the future of mind-machine interfaces. "This is where you can start to speculate straight away; in the very near future we should be able to operate computers without the need for a keyboard or a computer mouse," he explains. "It should be simply possible to type on your computer just by writing with your finger in the air."

This implant will not merely send signals to his computer, however; it will also receive them. The computer should be able to record and store sets of Warwick's

2 **transponder** device which transmits a signal on receiving a signal from another source
5 **Reading** ['redɪŋ]
8 **Big Brother** *(literary)* head of a regime that keeps its citizens under close surveillance, see Orwellian below
12 **evocative** *here:* which gives people ideas
14 **breezily** in a relaxed way
14 **to gloss over s.th.** not to mention the disadvantages of s.th.
14 **Orwellian** refers to the future described in George Orwell's (1903–50) antiutopian novel *1984* (1949)
23 **mind-machine interface** connection between the brain and a computer
25 **to muse** to speak in a thoughtful way

nervous signals and transmit them back at a later time; if all goes well, he'll be able to "play back" the motion of flexing his elbow or wiggling his fingers. He could even "re-experience" the nervous signals related to his emotions, "playing back" the signals his nervous core sent when he was feeling happy or stressed. "Will I feel the emotion I felt before, will I feel a different one, will it be better or will it be worse? We have no idea," he speculates. "The big worry is that while we'll be able to see what those transmissions will do to my fingers, they will also go back to the brain. What will my brain will of those signals? That's a smidgen dangerous. But it's extremely exciting." [...]

Perhaps the most peculiar aspect of Warwick's experimentation with robots and implants is his own cheerful acceptance of the dark side of his own research. "I think humans would be crazy and stupid to give machines the power to affect how the world operates," he explains. [...]

Warwick's implant systems – which could be used to "enhance" humans with sensory information – could also conceivably be employed to create races of super-humans or computer-controlled human slaves. While Warwick seems to have an eye on saving the world, it's a world that will partially be of his own making. He may even help change what it means to be a human.

That is, of course, if his predictions ever come true. But even if they don't, he says it's best to be prepared anyway.

"Yes, I believe in the doom and gloom, unfortunately – but that's evolution. Something is going to come along and surpass us at some time, and my feeling is that more than likely at some point it's going to be machines, intelligent machines," he matter-of-factly postulates. "Can anything be done about it? This type of implant should take us a long way down the road; but realistically we've got to have machine intelligence connected in some way to the human brain. It's a race against time."

From "Professor Cyborg" by Janelle Brown, salon.com, *October 20, 1999.*

51 **smidgen** *(informal)* a little bit

64 **doom and gloom** *here:* feeling that s.th. terrible will happen

Exploring the text

1 Why did Professor Warwick have transponders implanted under his skin?

2 How does he react to suggestions that implants could lead to an Orwellian society?

3 a) How does Professor Warwick judge the benefits and potential disadvantages of the implant?
b) In your opinion, do the disadvantages outweigh the advantages, or not?

A step further

a) Discuss the following issues in groups:
- Is it desirable to use computer implants to indicate the carrier's location or to allow the carrier to influence his / her surroundings?
- When is the use of computer implants justified? In what cases should their use not be allowed?

b) Put the results of your discussion on a transparency and present them to the other groups.

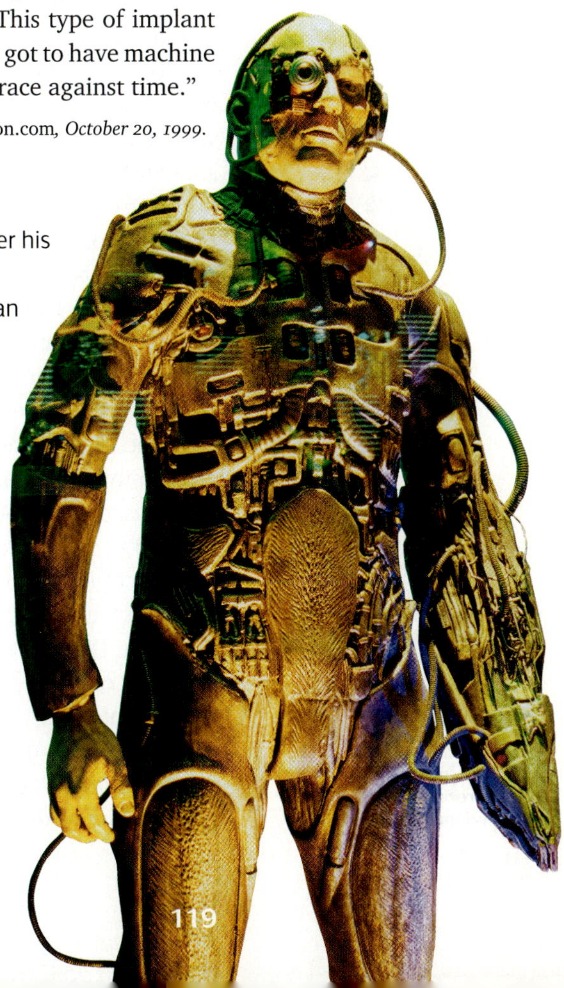

Before you read

- Working in groups, brainstorm for ideas about the following scientific areas: reproductive cloning – therapeutic cloning – stem cell therapy.
- What thoughts do you think are going through the head of the female shopper in the cartoon?

Shopping for humans

The reason most people have an almost instinctual repulsion to cloning is that deep down, they sense that it signals the beginning of a new journey where the "gift of life" is steadily marginalised and eventually abandoned all together. In its place, the new progeny becomes the ultimate shopping experience – designed in advance, produced to specification and purchased in the biological marketplace.

Cloning is, first and foremost, an act of "production", not creation. Using the new biotechnologies, a living being is produced with the same degree of engineering as we have come to expect on an assembly line. When we think of engineering standards, what immediately comes to mind is quality controls and predictable outcomes. That's exactly what cloning a human being is all about. For the first time in the history of our species, we can dictate the final genetic constitution of the offspring. The child is no longer a unique creation – one of a kind – but rather a reproduction. Human cloning opens the door wide to the dawn of a commercial eugenics civilisation, a brave new world where new technologies speed the process of "improving" our offspring, allowing us to create a second genesis. This time, each person can become a private god and make offspring in his or her own image.

In the future – certainly by the time today's babies reach adulthood – it will be possible to make genetic changes in the donor cell or embryo and begin creating customised variations of the original. Ian Wilmut, of the Roslin Institute, near Edinburgh, has already accomplished this feat in his second cloned sheep. Though less celebrated than Dolly, the birth of Polly is far more ominous. With Polly, Wilmut's team customised a human gene into a sheep cell and then cloned the sheep, making it the first truly "designer animal". Using the clone as a "standard model", scientists can now produce endless customised variations suited to the requisites of their clients.

Does anyone doubt for a moment that what Wilmut accomplished with Polly won't be made available by the biotech industry to parents who would like to produce cloned designer babies? Again, proponents argue, why not? If a prospective

1 **repulsion** [rɪˈpʌlsən] feeling that s.th. is unpleasant
3 **to marginalise s.th.** to make s.th. appear unimportant
14 **eugenics** [juːˈdjenɪks] improving humans, esp. by selective breeding (= *Züchtung*)
19 **customised** adapted
28 **proponent** *opp. of* opponent

parent knew they were likely to pass on a genetic predisposition for heart disease, or stroke, or cancer, wouldn't they feel obligated to spare their clone by eliminating those genes in the donor cell or embryo? But where does one draw the line? What if the parent knew he or she was likely to pass on a genetic predisposition for bipolar manic depression, or dyslexia, or growth hormone deficiency, or a cleft palate? Doesn't every parent want the best possible life for their child? In the future, some would argue, parental responsibility and intervention ought to begin at the design stage, in the donor cell or cloned embryo.

Customised human cloning offers the spectre of a new kind of immortality. Each generation of a particular genotype can become the ultimate artist, continually customising and upgrading new genetic traits into the model with the goal of both perfecting and perpetuating the genotype forever. It would be naive to believe that there aren't lots of people who would leap at the opportunity. Researchers at fertility clinics say that they are already besieged by requests to clone.

The real threat that human cloning represents is one that, as far as I know, is never talked about by scientists, ethicists, biotech entrepreneurs, or politicians. In a society where more and more people clone and eventually customise their genotype to design specifications and engineering standards, how are we likely to regard the child who isn't cloned or customised? What about the child who is born with a "disability"? Will the rest of society view that child with tolerance or come to see the child as an error in the genetic code – in short a defective product? Indeed, future generations might become far less tolerant of those who are not engineered and who deviate from the genetic standards and norms adhered to in the "best practices" of the bioindustrial marketplace. If that were to happen, we might lose the most precious gift of all, the human capacity to empathise with each other. When we empathise with another human being, it's because we feel and experience their vulnerability, their frailties and suffering, and their unique struggle to claim their humanity. But, in a world that comes to expect perfection in its offspring, can empathy really survive?

Human cloning represents the ultimate Faustian bargain. In our desire to become the architects of our own evolution, we risk the very real possibility of losing our humanity.

By Jeremy Rifkin, The Guardian, *March 29, 2001.*

32 **predisposition** *here:* being likely to have a certain genetic disorder
32 **bipolar manic depression** mental illness which causes mood swings
33 **dyslexia** reading or writing difficulties
33 **cleft palate** ['pælət] a gap in one's upper jaw (= *Kiefer*) from birth
40 **to perpetuate** to continue
42 **besieged** having more requests than one can deal with
44 **entrepreneur** s.o. who starts a business
51 **to adhere to** *here:* to follow
53 **to empathise** to understand s.o.'s feelings
55 **vulnerability** ability to be hurt
55 **frailty** weakness

Exploring the text

1 According to Jeremy Rifkin, why do most people find cloning unpleasant?
2 What are the differences between 'production' and 'creation'?
3 a) Why does Jeremy Rifkin refer to cloning as a "second genesis" (l. 15)?
b) What benefits of cloning for mankind does he mention?
4 What potential danger is Jeremy Rifkin most concerned about once cloning becomes more widespread?

A step further

- a) If you had to design a baby, what qualities would you like him / her to have?
  b) Do you think that the baby would be happier or more successful in life?
- "In our desire to become the architects of our own evolution, we risk the very real possibility of losing our humanity." Use the closing statement from the text as the motion in a debate on the pros and cons of cloning.

Based on the still from *Gattaca* on the right, what impression do you get of society in the film?

The brave new world of "Gattaca"

What is genetic engineering, after all, but preemptive plastic surgery? Make the child perfect in the test tube, and save money later. Throw in perfect health, a high IQ and a long life-span, and you have the brave new world of "Gattaca," in which the bioformed have inherited the earth, and babies who are born naturally get to be menial laborers.

This is one of the smartest and most provocative of science fiction films, a thriller with ideas. Its hero is a man who challenges the system. Vincent (Ethan Hawke) was born in the old-fashioned way, and his genetic tests show he has bad eyesight, heart problems and a life expectancy of about 30 years. He is an "In-Valid," and works as a cleaner in a space center.

Vincent does not accept his fate. He […] dreams of becoming a crew member on an expedition to one of the moons of Saturn. Using an illegal DNA broker, he makes a deal with a man named Jerome (Jude Law), who has the right genes but was paralyzed in an accident. Jerome will provide him with blood, urine samples and an identity. In a sense, they'll both go into space. "Gattaca" is the remarkable debut of a writer-director from New Zealand, Andrew Niccol, whose film is intelligent and thrilling – a tricky combination – and also visually exciting. His most important set is a vast office where genetically superior computer programmers come to work every day, filing into their long rows of desks like the office slaves in King Vidor's "The Crowd" and Orson Welles' "The Trial." (Why are "perfect" human societies so often depicted by ranks of automatons? Is it because human nature resides in our flaws?) Vincent, as "Jerome," gets a job as a programmer, supplies false genetic samples and becomes a finalist for the space shot.

The tension comes in two ways. First, there's the danger that Vincent will be detected; the area is swept daily, and even an eyelash can betray him. Second, there's a murder; a director of the center, who questions the wisdom of the upcoming shot, is found dead, and a detective (Alan Arkin) starts combing the personnel for suspects. Will a computer search sooner or later put together Vincent, the former janitor, with "Jerome," the new programmer?

1 **preemptive** which stops s.th. from happening
4 **bioformed** *here:* created by biotechnology
5 **menial laborer** s.o. who does low-skilled or unskilled work

Vincent becomes friendly with Irene (Uma Thurman), who works in the center but has been passed over for a space shot because of low scores in some areas. They are attracted to one another, but romance in this world can be dangerous; after kissing a man, a woman is likely to have his saliva swabbed from her mouth so she can test his prospects. Other supporting characters include Gore Vidal, as a mission supervisor, and Tony Shalhoub as the broker ("You could go anywhere with this guy's helix under your arm").

Hawke is a good choice for the lead, combining the restless dreams of a "Godchild" with the plausible exterior of a lab baby. The best scenes involve his relationship with the real Jerome, played by Law as smart, bitter, and delighted to be sticking it to the system that has grounded him. (He may be paralyzed from the waist down, but after all, as the movie observes, you don't need to walk in space.) His drama parallels Vincent's, because if either one is caught they'll both go down together.

Science fiction in the movies has recently specialized in alien invasions, but the best of the genre deals with ideas. At a time when we read about cloned sheep and tomatoes crossed with fish, the science in "Gattaca" is theoretically possible. When parents can order "perfect" babies, will they? Would you take your chances on a throw of the genetic dice, or order up the make and model you wanted? How many people are prepared to buy a car at random from the universe of all available cars? That's how many, I suspect, would opt to have natural children.

Everybody will live longer, look better and be healthier in the Gattacan world. But will it be as much fun? Will parents order children who are rebellious, ungainly, eccentric, creative, or a lot smarter than their parents are? There's a concert pianist in "Gattaca" who has 12 fingers. Don't you sometimes have the feeling you were born just in time?

By Roger Ebert, Chicago-Sun Times, *www.suntimes.com/ebert/ebert_reviews/1997/10/102403.html.*

35 **broker** s.o. who buys and sells things
38 **Godchild** *(from Gattaca)* s.o. who was not genetically manipulated as an embryo
40 **to stick it to s.o. / s.th.** *(informal)* to trick s.o. / s.th.
40 **to ground s.o.** to stop s.o. doing what they want to
52 **ungainly** clumsy

Exploring the text

1 a) Describe the dreams and ambitions of the film character Vincent.
b) How does the society he lives in make it almost impossible to fulfil his dreams?

2 What does Roger Ebert mean when he writes that "human nature resides in our flaws" (ll. 21 – 22)? Would you agree with this idea, or not?

3 How would you answer the questions in ll. 46 – 49?

Meet the media

- Societies in science fiction
  According to Roger Ebert "perfect human societies" are "often depicted by ranks of automatons" and the best science-fiction films deal with ideas, not alien invasions.
  a) Think of films and TV series that support or contradict these points of view.
  b) Are the societies in these films and TV series utopian (i.e. free, happy, well-ordered) or dystopian (i.e. well-structured, yet depressed and unhappy)?
- *Gattaca* – scene analysis
  Watch the scene in *Gattaca* in which Vincent's parents discuss the genetic characteristics of their second child with a geneticist (cf. skills files, p. 184).
  1 a) Study the setting of the scene. What atmosphere does it convey?
  b) How do the dialogue and characters' body language contribute to this?
  2 What choices is the couple left with? How do they feel about these choices?
  3 Imagine and act out the conversation they had before meeting the geneticist.

Forests for life

Before you watch

- Imagine you are a member of Greenpeace. In groups, plan a commercial protesting against deforestation to be shown in cinemas and on TV. Discuss these points:
  - What is the message?
  - Who is the target audience? What motifs will make the biggest impression?
  - What kind of film material do you want to use?
  - What kind of information do you want to include, and how will you present it?

  Present the results in class and then discuss which ideas are the best.

Watching and thinking

Step 1 Watch the commercial "Forests for life" and share your first impressions with the rest of the class, e.g. What impressed you most / least?

Step 2 Watch the commercial again. Divide it into sense units.

Step 3 Working in groups focus on one sense unit. Analyse its function and the means used to convey its message.

- Examine the function of cuts, speed, montage and field sizes (cf. page 184).
- Analyse the function of the voice-over.
- Sum up the message in one sentence as if it were a tagline in a printed advert.

Step 4 Present the results in class.

A step further

- Devise a campaign for your school or community in response to the commercial.
- Set up a Greenpeace group in your school. Check their website for information about what they do. Then think up a campaign to recruit members.

Talking about GM food

pesticide use – herbicide use – biotech crops – farm income – reduced acreage – to plant – pest resistant – famine – better diets – world population

Before you read

- Think of arguments for and against GM food (= genetically modified).
- a) Look at the cartoon on the left. What potential problem with GM produce does the cartoonist point out? How important is this issue for consumers?

  b) How do you personally feel about GM food?

Nothing's labeled. How are we supposed to know which fruit has been genetically engineered?

The view from Ghana

George Acquaah of Ghana describes how biotechnology can benefit the people of Africa.

As a native of Ghana, and a professor at Langston University in Oklahoma, I see both the enormous challenges facing the people of Africa and the potential solutions. Growing up in Africa, I saw firsthand so many of the problems that people in the United States only read about: chronic hunger, children going blind from malnutrition and people dying from treatable diseases. As a scientist, I find biotechnology a challenging field, but as an African, I am genuinely encouraged by its potential to help alleviate these problems that plague Africa and developing countries around the world.

"Vitamin A deficiency leads to approximately half a million cases of permanent childhood blindness and 1 million to 2 million deaths."

5 **malnutrition** being ill from too little food
7 **to alleviate** to ease

One of the gravest health issues facing Africa is malnutrition and the diseases it spawns. For example, vitamin A deficiency leads to approximately half a million cases of permanent childhood blindness and 1 million to 2 million deaths each year. Part of the reason is that the staple foods of many Africans are starchy crops like rice and cassava that do not provide enough nutrients. Now there is real hope in a new type of rice called "golden rice" that is fortified through biotechnology with beta-carotene, the nutrient the body uses to make vitamin A. This technology could soon be used to increase the levels of vital nutrients in other crops as well.

Food storage is another significant problem in Africa because of the lack of refrigeration. Tons of food rot before they get to the market. Biotechnology could help to prevent these losses by producing crops that ripen more slowly. If crops ripened more gradually, there would be more time to get them to market before they spoil, and far less food would go to waste. […]

Biotechnology could also help reduce hunger by decreasing the amount of food lost to pests and disease before it is harvested. In East Africa, a virus can destroy an entire maize crop, and between 20 percent and 80 percent of the sweet potato crop is lost to pests and disease every year. Scientists have already developed some types of crops that resist insects and disease, and more are on the way. Less food lost means less hunger.

Helping farmers in developing countries grow more food will go a long way toward reducing hunger and, by developing crops that can grow in difficult conditions like poor soil, extreme heat and drought that are common in much of Africa, biotechnology could help local farmers grow more food. […]

Biotechnology has benefits for Africans that go beyond food, too. Vaccines to prevent diseases like cholera and hepatitis B may someday be grown in fruits and vegetables. Currently, too many Africans die of preventable diseases because vaccines are too expensive or inaccessible. Often the refrigeration needed to preserve them is not available. The edible vaccines that biotechnology researchers are developing could be produced for pennies and would not need the extensive purification and refrigeration that injectable vaccines require.

For Americans, biotechnology offers great benefits – from more flavorful and healthful foods for consumers to insect resistant crops for farmers. But for Africans, biotechnology could be the difference between health and illness, or life and death.

By George Acquaah, Council for Biotechnology Information, 2002, www.whybiotech.com/index.asp?id=1263

12 **to spawn** *here:* to cause
14 **staple foods** the kinds of food people usually eat
14 **starchy** *stärkehaltig*
15 **cassava** tropical plant grown for its roots *(Maniok)*
16 **to fortify** to improve
32 **drought** long period of hot, dry weather
38 **edible** *here:* that can be taken orally
38 **vaccine** *Impfstoff*

Exploring the text

1 According to the text, what problems do many Africans face and what causes these problems? How can biotechnology provide solutions? Record your ideas in a grid like the one below.

Problems	Causes	Biotechnological solutions
Vitamin A deficiency	*childhood blindness*	...

2 How do attitudes in the US towards biotech foods differ to those in Africa?

A step further

- In groups, design an advert promoting GM foods. Include a photo, tagline and copy in your advert. Cf. skills file, "Adverts", page 187 for ideas.

What happens if you drink GM coffee.

You have been warned: GM ripening-controlled coffee has some serious side effects. Up to 60 million people could be permanently harmed by drinking it.

So what makes GM coffee so destructive?

In nature, coffee beans don't all ripen at the same time, making any mechanised picking inefficient. No wonder then that 70 % of all coffee is grown by smallholder farmers in developing countries around the world. Changing the way coffee is grown would wipe out the livelihoods of these poor farmers and push millions of people further into poverty.

Frighteningly, a US company, ICTI, is developing genetically modified coffee beans, which can be made to ripen all at the same time. These GM coffee beans can be sprayed with a chemical which 'switches them on' making them perfect to be mass machine-harvested.

There is no doubt that GM ripening-controlled coffee is being developed for large plantations. They will be able to increase the size of their operations and drastically reduce the size of their workforce.

Up to seven million poor farmers won't be able to afford the chemical or compete with the big companies. As a result many will go out of business, be forced to move their families to the cities in search of work and plunged into conditions of appalling health, squalor and the inescapable unemployment of the urban developing world.

Now, we at ActionAid are not against technology being used to make food more productive, it's just that we are horrified that GM coffee will destroy the lives of poor coffee farmers and their families, rather than improve it.

What can you do? (Apart from getting angry.)

UK supermarkets and coffee retailers have the power to stop the development of GM coffee. They rely on your business and if they know you won't swallow GM coffee, then they won't stock it. There will then be little point in growing it.

As a consumer you have a powerful voice. Use it.

Call us today on **0800 482 400** or return the coupon to find out how you can make the UK supermarkets and coffee retailers wake up and smell the GM coffee.

Please send me information on how I can help stop this GM coffee being developed. Or call 0800 482 400 now.

Mr/Mrs/Miss (PLEASE PRINT) ____________________

Address ____________________

____

Postcode ____________________

Tel. (day) __________ (eve) __________

Date of birth (if under 24) ____/____/____

Return to ActionAid, Freepost BS4868, Chard, Somerset, TA20 1BR.
Visit us at www.actionaid.org.uk

0 **GM** *short for* genetically modified (= changed)
8 **smallholder** having a small piece of land for farming purposes
27 **to plunge s.o. into s.th.** to force s.o. into a certain position
36 **retailer** *here:* shop
43 **to wake up and smell the coffee** to notice what is happening

What happens if you drink GM coffee

Looking and thinking

1 Study the advert campaigning against GM coffee on page 126. What effect do the photo, tagline and first four lines of the ad copy have on you the reader?
2 What aspect(s) of GM coffee does ActionAid criticize in the advert?
3 What devices does the advertiser use to convey ActionAid's message to readers and then to get them to take action? Refer to skills file on page 187 for ideas.

A step further

- Compare the mood evoked in George Acquaah's text on GM food (pp. 124–125) with that in the advert.

Internet project

- Choose an issue related to genetic engineering that you would like to explore in greater detail, for example, therapeutic cloning, human cloning, GM food.
  - Find websites which deal with the topic of your choice (cf. the box on the right or type key words into a search engine such as www.google.de);
  - Select relevant texts and reorganise the information so that you can present the topic either in a talk (skills file, pp. 182–183) or an essay (skills files, p. 187).

Talking about adverts

The ad copy is objective / subjective / provocative / …

The … catches the reader's interest / draws the reader's attention to …

The … makes the reader feel …

The … appeals to / calls on the reader …

The advertiser wants to emphasize / underline / stress …

Websites

www.whybiotech.com/
www.greenpeace.org/homepage/
www.actionaid.org/

The challenge of change

Before you watch

- Which of the key words in the box on the right do you associate with globalization? Give reasons for your choice.

While viewing

1 According to Tony Blair, why is the era we live in the most "dramatic and unpredictable" in history?
2 a) What changes in everyday life does he find frightening?
b) Are these changes exclusively related to globalization, or not?
3 a) What methods does Tony Blair mention of coming to terms with globalization?
b) In your opinion, which method, if any, is satisfactory?

A step further

- "There is greater individual freedom, yet greater interdependence". Think of examples to support this statement and write a comment (cf. skills file, page 188).
- Do you think it is appropriate to call our age the "age of anxiety", or not? Give reasons for your answer.

Talking about globalization

Industrialised countries
prosperity – trade expansion – international investment – access to markets – trade agreement – e-commerce – communication technology – unemployment

Third World countries
cultural imperialism – the global divide – cultural diversity – poverty – technologically underdeveloped – global migration – economic dependence – military conflicts – multinational corporations – survival of the fittest – gap between rich and poor

Globalization – the key issues

Listen to the commentary on globalization by social theorist, Anthony Giddens.

Before you read

- What ideas does the term 'global village' evoke?

In the following extract from No Logo, *the writer Naomi Klein tells of encounters with factory workers in developing countries who produce consumer goods for the developed world.*

The other side of the global village

JAKARTA – "Ask her what she makes – what it says on the label. You know – label?" I said, reaching behind my head and twisting up the collar of my shirt. By now these Indonesian workers were used to people like me: foreigners who come to talk to them about the abysmal conditions in the factories where they cut, sew and glue for multinational companies like Nike, the Gap and Liz Claiborne. But these seamstresses looked nothing like the elderly garment workers I meet in the elevator back home. Here they were all young, some of them as young as fifteen; only a few were over twenty-one.

On this particular day in August 1997, the abysmal conditions in question had led to a strike at the Kaho Indah Citra garment factory on the outskirts of Jakarta in the Kawasan Berikat Nusantar industrial zone. The issue for the Kaho workers, who earn the equivalent of US $ 2 per day, was that they were being forced to work long hours of overtime but weren't being paid at the legal rate for their trouble. After a three-day walkout, management offered a compromise typical of a region with a markedly relaxed relationship to labor legislation: overtime would no longer be compulsory but the compensation would remain illegally low. The 2,000 workers returned to their sewing machines; all except 101 young women who – management decided – were the troublemakers behind the strike. "Until now our case is still not settled," one of these workers told me, bursting with frustration and with no recourse in sight.

I was sympathetic, of course, but, being the Western foreigner, I wanted to know what brand of garments they produced at the Kaho factory – if I was to bring their story home, I would have to have my journalistic hook. So here we were, ten of us, crowded into a concrete bunker only slightly bigger than a telephone booth, playing an enthusiastic round of labor charades.

"This company produces long sleeves for cold seasons," one worker offered.

I guessed: "Sweaters?"

"I think not sweaters. If you prepare to go out and you have a cold season you have a ..."

I got it: "Coat!"

"But not heavy. Light."

"Jackets!"

"Yes, like jackets, but not jackets – long."

You can understand the confusion: there isn't much need for overcoats on the equator, not in the closet and not in the vocabulary. And yet increasingly, Canadians get through their cold winters not with clothing manufactured by the tenacious seamstresses still on Spadina Avenue but by young Asian women working in hot climates like this one. In 1997, Canada imported $ 11.7 million of anoraks and ski jackets from Indonesia, up from $ 4.7 million in 1993. That much I already knew. But I still didn't know what brand of long coats the Kaho workers sewed before they lost their jobs.

"Long, yes. And what's on the label?" I asked again.

There was a bit of hushed consultation, and then, finally, an answer: "London Fog."

A global coincidence, I suppose. I started to tell the Kaho workers that my apartment in Toronto used to be a London Fog coat factory but stopped abruptly when it became clear from their facial expressions that the idea of anyone choosing

1 **label** tag on clothes showing where they were made, by whom, etc.
2 **collar** band around the neck of a piece of clothing
4 **abysmal** [ə'bɪzməl] *(informal)* terrible
5 **seamstress** woman whose job it is to make clothes
6 **garment** clothing
15 **compulsory** s.th. which has to be done
19 **recourse** source of help
21 **brand** type of product made by a company
22 **journalistic hook** story based on personal experience to catch readers' attention
24 **charades** [ʃə'rɑːdz] game; one player describes s.th. and the others guess what it is
34 **closet** *(AE)* cupboard one puts clothes into
35 **tenacious** [tɪ'neɪʃəs] *here:* who try hard to hold onto their jobs
36 **Spadina Avenue** former centre of the clothing industry in Toronto
42 **hushed consultation** quiet discussion in a group

to live in a garment building was nothing but alarming. In this part of the world, hundreds of workers every year burn to death because their dormitories are located upstairs from firetrap sweatshops.

Sitting cross-legged on the concrete floor of the tiny dorm room, I thought of my neighbours back home: the Ashtanga yoga instructor on two, the commercial animators on four, the aromatherapy candle distributors on eight. It seems the young women in the export processing zone are our roommates of sorts, connected, as is so often the case, by a web of fabrics, shoelaces, franchises, teddy bears and brand names wrapped around the planet. Another logo we had in common was Esprit, also one of the brands manufactured in the zone. As a teenager I worked as a clerk in a store that sold Esprit clothes. And of course, McDonald's: an outlet had just opened near Kaho, frustrating workers, because this so-called bargain food was squarely out of their price range.

Usually, reports about this global web of logos and products are couched in euphoric marketing rhetoric of the global village, an incredible place where tribes-people in remotest rain forests tap away on laptop computers, Sicilian grandmothers conduct E-business, and "global teens" share, to borrow a phrase from a Levi's Web site, "a world-wide style culture." Everyone from Coke to McDonald's to Motorola has tailored their marketing strategy around this post-national vision, but it is IBM's long-running "Solutions for a Small Planet" campaign that most eloquently captures the equalizing promise of the logo-linked globe.

It hasn't taken long for the excitement inspired by these manic renditions of globalization to wear thin, revealing the cracks and fissures beneath its high-gloss façade. More and more over the past four years, we in the West have been catching glimpses of another kind of global village, where the economic divide is widening and cultural choices narrowing.

This is a village where some multinationals, far from leveling the global playing field with jobs and technology for all, are in the process of mining the planet's poorest back country for unimaginable profits. This is the village where Bill Gates lives, amassing a fortune of $55 billion while a third of his workforce is classified as temporary workers, and where competitors are either incorporated into the Microsoft monolith or made obsolete by the latest feat in software bundling. This is the village where we are indeed connected to one another through a web of brands, but the underside of that web reveals designer slums like the one I visited outside Jakarta. IBM claims that its technology spans the globe, and so it does, but often its international presence takes the form of cheap Third World labor producing the computer chips and power sources that drive our machines. On the outskirts of Manila, for instance, I met a seventeen-year-old girl who assembles CD-ROM drives for IBM. I told her I was impressed that someone so young could do such high-tech work. "We make computers," she told me, "but we don't know how to operate computers." Ours, it would seem, is not such a small planet after all.

48 **dormitory** ['dɔːmɪtrɪ] room where several people sleep
49 **sweatshop** factory where people work for little money in bad conditions
51 **commercial animator** artist who produces cartoons
59 **squarely** *here:* completely
60 **to couch** *(formal)* to express an idea in a particular way
65 **to tailor s.th.** to adapt s.th. for one's own uses
68 **manic rendition** energetic presentation
69 **to wear thin** *here:* to decrease
73 **to level** *here:* to create equal opportunities
76 **to amass** to gather
78 **monolith** *(negative)* huge static organisation
78 **obsolete** out of date
78 **feat** achievement
78 **software bundling** package of programmes; the advantage is that customers can buy all of the programmes from one supplier

From No Logo *by Naomi Klein, London: Flamingo, 2001, pp. xv–xvii.*

Exploring the text

1 a) Why did the workers at the clothing factory in Jakarta go on strike?
b) What does the management's response reveal about labour legislation there?

2 Why do the factory workers seem to have problems with the products they make?

3 What picture does marketing often convey of the "global village" (l. 61)?

4 According to the writer, who has not benefited from the global village?

A step further

- Choose an international company and visit its website to find out about: its philosophy – its marketing strategy – where and how its products are produced.

Read the following text and think of ways of dealing with it in groups.

Over to you

13 **ramen** noodle dish
14 **ubiquitous** which seem to be everywhere
17 **globality** a worldwide, interconnected economy that ignores national boundaries

Globalization

"Globalization" – lots of people seem to think it means that the world is turning into some consumer colony of America. Coke, CNN, McDonald's, Levi's, Nikes – if they haven't taken over the world yet, the feeling goes, they will soon. (Odd: Japan is the world's second largest economy, and yet I've never heard of anyone who buys Sony or eats sushi believing that it's part of some plot to turn the world into Japan.)

But regardless of whether you're buying or selling, in the past 20 years much of the world's economy has become increasingly integrated and foreign direct investment has grown three times as fast as total domestic investment. From 1980 to 1995 the value of trade worldwide rose dramatically, with the total value of world exports estimated at U.S. $ 5.1 trillion in 1995, up from U.S. $ 2 trillion in 1980.

Yet the globalization phenomenon is more than the mere transfer of goods, the fact that, for instance, you can buy French mineral water and Danish beer in Shanghai airport or eat Japanese ramen out of your suburban microwave. It's the advent of cheap and ubiquitous information technologies that is dissolving our sense of boundaries. More and more television channels and the Internet have contributed to what expert Daniel Yergin calls a "woven world."

When we talk about "globality" (a new buzzword), we're trying to define a world in which cultures meet and, rather than fight, they blend. As observer Frederick Tipson notes, "More like a thin but sticky coating than a powerful acid, this cosmopolitan culture of communications networks and the information media seems to overlay rather than supplant the cultures it interacts with." Because when cultures receive outside influences, they ignore some and adopt others, and then almost immediately start to transform them.

That's how you end up listening to something called "bhangra pop" in India, to take an example at random: sounds like Jamaican reggae played on traditional Indian instruments, then amplified. "As things get more global," commented Norman Klein, a communications professor in Los Angeles, "they're actually becoming more localized." […]

McDonald's may be the most notorious name in the whole complex business of American culture going abroad. There are approximately 24,500 McDonald's restaurants in over 115 countries; a new McDonald's opens somewhere in the world every six hours. […]

"That's no mirage – they have outlets everywhere!"

But McDonald's has actually been remarkably responsive to the local cultures; they offer ayran (a popular chilled yogurt drink) in Turkey; McLaks (a grilled salmon sandwich) in Norway, and teriyaki burgers in Japan. […] The fact that the staff are all local people means that the restaurant, though obviously foreign, isn't instantly perceived as being American. In New Delhi, as in Brazil or Manila, you may well buy your burger from the kid down the street who speaks the local dialect. "People call us multinational. I like to call us multilocal," commented James Cantalupo, president and CEO of McDonald's International.

"Culture," anthropologist James Watson has commented, "is not something that people inherit as an undifferentiated bloc of knowledge from their ancestors. Culture is a set of ideas, reactions, and expectations that is constantly changing as people and groups themselves change."

Which brings us around to the subject of America. […]

Those who are quick to criticize America often seem unaware that America is not some monolithic one-size-fits-all culture, but arguably the most multicultural society on Earth. Thousands of things that we think of as American came from somewhere else: Christmas trees, hot dogs and beer, denim. An elderly Indian professor of sociology named Yogendra Singh understands this […].

"What is Western culture?" he asked as he sat barefoot in his New Delhi living room. "There's very little understanding of the diversity of Western cultures. But American culture draws on so many other cultures. America could be the best example of how cultures appreciate each other."

Americans are so quick to adopt foreign food, phrases, clothing, that it may be hard to see them as foreign for long. […]

People forget where certain things came from, and they don't care. Americans say "ciao" and "glitch," dance to salsa (and eat it too), drink vodka, and on and on, but don't think this makes them Italian, Jewish, Hispanic, Russian, or whatever. We adopt elements of myriad immigrant cultures because they help us express ourselves better. This, I think, is the essence of cultural interchange: not adopting foreign things wholesale, but choosing them according to the values and ideas of your own culture.

By Erla Zwingle, National Geographic, *2000.*

42 **teriyaki** grilled beef, chicken, or fish in soy sauce
47 **CEO** *short for* **Chief Executive Officer**
67 **myriad** ['mɪrɪəd] a large number

Shakespeare & love

Shakespeare's words

Looking and thinking

1 In small groups focus on **one** of the quotations below and complete these tasks:
 - Explain in your own words what Shakespeare writes about love and life.
 - Do you agree with the quotation, or not?
 - Who might have said this in a play, and in what kind of situation?
 - Practise saying the quotation. Then walk around the classroom until you establish eye contact with someone. Recite your quotation and listen to theirs. Then move on.

2 What impression of Shakespeare's language do the quotations convey?

If thou remember'st not the slightest folly
That ever love did make thee run into,
Thou hast not lov'd.
As You Like It, Act II, Scene 4

Then come kiss me, sweet and twenty,
Youth's a stuff will not endure.
Twelfth Night, Act II, Scene 3

Sigh no more, ladies, sigh no more!
Men were deceivers ever,
One foot in sea, and one on shore;
To one thing constant never.
Much Ado About Nothing, Act II, Scene 3

Love is [...] a fire sparkling in lovers' eyes
[...] a sea nourished with lovers' tears;
What is it else? A madness most discreet
Romeo and Juliet, Act I, Scene 1

Life's but a walking shadow, [...] it is a tale
Told by an idiot, full of sound and fury,
Signifying nothing.
Macbeth, Act V, Scene 5

Love is blind and lovers cannot see
The pretty follies that they themselves commit.
The Merchant of Venice, Act II, Scene 6

thou *(old)* you *(subject)* – **folly** s.th. stupid one does – **thee** *(old)* you *(object)* – **to endure** [ɪn'djʊə] to last a long time – **but** *here:* only

Shakespeare and his times

1547 King Henry VIII dies.

1558 Henry's daughter Elizabeth I assumes the throne.

1564 William Shakespeare is born, the first son of a prominent businessman. Over 20,000 people die of the plague in London.

1577 English sailor, Francis Drake sails around the world.

1582 Marries Anne Hathaway, a 26-year old farmer's daughter. The first child is born 6 months later.

1585 Twins are born; Shakespeare disappears for seven years, the "Lost Years".

1588 England defeats the Spanish Armada, a great fleet of ships sent by Phillip II to attack the country.

1592 Established in the London theatre world as an actor, playwright, poet

1593/'94 Theatres in London close because of the plague.

1593 First publication (a narrative poem)

1594 Founding member of an acting company

1595/'96 *Romeo and Juliet*, *A Midsummer Night's Dream* are published.

1597 Buys 'New Place', the second-largest house in Stratford

1599 The Globe Theatre is built in London; Shakespeare is part owner.

1603 Queen Elizabeth dies and is succeeded by James I.

1605 Shakespeare's acting company, The King's Men, performs eleven times before the king, seven of the performances are plays by Shakespeare.

1606 *Macbeth* is published.

1609 The sonnets are published.

1610 Leaves London, settles in Stratford a rich man

1616 Dies, having written 38 plays

1623 *The First Folio* (complete collection of Shakespeare's works) is published.

At the time, a promise to marry was considered binding and the couple was free to act as if they were married; one in every three Elizabethan brides was pregnant on her wedding day.

According to the most commonly told story, he left Stratford to escape prosecution for poaching deer.

prosecution being taken to court – **to poach** to steal

Apparently Anne and the children remained in Stratford while Shakespeare worked in London. Back then, the trip from London to Stratford took about four days on foot and two on horseback.

Exploring the text

1 What impression does the timeline convey of Shakespeare's life and times?
2 Who could you interview to find out more? What questions would you ask?

Shakespeare's early years

What details from the documentary extract would you add to the timeline, and how?

A step further

- Start a mind map or fact file about Shakespeare. Search the internet and look at pp. 134–135 for key words and ideas.

Shakespeare's birthplace in Stratford-upon-Avon

1 **sceptered** ['septəd] royal
3 **demi-** like
4 **fortress** place which is difficult to attack
5 **infection** *here:* negative influence
6 **breed** *here:* group with specific characteristics
7 **precious** ['preʃəs] valuable
9 **moat** *(old)* channel of water around a building
11 **realm** [relm] kingdom
16 **gallows** *(old)* place of execution
25 **bear and bull-baiting** dogs attacked a bear or bull tied to a wooden post
25 **cockfighting** *Hahnenkämpfe*
27 **matchmaking** finding a husband or wife for s.o.
34 **suffocation** *here:* death caused by blocking the air passages

Elizabethan England

This royal throne of kings, this sceptered isle,
This earth of majesty, this seat of Mars,
This other Eden, demi-paradise,
This fortress built by nature for herself
Against infection and the hand of war,
This happy breed of men, this little world,
This precious stone set in the silver sea,
Which serves it in the office of a wall,
Or as a moat defensive to a house,
Against the envy of less happier lands,
This blessed plot, this earth, this realm, this England. *Richard II*, Act II, Scene 1

Politics and religion Politics and religion were closely linked in the England of the Tudor kings and queens: The Church changed from being Catholic to Protestant under Henry VIII, back to Catholic under Queen Mary and back to Protestant again under Elizabeth I. The people had to accept the changes: anyone who criticized the Church risked being marched off to the nearest gallows.

Hierarchy and order To an Elizabethan, anything out of the ordinary – floods, storms, unexpected deaths – signalled a violation of order. In the Chain of Being all phenomena were interrelated in a well-balanced hierarchy with God at the top, then came the angels and spirits, the king and nobility, the lower classes, animals, plants, rocks and minerals. Many people felt that all would be well with society if people knew their duty and kept their places. In Shakespeare's tragedy *Macbeth*, the consequences of ignoring this god-given order were disastrous for Macbeth himself.

Fun and games The leading amusements of the day are theatre (Shakespeare is a big favourite.), bear and bull-baiting, cockfighting (with a lot of flying feathers and blood), drunken fights and riots, and witch burnings and public executions.

Love and marriage For many matchmaking parents, wealth and property were the only considerations. Equality of status, religion and age were important, too. In Shakespeare's tragedy *Othello*, Desdemona's marriage to the dark-skinned Moor Othello shocks and angers her father, who feels that an Elizabethan father has an absolute right to decide who his daughter marries. The marriage age was surprisingly late (between 25 and 28); teenage brides like Juliet in *Romeo and Juliet* were an exception. Unmarried mothers often lost their jobs or were refused help by midwives. Infanticide by poisoning or suffocation was common.

Just as the king ruled over the kingdom, a man ruled over his wife and children. Husbands were expected to provide for their families and wives were expected to be patient, obedient and quiet. Children were brought up to fear and respect their parents, e.g. they called their father "Sir" and stood in his presence.

Working with the fact file

1. a) What picture do we get of England at the end of the 16th century?
   b) Explain the images used in the lines from *Richard II*.
2. Use the information to write the diary entry of a citizen in the Elizabethan era.
3. Write a monologue or funny sketch about an Elizabethan who travels to our age.
4. Use a search engine to find out about the plays mentioned. Write plot summaries.

All the world's a stage – Shakespeare's theatre

All the world's a stage,
And all the men and women are merely players.
They have their exits and their entrances,
And one man in his time plays many parts

As You Like It, Act II, Scene 7

- In 1576, carpenter-turned-actor James Burbage built England's first permanent theatre.
- Despite being popular with the people, actors were considered to be rogues and vagabonds by those in power. However, they still regularly performed at court.
- Whereas in the Middle Ages drama mainly had religious themes, the London theatre was the first place to show the common man, war and everyday life.
- The Globe Theatre opened in 1599. Shakespeare's Chamberlain's Men (later the King's Men) became London's premier company of actors. By 1600, London had more theatres than any other European capital.
- Shakespeare had a 10 percent share in the Globe's profits, i.e. about £200–£250 per year, quite a large sum by Elizabethan standards. The entrance fee was collected in a box at the door (hence the term 'box office').
- The Globe was round and partly open to the sky. It was small enough for the actors to be heard but large enough to take up to 3,000 people.
- The stage was about 1,5 metres high to keep the audience from climbing onto it and projected into the circle. An overhead canopy, representing the sky, kept the actors dry. A trapdoor in the stage led to the 'hell'.
- The Globe was situated in a run-down area, surrounded by brothels and taverns. All kinds of criminals operated outside the box office.
- After being destroyed by fire in 1613, the Globe was immediately rebuilt. It closed in 1642. In 1997, the Globe was rebuilt at its original site in London.
- As there were no lights, performances ran from 2:00 to 5:00 p.m. People did not sit still for the full three hours, however, so that the atmosphere at an Elizabethan play was like that at a modern football match. If the audience did not like the play, they made loud comments or threw things at the actors.
- Ticket prices depended on the location of the seat. The people standing in front of the stage were called groundlings; they were nearer the action but became wet when it rained. People paid more to sit in the covered galleries, especially if they had a cushion.
- As scenery and props were minimal and the only special effects were provided by the musicians, audiences had to use their imagination. Costumes and props were quite elaborate.
- Women were forbidden to act in public, and female roles were played by men and boys. The ban ended in 1660.

7 **rogue** [rəʊg] a dishonest person
8 **vagabond** s.o. without a fixed place to live or a proper job
22 **brothel** place where prostitutes work
34 **cushion** s.th. soft one sits on
35 **prop** object used on stage, e.g. a chair, knife

The New Globe Theatre, London

Working with the fact file

1. What made the theatre attractive to all classes of Elizabethan society?
2. List differences between Elizabethan theatre and theatre today.
3. Watch the first half of the film *Shakespeare in Love*. Which of the above aspects are shown on screen? What other details are given about theatre then?

Shakespeare's love poetry

Before you read

a) Listen to the recording of Sonnet 18 twice. Then say in your own words what you think it is about.

b) What impression does the poem make on you? Speculate as to why the 400-year-old text is famous.

2 **temperate** mild, calm
3 **darling buds** young, lovely flowers
4 **lease** *(legal)* the right to use s.th. for a certain time
4 **date** *here:* duration
5 **eye of heaven** *(fig.)* sun
6 **complexion** *here:* appearance
8 **nature's changing course untrimmed** the changing state of nature which is not controlled by anything
10 **to owe** *(archaic)* to own, to possess
11 **to brag** to speak proudly of s.th. which may not be true
12 **eternal lines** immortal verses
12 **to time thou grow'st** you and time become one, i.e. eternal

Sonnet 18

Shall I compare thee to a summer's day?
Thou art more lovely and more temperate:
Rough winds do shake the darling buds of May,
And summer's lease hath all too short a date:
Sometime too hot the eye of heaven shines,
And often is his gold complexion dimmed,
And every fair from fair sometime declines,
By chance, or nature's changing course untrimmed:
But thy eternal summer shall not fade,
Nor lose possession of that fair thou ow'st,
Nor shall death brag thou wander'st in his shade,
When in eternal lines to time thou grow'st,
So long as men can breathe, or eyes can see,
So long lives this, and this gives life to thee.

Talking about time

permanent – constant – eternal – immortal – for ever

short-lived – transitory – fleeting – changeable – mortal – temporary – limited

Exploring the text

1 a) Follow the speaker's train of thought by answering these three questions:
- How is the speaker's initial question answered?
- What characteristics of summer are referred to in the images used?
- What problem does the speaker face, and what solution does he offer?

b) Sum up how the speaker's line of argument develops (cf. the box on the left).

2 What is the speaker referring to when he talks about "thy eternal summer" (l. 9) and "his shade" (l. 11)?

3 Find examples of the characteristics of a Shakespearean sonnet (cf. box below).

Shakespearean sonnet
A sonnet is a fourteen-line poem written in iambic pentameter, i.e. an unstressed syllable is followed by a stressed syllable five times. A Shakespearean sonnet is usually made up of three quatrains (four lines of verse) and a concluding couplet of two lines, sometimes written 4 + 4 + 4 + 2, which form clear units in a line of argument and rhyme abab cdcd efef gg.

4 Try to translate the concluding couplet into poetic German. Keep as close as possible to the original words and syntax; the two lines do not have to rhyme.

5 a) Would you consider the tone of the poem to be sincere or exaggerated?

b) Listen again to the recording of the sonnet and comment on it. Experiment with alternative readings in small groups. Then make and present your own recording in class.

Before you read

- What is true / perfect love? Approach the topic using **one** of these methods:
  - In groups, make a list of its characteristics and then agree on a top three.
  - What should **not** happen in a loving relationship? In pairs, make a list of ideas.
  - What would your photo of true / perfect love look like? Think of a few variations.
  - Explain true love poetically using similes and metaphors: True love is (like) …
- Listen to the recording of Sonnet 116. What does Shakespeare say about true love?

Sonnet 116

Let me not to the marriage of true minds
Admit impediments. Love is not love
Which alters when it alteration finds,
Or bends with the remover to remove:
O, no! it is an ever-fixed mark,
That looks on tempests and is never shaken;
It is the star to every wand'ring bark,
Whose worth's unknown, although his height be taken.
Love's not Time's fool, though rosy lips and cheeks
Within his bending sickle's compass come;
Love alters not with his brief hours and weeks,
But bears it out even to the edge of doom.
If this be error and upon me prov'd,
I never writ, nor no man ever lov'd.

1 **true** *here:* faithful
1 **marriage** *here:* union
2 **to admit** *here:* to allow to enter
2 **impediment** s.th. that stops a development
4 **to bend … to remove** to change when the other person's love changes
5 **mark** *here:* signal for ships
6 **tempest** *(old)* storm
7 **bark** sailing ship with three masts
8 **to take a height** *here:* to measure a position
10 **sickle** *Sense*
10 **compass** *here:* reach
12 **to bear s.th. out** to be patient and loyal despite difficulties
12 **edge of doom** end of the world; death
13 **to prove** *here:* to demonstrate
14 **writ** *(old)* wrote

Exploring the text

1. a) What "impediments" (l. 2) does the speaker refer to in the sonnet? How does he feel about these impediments?
   b) Do these impediments still cause problems between couples today?
2. Find and explain the positive metaphors for love in the sonnet. Cf. example on the right for one way of doing this.
3. Which phrases or lines in the sonnet appeal to you most? Which ones do you find particularly difficult?

Love = a madness
↘ ↙
illogical, unpredictable

A step further

- Suggest appropriate titles for the two sonnets.
- Compare the attitudes to love expressed in the two sonnets.
- Imagine you have received an anonymous e-mail with one of the two sonnets on these pages from a secret admirer. Write a humorous reply.
- Dramatisation
  In pairs, dramatise one of the sonnets in the following way: One speaker recites the full text of the sonnet stopping after each line. The other speaker makes a short comment in modern (informal) English on the line which has just been recited. Feel free to make humorous or critical remarks.
- Write a modern sonnet about a subject of your choice. You could base your text on Sonnet 18 and start with "Shall I compare life / school / etc. to a …?"

The world's most famous love story

Getting started

1 Put the pieces of the plot of *Romeo and Juliet* in the correct order.

1. Meanwhile Capulet, who knows nothing about the secret wedding, arranges a marriage between Juliet and a nobleman, Paris. Juliet asks Friar Lawrence for help. He gives her a drug which will make her seem dead for two days. In that time, her body will be taken to the family tomb, thus giving Romeo the chance to return to Verona and rescue her when she wakes up.

2. For many years there has been a bitter quarrel between two important families of Verona, the Montagues and Capulets. Members of the two families fight whenever they meet. The Prince of Verona declares that any further fighting will be punished by death.

3. That night Romeo steals into the Capulets' garden. Standing below Juliet's balcony, he hears her say that she is in love with him. Although well aware of the feud between their families, they decide to marry in secret.

4. Almost immediately, Juliet awakes expecting to find Romeo. When she sees his dead body, she stabs herself with Romeo's dagger. The play ends with the two families reconciled by their children's death.

5. Outside the Capulet tomb, Romeo is challenged by Paris. They fight and Paris is killed. Romeo enters the tomb and finds Juliet. Believing her to be dead, Romeo takes the poison and dies.

6. Romeo Montague and Juliet Capulet are the children of the two feuding families. They meet and fall in love at a masked ball given by the Capulets. Juliet's cousin, Tybalt, recognizes Romeo and is insulted by his presence; he swears to have revenge.

7. The lovers persuade a friendly priest, Friar Lawrence, to marry them. Shortly after the wedding Tybalt meets Romeo in the street and he challenges him. Romeo refuses to fight for Juliet's sake. His friend Mercutio takes up Tybalt's challenge and is fatally wounded. Romeo is overcome by anger and takes revenge for his friend's death by killing Tybalt.

8. Juliet takes the drug and is discovered 'dead' on the morning of her wedding to Paris. Friar Lawrence tries to inform Romeo of the plan, but the message does not reach him. Romeo only learns that Juliet is dead. Heartbroken, he buys some poison and goes back to Verona intending to kill himself by Juliet's side.

9. The Prince decides not to sentence Romeo to death for taking part in the fight. Instead he banishes Romeo from Verona for ever. Before leaving Verona for Mantua the next morning, Romeo spends the night secretly with Juliet.

2 a) Look at the poster on the left of a 1996 film production of Romeo and Juliet. Which events in the play are the stills probably based on?
b) The four key words on the poster (hope, vengeance, etc.) refer to themes in the play. Explain their significance by referring to the plot summary above.

The Prologue

Romeo and Juliet *begins with a prologue (= an introductory poem) spoken by the Chorus.*

The Prologue
Two households, both alike in dignity,
In fair Verona, where we lay our scene,
From ancient grudge break to new mutiny,
Where civil blood makes civil hands unclean.
From forth the fatal loins of these two foes
A pair of star-crossed lovers take their life;
Whose misadventured piteous overthrows
Do with their death bury their parents' strife.
The fearful passage of their death-marked love,
And the continuance of their parents' rage,
Which but their children's end nought could remove,
Is now the two hours' traffic of our stage;
The which if you with patient ears attend,
What here shall miss, our toil shall strive to mend. *The Prologue, ll. 1–14*

chorus *(Elizabethan theatre)* actor who speaks the opening and closing lines of the play
1 **dignity** *(old use)* of a high social standing
3 **grudge** reason for a conflict
3 **mutiny** *here:* violence
4 **civil blood** fighting between people of the same town
5 **From forth … foes** refers to the enemies' children
6 **star-crossed** *here:* whose love is ruined by the stars / fate
7 **misadventured piteous overthrows** unlucky tragic accidents
8 **strife** [straɪf] bitter conflict
11 **but** except for
11 **nought** [nɔːt] nothing
14 **toil** hard work
14 **to strive** [straɪv] to try hard

Exploring the text

1 a) How much does the Chorus reveal about the play?
b) What details does the Chorus **not** mention? Refer to the summary on page 138.
2 a) Try to identify the poetic form used by the Chorus. Look at page 136 for help.
b) Can you think of reasons why Shakespeare starts his tragedy this way? Consider in particular the situation in theatres at Shakespeare's time (cf. page 135 for ideas).
3 a) How would you present the Prologue in a modern version of *Romeo and Juliet*?
b) Rewrite the text in modern English, either in a poetic form or a prose text.
4 Practise a version of the Prologue in groups, e.g. different students could perform certain sections or lines.

The first meeting of the lovers

This is what Romeo says when he sees Juliet for the first time at a masked ball:

Romeo O she doth teach the torches to burn bright!
It seems she hangs upon the cheek of night
As a rich jewel in an Ethiop's ear –
Beauty too rich for use, for earth too dear:
So shows a snowy dove trooping with crows,
As yonder lady o'er her fellows shows.
The measure done, I'll watch her place of stand,
And touching hers, make blessèd my rude hand.
Did my heart love till now? Forswear it, sight!
For I ne'er saw true beauty till this night. *Act I, Scene 5, ll. 41–52*

1 **torch** *(old use)* piece of burning wood used to give light
5 **dove** *Taube*
5 **crow** *Krähe*
7 **measure** *(old)* dance
8 **rude** *here:* rough
9 **to forswear s.th.** to swear s.th. that is not true

Exploring the text

1 Describe Romeo's reaction when he first sees Juliet.
2 How does Romeo underline Juliet's "brightness" in the passage?

When Romeo addresses Juliet (Act I, Scene 5, ll. 92 – 105), the dialogue takes the form of a sonnet.

1 **to profane s.th.** [prə'feɪn] to be disrespectful to s.th. holy
2 **holy shrine** *here:* Juliet's hand
2 **fine** penalty
6 **mannerly devotion** respectful behaviour towards s.th. holy
8 **palm** flat inside part of the hand
9 **palmer** pilgrim to Jerusalem who brought back palm leaves
12 **to grant** *here:* to give in
12 **lest** if not
13 **to move** *here:* to take the initiative
14 **effect** *here:* result (i.e. a kiss)

Romeo *(To Juliet)* If I profane with my unworthiest hand
This holy shrine, the gentle fine is this:
My lips, two blushing pilgrims, ready stand
To smooth that rough touch with a tender kiss.
Juliet Good pilgrim, you do wrong your hand too much,
Which mannerly devotion shows in this;
For saints have hands that pilgrims' hands do touch,
And palm to palm is holy palmers' kiss.
Romeo Have not saints lips, and holy palmers too?
Juliet Ay, pilgrim, lips that they must use in prayer.
Romeo O then, dear saint, let lips do what hands do:
They pray, grant thou, lest faith turn to despair.
Juliet Saints do not move, though grant for prayers' sake.
Romeo Then move not, while my prayer's effect I take. *Kissing her.*

3 a) In a close reading of these lines, explain the religious imagery used.
b) What impression do you get of Romeo? How might Juliet feel?

4 Work out Romeo's and Juliet's movements from what they say. Then, in pairs, read the dialogue in a suitable tone, using actions you feel are appropriate to the words.

5 Explain in which way Romeo and Juliet share this sonnet between them (cf. definition, page 136). How do the lines express their emotions and reactions?

The balcony scene

After the ball, Romeo climbs a wall into the Capulet's orchard. He speaks aloud of his love for Juliet, thinking that he is alone. Then Juliet appears at a window above him.

Romeo But, soft! what light through yonder window breaks?
It is the east, and Juliet is the sun.
Arise, fair sun, and kill the envious moon,
Who is already sick and pale with grief,
That thou her maid art far more fair than she:
Be not her maid, since she is envious; [...]
It is my lady, O, it is my love!
O that she knew she were! [...]
She speaks.
O, speak again bright angel! for thou art
As glorious to this night, being o'er my head
As is a wingèd messenger of heaven
Unto the white-upturned wondering eyes
Of mortals that fall back to gaze on him
When he bestrides the lazy puffing clouds
And sails upon the bosom of the air.
Juliet O Romeo, Romeo, wherefore art thou Romeo?
Deny thy father and refuse thy name;
Or if thou wilt not, be but sworn my love,
And I'll no longer be a Capulet.

4 **grief** sadness
5 **her maid** the moon's servant (In mythology, virgins were servants to Diana, goddess of the moon.)
14 **to fall back** to throw one's head back
14 **to gaze** to look for a time
15 **to bestride, bestrode, bestridden** to sit on
16 **bosom** *(here fig.) Brust*
17 **wherefore art thou Romeo?** why is your name Romeo? (it shows he is a Montague)
18 **Deny ...** refuse to acknowledge your family

Romeo *(Aside)* Shall I hear more, or shall I speak at this?
Juliet 'Tis but thy name that is my enemy;
Thou art thyself, though not a Montague.
What's Montague? It is nor hand, nor foot,
Nor arm, nor face, nor any other part
Belonging to a man. O be some other name!
What's in a name? That which we call a rose
By any other name would smell as sweet;
So Romeo would, were he not Romeo called,
Retain that dear perfection which he owes
Without that title. Romeo, doff thy name,
And for thy name which is no part of thee,
Take all myself. *Act II, Scene 2, ll. 2–48*

21 **aside** *(theatre)* s.th. an actor says for the audience, not for the other characters
30 **to retain** to keep
30 **to owe** to own
31 **to doff** to take off (like clothes)

Exploring the text

1 With a partner, write down the phrases Romeo uses to talk about Juliet. Compare your findings with what he said when he first saw her at the ball (cf. page 139).
2 Explain Juliet's line of argument in ll. 22–33. Does it make sense, or not?
3 Think of people, countries or institutions whose names have been changed. Why was this done? How important is a name?

"Farewell, farewell!"

The scene (Act III, Scene 5) takes place when Romeo visits Juliet (cf. page 138, part 9).

Juliet Wilt thou be gone? It is not yet near day:
It was the nightingale, and not the lark,
That pierced the fearful hollow of thine ear;
Nightly she sings on yond pomegranate tree:
Believe me, love, it was the nightingale.
Romeo It was the lark, the herald of the morn,
No nightingale. Look, love, what envious streaks
Do lace the severing clouds in yonder east:
Night's candles are burnt out, and jocund day
Stands tiptoe on the misty mountain tops.
I must be gone and live, or stay and die.
Juliet Yon light is not daylight, I know it, I:
It is some meteor that the sun exhaled,
To be to thee this night a torch-bearer,
And light thee on thy way to Mantua:
Therefore stay yet; thou need'st not to be gone.
Romeo Let me be tane, let me be put to death;
I am content, so thou wilt have it so.
I'll say yon grey is not the morning's eye,
'Tis but the pale reflex of Cynthia's brow;
Nor that is not the lark whose notes do beat
The vaulty heaven so high above our heads:
I have more care to stay than will to go:

2 **nightingale** Nachtigall
2 **lark** *Lerche*
3 **to pierce** *here:* to reach
6 **herald** sign that s.th. will happen
8 **to lace** *here:* to shine from behind the cloud
8 **severing** *here:* which are moving apart
9 **jocund** cheerful
14 **torch-bearer** *(old)* s.o. who carries a light
17 **tane** captured
20 **reflex of Cynthia's brow** reflection of part of the moon
23 **care** *here:* desire

28 **harsh discords** shrill notes
29 **division** *(old)* music
31 **loathed** much hated
31 **toad** *Kröte*
33 **to affray** *(old)* to frighten
34 **hunt's-up** music played to wake hunters in the morning
36 **woe** *(old)* sadness, trouble

Look at the photo below and on p. 141, and the poster on p. 138. What impression do you get of the film versions of *Romeo and Juliet*?

Come, death, and welcome! Juliet wills it so.
How is't, my soul? let's talk, it is not day.
Juliet It is, it is: hie hence, be gone, away!
It is the lark that sings so out of tune,
Straining harsh discords and unpleasing sharps.
Some say the lark makes sweet division;
This doth not so, for she divideth us:
Some say the lark and loathed toad change eyes;
O, now I would they had changed voices too,
Since arm from arm that voice doth us affray,
Hunting thee hence with hunt's-up to the day,
O, now be gone; more light and light it grows.
Romeo More light and light; more dark and dark our woes!
Enter Nurse, hastily.
Nurse Madam!
Juliet Nurse?
Nurse Your lady mother is coming to your chamber.
The day is broke; be wary, look about. *Exit*
Juliet Then, window, let day in, and let life out.
Romeo Farewell, farewell! one kiss, and I'll descend. *He goeth down.*

Exploring the text

1 Outline what happens in the scene in your own words.
2 Describe how the mood of the two main characters changes during the exchange.
3 Which symbols and images are used to refer to day and night?

A step further

- Read the scene from the *Shakespeare in Love* screenplay on page 143 (ll. 1 – 16). How is it linked to the scene you have just read?

Using your skills

Projects: Romeo and Juliet

- **Mini-performance**
  Form groups of 5 – 7 students. Each group does the following:
  – Use the plot summary (p. 138) and a copy of the full text to find more key scenes which relate directly to the love story.
  – Turn your findings into a version of the play which focuses on the two main characters. A narrator (= Chorus) could link the scenes and minor characters could present their perspectives in short monologues (Find suitable statements in the play for the parents, the nurse, the friar, etc.). Write a script for your play.
  – Decide who is to play which role (director, Romeo, Juliet, other characters, scriptwriter/ prompter, narrator / Chorus). Then rehearse your play – you will have to learn your texts by heart – and perform it in class.
- **Key scenes on film**
  In groups, examine the extracts from *Romeo and Juliet* on pp. 139 – 142 and consider how to present them on film. First discuss your options regarding language, setting and cast. Then decide which cinematic devices to use (cf. glossary, page 184). Present your ideas in class (cf. skills file, page 182).

Before you read

Do task a) if you do **not** know the film *Shakespeare in Love* and do task b) if you do. The words in the box on the right will be useful for both tasks.

a) Find out about the plot and characters in *Shakespeare in Love*. You could check the internet. Then write a short summary of your findings.

b) Which characters from the film are shown in the still below and on page 145, and in what situations?

Talking about love

to fall head over heels (in love)
to be madly in love
to be infatuated with s.o.
love at first sight
a passionate love affair
a loveless relationship
love against the odds

The film Shakespeare in Love *is set in Elizabethan England, where young playwright William Shakespeare is working on his new play,* Romeo and Juliet. *Will meets and falls in love with Viola de Lesseps, a rich man's daughter. Viola also falls in love with Will but unfortunately she is to be married to Lord Wessex. Wessex hopes to solve his financial problems by trading his title for Viola's father's money. He suspects that he has a rival but he still proceeds with the arranged marriage. The next step is to gain Queen Elizabeth's consent.*

Shakespeare in love

INT. DE LESSEPSES' HOUSE: VIOLA'S BEDROOM. MORNING.

(A sunbeam wakes the lovers. Sunday morning. Church bells. Viola wakes with a start. Something is bothering her, she can't think what. Will calms her.)

Will Sunday … it is Sunday. *(He brings her back down to the pillow.)*

Will *(Cont'd)* I found something in my sleep. The Friar who married them will take up their destinies.

Viola Oh, but it will end well for love?

Will In heaven, perhaps. It is not a comedy I am writing now. A broad river divides my lovers – family, duty, fate – as unchangeable as nature.

Viola *(sobered)* Yes, this is not life, Will. This is a stolen season.

(Suddenly there is a great racket heard from downstairs … a man shouting.)

Wessex *(O.S.)* Not ready? Where is she?

Nurse *(O.S.)* Be patient, my lord, she is dressing.

Wessex *(O.S.)* Will you ask Her Majesty to be patient?

(Viola remembers. She jumps up and gives a cry.)

Viola Sunday! Greenwich! […]

1 **INT.** *short for* **interior**, *here:* inside a building
2 **start** *here:* sudden movement
5 **Cont'd** *short for* **continued**
5 **to take up** *here:* to influence
10 **sobered** *here:* seriously
12 **O.S.** *short for* **off screen**, i.e. s.o. is speaking who is not visible on screen

EXT. GREENWICH PALACE. NIGHT.

(Fireworks explode in the evening sky over Greenwich, a royal palace, crowded now with noble guests.)

EXT. GREENWICH PALACE. TERRACE. NIGHT.

(The way these royal routs work is that the guests mill about, chatting, bowing and generally behaving gallantly, while Queen Elizabeth creates a vortex around her as she passes through the throng, occasionally honouring somebody with a couple of words, until she arrives thankfully at the best chair … where she establishes a headquarters. Her current Lord in Waiting ferries the lucky few forward to a brief audience with the Queen, each giving way to the next. Viola and Wessex are respectively dipping and bowing, as they are greeted by people who know them … […] The Queen's Lord in Waiting plucks Wessex's sleeve.)

Wessex *(to him)* Now?

Lord in Waiting Now.

Wessex *(to Viola)* The Queen asks for you. Answer well.

(The Lord in Waiting ushers Viola through the crowd.) […]

(Angle on the Queen.)

(The Lord in Waiting has presented Viola. Viola speaks from a frozen curtsey.)

Viola Your Majesty.

Queen Stand up straight, girl.

(Viola straightens. The Queen examines her.)

Queen *(Cont'd)* I have seen you. You are the one who comes to all the plays – at Whitehall, at Richmond.

Viola *(agreeing)* Your Majesty.

Queen What do you love so much?

Viola Your Majesty …

Queen Speak out! I know who I am. Do you love stories of kings and queens? Feats of arms? Or is it courtly love?

Viola I love theatre. To have stories acted for me by a company of fellows is indeed –

Queen *(interrupting)* They are not acted for you, they are acted for me.

(Viola remains silent, in apology.

Angle on Will.

He is watching and listening. He has never seen the Queen so close. He is fascinated.)

Queen *(Cont'd)* And – ?

Viola And I love poetry above all.

Queen Above Lord Wessex?

(She looks over Viola's shoulder and Viola realises Wessex has moved up behind her. Wessex bows.)

Queen *(Cont'd) (to Wessex)* My lord – when you cannot find your wife you had better look for her at the playhouse.

(The Courtiers titter at her pleasantry.)

Queen *(Cont'd)* But playwrights teach nothing about love, they make it pretty, they make it comical, or they make it lust. They cannot make it true.

Viola *(blurts)* Oh, but they can!

(She has forgotten herself. The Courtiers gasp. The Queen considers her. Wessex looks furious. Will is touched.)

17 **EXT.** *short for* **exterior**, *here:* outside a building
21 **rout** *here:* evening reception
22 **vortex** empty space
25 **Lord in Waiting** *Zeremonienmeister*
25 **to ferry** *here:* to guide
26 **to dip** *here:* to lower the body by bending one knee; a sign of respect
34 **curtsey** *(old)* cf. **to dip** above
39 **Whitehall, Richmond** reference to royal palaces
43 **feat of arms** impressive use of weapons
48 **angle** *here:* camera
57 **to titter** to laugh nervously
61 **to gasp** to take in a breath loudly, e.g. in shock

Viola *(Cont'd)* I mean … Your Majesty, they do not, they have not, but I believe there is one who can –

Wessex Lady Viola is … young in the world. Your Majesty is wise in it. Nature and truth are the very enemies of playacting. I'll wager my fortune.

Queen I thought you were here because you had none.

(Titters again. Wessex could kill somebody.)

Queen *(Cont'd) (by way of dismissing him)* Well, no one will take your wager, it seems.

Will Fifty pounds!

(Shock and horror. Queen Elizabeth is the only person amused.)

Queen Fifty pounds! A very worthy sum on a very worthy question. Can a play show us the very truth and nature of love? I bear witness to the wager, and will be the judge of it as the occasion arises. *(Which wins a scatter of applause. She gathers her skirts and stands.)* I have not seen anything to settle it yet. *(She moves away, everybody bowing and scraping.)* So – the fireworks will be soothing after the excitements of Lady Viola's audience. *(And now she is next to Wessex who is bowing low. Intimately to him.)* Have her then, but you are a lordly fool. She has been plucked since I saw her last, and not by you. It takes a woman to know it …

From Shakespeare in Love *by Marc Norman and Tom Stoppard, Stuttgart: Reclam, 2000, pp. 87–88, 90–94.*

67 **to wager one's fortune** *(old)* to risk all of one's money in a bet *(= Wette)*
77 **to bear witness** *here:* to say later that a bet was taken
79 **scatter** *here:* from a few people
80 **to bow and scrape** to show too much respect
83 **to pluck** *here:* to have sexual relations

Exploring the text

1 What kinds of love are either mentioned or demonstrated in the two scenes?

2 a) How do the screenwriters use comic elements and characterization to make the scenes more entertaining?
b) At which points could the director further emphasise comedy in the scenes by means of cinematic effects, e.g. camera operations? (Cf. glossary, page 184.)

3 What hints do we get in the course of the scenes about future plot developments?

Close-up: language

Based on the two scenes, what makes the language of *Shakespeare in Love* both ideally suited to the screen and also at times reminiscent of Shakespearean English?

A step further

- a) View the scenes in the film which correspond to the screenplay extracts. What additional stage directions did the author give to the actors / actresses and cameramen?
b) Write the director's commentary in which you explain why the scenes were filmed in this way. If the film is available on DVD, you could compare your version with the original commentary by John Madden.
- Watch selected scenes from *Shakespeare in Love*. What impression do you get of Shakespeare the man and of life in Elizabethan times? Compare your findings with the information on pp. 134–135.

Shakespearean idioms

green-eyed jealousy
to knit your brows
to make a virtue of necessity
not to sleep a wink
to give s.o. or to get short shrift
cold comfort

3 **by a head** *here:* by a few votes
12 **thereabouts** *here:* having a particular placing
20 **National Curriculum** *(GB)* subjects taught in state schools
21 **RSC** *short for* **Royal Shakespeare Company** classical theatre company

Before you read

- Who would you nominate as the 'German Personality of the Millennium'? What kind of personality should this be? Argue the case for the person of your choice.
- a) Explain the idioms in the box on the left with the help of a dictionary.
  b) Write a monologue which includes one or two of these phrases.

Shakespeare, man of the Millennium

William Shakespeare was elected British Personality of the Millennium by listeners to Radio Four's *Today* programme.

The man whose poetry and plays enriched the English language won by a relatively short head over Sir Winston Churchill, gaining 11,717 telephone votes to 10,957 for the statesman who led Britain during its "finest hour". Third place was taken by William Caxton, who learnt the art of printing in Cologne and brought it to England. He gained 7,109 votes.

Charles Darwin, author of *The Origin of the Species*, came fourth with 6,337, while Isaac Newton (4,664) and Oliver Cromwell (4,653) were almost equal in last place.

Rod Liddle, Editor of *Today*, said: "Even though many thousands of listeners voted for other nominees I think most people would agree that Shakespeare should be there or thereabouts."

The news was greeted with pleasure on the programme by Dame Judy Dench, the actress whose latest part is as Queen Elizabeth in the film *Shakespeare in Love*. She said: "He is known in our house as 'the gentleman who pays the rent'."

Shakespeare's poetry and plays have been translated into more than 100 languages and his coinages and metaphors salt the tongues of the English speaking world. Common phrases like green-eyed jealousy, knitted brows, a virtue of necessity, haven't slept a wink, short shrift and cold comfort all derive from him. He is the one compulsory author on the National Curriculum.

Ian Rowley, spokesman for the RSC, said: "Last year the Royal Shakespeare Company took him to five continents, including Japan and Pakistan. He's a better international currency than the Euro. The Japanese see more Shakespeare and put on more productions of his plays than we do in Britain." At one point there were 12 productions of *Hamlet* playing at the same time in different theatres in Tokyo.

Jonathan Bate, King Alfred Professor of English at the University of Liverpool and author of *The Genius of Shakespeare* (Picador), attributes some of his influence to the simple fact that the British Empire took the language he wrote in to distant outposts of the globe. He said: "But he is also important in other European countries. He provided a model for a national poet, a writer creating a sense of a national identity and national history."

Each generation has found a new relevance in his plays. The story of Romeo and Juliet, for example, was translated to Los Angeles by Baz Luhrmann for his recent film starring Leonardo DiCaprio and Claire Danes, with the Montague and Capulet gangs battling it out in Shakespeare's words but with modern weapons. Indeed, the *Guinness Books of Records* describes Shakespeare as the most filmed author, with 309 straight or fairly straight versions of his plays on film and 41 loosely based on his works.

Prof Bate believes that Shakespeare's willingness to present conflicts without giving answers is one of the reasons why his work continues to fascinate each generation, and why his plays have the capacity to keep on evolving.

Stanley Wells, Emeritus Professor of Shakespeare Studies at the University of Birmingham, who received the award from *Today* on Shakespeare's behalf, said: "He's in the water supply so far as language goes." He also emphasised the flexibility of Shakespeare's plays. "Even if you lose the language you can make ballets out of them, because they're not only highly literary and poetic, they are also highly dramatic. They have taken on the quality of myth."

An educated person in the last century would have been grounded in the classics, mainly Roman, but also Greek. In this century, Shakespeare has to a large extent taken the place of the classics.

One of the reasons he is so popular in translation, said Professor Wells, is that: "In a sense it's easier, the Elizabethan English is translated into modern languages." But the deepest reasons for his appeal is, he believes, that Shakespeare is a deeply humane writer and that "he is a religious writer in the profoundest sense, one who is concerned with a world elsewhere; the ghost, the supernatural, the fairy world". He said: "He has an awareness of man in relation to the universe, in relation to the unknown."

42 **emeritus** who is no longer employed full-time at the university
44 **he is in the water supply** *(here fig.)* he is an essential part of modern English
54 **profound** deep

By Sandra Barwick, The Telegraph, *January 2, 1999.*

Exploring the text

1 What reasons are given for electing Shakespeare British Personality of the Millennium?

2 a) Compare Shakespeare's achievements to those of the other candidates. Do you find the arguments in favour of Shakespeare convincing, or not?
b) What further arguments can you think of in Shakespeare's favour?

3 Turn the *Telegraph* article into a short article for a popular newspaper. First, list the features of this kind of text (cf. skills file, p. 188). Use indirect speech, not quotes.

4 In your opinion, should German pupils have to study Shakespeare? Refer to arguments from the text in your answer.

A step further

- Panel discussion

Conduct a panel discussion on whether Shakespeare should also be 'International Personality of the Millennium'. Your guest list should include two or three of the people quoted in the text as well as speakers with other suggestions.
In groups, prepare statements for one of the panellists or the moderator. Choose a representative from each group at random to participate in the discussion.

Meet the media

- TV news item

Turn the information and opinions in the article into a TV news item. Write a script for the newsreader, and prepare short interviews and a concluding comment. What visual material could you use? Broadcast your item live in class.

Shakespeare – a great author

1 What arguments, put forward by the speakers, show that Shakespeare is a major historic personality? Compare your findings with evidence in the article.

2 What features of a documentary do the video clips reveal? (Cf. skills file, p. 185.)

Using your skills

Setting
the time and place which characterise a work of literature or a film

Romeo and Juliet on film

The film William Shakespeare's Romeo and Juliet *(1997), directed by Baz Luhrmann, closely follows the original play as regards the order of the scenes and the text. The major difference between the original play and the film is the* setting*: Luhrmann moved the location from Renaissance Verona to a contemporary, urban Verona Beach in the US. Montague and Capulet have become the warring heads of two huge companies. Baz Luhrman also incorporated elements of other genres into his film, notably those typical of Westerns.*

Viewing log

Keep a viewing log as you watch the film.

- Choose two or three important scenes to examine more closely (cf. below). These will provide you with a basis for your own personal review once you have watched all of the film.
- You could make notes about the following points as you watch the key scenes: setting – sequence of events – main characters, their costumes and characteristic actions – striking cinematic devices (cf. glossary, p. 184) – your own observations and comments. Cf. skills file, "Film scene analysis", pp. 184 – 185 for ideas.

Overhead shot
this camera position gives a 'bird's eye view' of s.th.
Flashforward
a scene that breaks the chronological order of the plot. It shows future events.

Focus on: The Prologue [0.00 – 2.24]

1 What kind of TV format is used to start the film? What might its purpose be?
2 What picture do we get of Verona Beach from the *overhead shots*?
3 What impression do the *flashforwards* at the end of the prologue convey of the plot?

Focus on: The encounter between the Montagues and Capulets at the petrol station [2.25 – 9.07]

1 a) Describe the atmosphere at the beginning of the scene.
b) At what point does it change? How is the viewer made aware of this change?
2 The shootout at the petrol station is presented in a series of *fast cuts*. What effect do these cuts have on the atmosphere in the scene?
3 Make a list of at least five *close-ups* which you find striking and then explain their significance.
4 What elements of a Western are included in the fight scene?
5 How is Tybalt characterized by what he says, his body language and costume, camera movement and angles?

Fast cut
rapid switch from one image to the next
Close-up
the camera is held very close to the subject

A step further

- Film review
After you have watched all of the film *Romeo and Juliet*, write a review which includes a short introduction with some detail about the plot, a detailed discussion of two or three scenes, an evaluation of the actors' performances, a comment on whether Luhrman's has been successful or not in adapting Shakespeare to a modern setting and a concluding statement which includes your opinion of the film. Cf. skills file, "Film reviews" on page 189 for further ideas.

The music of love

Before you watch

- Write definitions for the types of love in the box on the right. Check any unknown words in a dictionary. Then find links between the different types of love.
- What music video clips to do with 'love' can you think of? What types of love do they deal with? What do you like / dislike about them?

Types of love

romantic love
unrequited love
ill-fated love
puppy love
undying love

Love is a stranger (Eurythmics)

Before you watch

- a) Read the lyrics on the right. Working in two groups, brainstorm for ideas about the personification of love in line 1 or the metaphor for love in line 3.
  b) In pairs, compare your connotations with a partner from the other group.
  c) What mood would you expect a music video clip of the song to convey?

"Love is a stranger in an open car
To tempt you in and drive you far away [...]
Love is a danger of a different kind
To take you away and leave you far behind."

From Love is a stranger *by the Eurythmics*

Watching and thinking

1 Watch the video clip of "Love is a stranger" to see if it meets with the expectations you had in "Before you watch", or not. What kind of mood was conveyed?
2 Before you watch the clip again decide which of the following aspects you wish to observe and report back to the class about later (cf. skills file, p. 186 for ideas): the roles lead singer Annie Lennox adopts – the roles of the male characters – settings and costumes – links between lyrics and images – discrepancies between lyrics and images – elements of plot vs. a chain of associations.

All woman (Lisa Stansfield)

Before you watch

- In the role of either the man or woman in the lyrics on the right, explain your side of the story to a friend.
- Write storylines based on the lyrics and present them in class.

"He's home again from another day
She smiles at him as he walks through the door
She wonders if it will be okay
It's hard for her when he doesn't respond

He says babe you look a mess
You look dowdy in that dress
It's just not like it used to be [...]"

From All Woman *by Lisa Stansfield*

Watching and thinking

1 a) Watch the music video clip with the sound turned off. What do you find out about the couple's relationship?
  b) Describe the special effects used in the clip and the mood they convey.
2 Watch the clip again, this time with sound. Discuss whether the lyrics or the film material are more important.
3 Compare the film material and the lyrics. Is the ending happy, or not?

A step further

- In groups, work out differences between the making of the two clips and the clips you thought of in "Before you watch", task 2. Then present the results in class.

Talking about the speaker

The speaker …
reveals his / her attitude towards …
conveys his / her feelings about …
poses the question if … /
appeals to … to …
argues that …
aims to convince … of …
arouses compassion / sympathy for …

The poetry of modern love

Before you read

a) Listen to the recordings of the poems on these pages and label the type or phase of love expressed in them.
b) Describe the tone in which they are read.

Exploring the texts

1 What do you learn about the speakers in the five poems? Consider attitudes to / experiences with love, possible ages and genders. (Note: the poet is not necessarily identical with the speaker.)

Unfortunate Coincidence

By the time you swear you're his,
Shivering and sighing,
And he vows his passion is
Infinite, undying –
Lady, make a note of this:
One of you is lying.

Dorothy Parker (1893–1967)

Coat

Sometimes I have wanted
to throw you off
like a heavy coat.

Sometimes I have said
you would not let me
breathe or move.

But now that I am free
to choose light clothes
or none at all.

I feel the cold
and all the time I think
how warm it used to be.

Vicki Feaver (b. 1943)

Symptoms of Love

Love is a universal migraine,
A bright stain on the vision
Blotting out reason.

Symptoms of true love
Are leanness, jealousy,
Laggard dawns;

Are omens and nightmares –
Listening for a knock,
Waiting for a sign:

For a touch of her fingers
In a darkened room,
For a searching look.

Take courage, lover!
Could you endure such grief
At any hands but hers?

Robert Graves (1895–1985)

2 Select effective images and explain them in the context of the poem.

3 a) Compare and rank the poems according to tone (most to least positive), language (most to least complex) and the most effective use of poetic devices.
b) Which poem do you like best / least? Why?

A step further

- What kind of photo(s) would you use to illustrate each of the poems?
- Turn one of the five poems into a mini-saga. It may be only loosely based on the poem, i.e. you can reuse ideas and phrases but feel free, for example, to invent a surprise ending.

Talking about tone I

A tone reveals / reflects the speaker's feelings.
It may be:
matter-of-fact / detached
melancholy / sad
cheerful / enthusiastic
humorous / joking / playful
emotional / harsh / accusing
ironic / sarcastic / cynical
or:
It signals resignation / frustration
It suggests / indicates disappointment / anger

After the Lunch

On Waterloo Bridge, where we said our goodbyes,
The weather conditions bring tears to my eyes.
I wipe them away with a black woolly glove
And try not to notice I've fallen in love.

On Waterloo Bridge I am trying to think:
This is nothing. You're high on the charm and the drink.
But the juke-box inside me is playing a song
That says something different. And when was it wrong?

On Waterloo Bridge with the wind in my hair
I am tempted to skip. *You're a fool.* I don't care.
The head does its best but the heart is the boss –
I admit it before I am halfway across.

Wendy Cope (b. 1945)

Sonnet XLII

What lips my lips have kissed, and where, and why,
I have forgotten, and what arms have lain
Under my head till morning; but the rain
Is full of ghosts tonight, that tap and sigh
Upon the glass and listen for reply,
And in my heart there stirs a quiet pain
For unremembered lads that not again
Will turn to me at midnight with a cry.
Thus in the winter stands the lonely tree,
Nor knows what birds have vanished one by one,
Yet knows its boughs more silent than before:
I cannot say what loves have come and gone,
I only know that summer sang in me
A little while, that in me sings no more.

Edna St. Vincent Millay (1892–1950)

Lessons in love

Before you watch

- What situation might the still on the left be taken from?

Watching and thinking I

- Take notes about the parts of the sketch which make you laugh, and why.
- In pairs, compare notes. What basic comic effects are used?

Watching and thinking II

- Make a grid with the situations in one column and the speakers' advice in the other.
- Describe the speaker's appearance and body language.
- Describe Rowan Atkinson's body language. You could refer to a dictionary for help.

A step further

- Evaluate the performances and the entertainment value of the sketch.

Stereotypes

a womanizer – a lonely heart – a Latin lover – a wallflower – a flirt – a libertine – a Casanova – a henpecked husband

Before you read

- Collect collocations with the noun 'relationship', e.g. to have a relationship with …
- a) Describe the stereotypes in the box on the left as regards their attitudes to love.
  b) Improvise a situation in which two of these characters meet.
- If you did a survey on people's attitudes to love, what questions would you ask?

The four stages of love

John Robert's romantic history was varied, but – he found – not unique

It is quite rare to read of a survey in which one can recognise oneself, but it happened to me yesterday when I saw the headline: "Men cannot help falling in love at 50". We are biologically programmed, said the study by the Institute of Psychology in Rome, not for "passing lust" but for a "genuine resurgence" of our emotional life. The programme, the survey found, begins when we first fall in love in our teens. Well, of course: it was at university in another country and it ended in tears. In stage two, in our twenties, we form "serious and purposeful attachments leading to marriage". Mine was ill-judged but very purposeful: we both wanted to be married and to have children.

In stage three, in our thirties and forties, we "enter a libertine period" in which our "main interest is in exploring sex, both within and outside marriage".

Guilty on all counts. By my mid-thirties, with two young children, my marriage was over, the incompatibilities of the relationship having become insuperable. I didn't, though, immediately plunge into the libertine phase. Instead, I returned to my original love, savouring the echoes of that time when we were young and careless in another country. Once again, it ended in tears.

Bachelor life was fun for a while: enough money and confidence to attract the attractive, and the heady relief of not having to account for one's actions or whereabouts. Having enough time to change the bedding between engagements and

5 **passing** *here:* lasting for a short time
5 **resurgence** increase in activity
9 **ill-judged** badly planned
16 **to savour** ['seɪvə] **the echoes** *here:* to enjoy the memories

remembering when to unplug the phone seemed to be my principal worries.

But, oh, how it palls! The superficiality, the meaninglessness, and, most of all, the loneliness. By my late forties, I was ready – all too ready, as it turned out – for stage four, "falling in love again". But that is not quite as straightforward as the institute in Rome implies.

The assumption is that you will get it right this time. Knowing yourself better and being a better judge of others, you will choose more wisely. But, as the institute points out, you are also driven – not that you would ever admit it – by "fears that time is running out, by panic at the thought of old age and death".

For me, the consequences were disastrous. I chose once and then twice with all the panache of an awkward teenager. I had learnt nothing and remembered nothing. By my 51st birthday, I was ready to abort the programme: chastity, solitude and long hours at work seemed the only answer left. In the state I was in, I was a danger to others.

However, the drive doesn't give up. As a last resort, I – like, presumably, thousands of others – started reading the lonely hearts columns. Sunday afternoons were spent drafting letters that never reached a convincing conclusion.

And then, five years ago, my jaundiced eye fell on an ad that began, uniquely, with the words: "Well educated …"

The reply flowed from my pen and was posted on the Monday. After a halting phone conversation, we arranged to meet on the bridge over the Thames at Windsor. We came from different professional worlds and knew no one in common. We knew nothing about each other but what was in front of us. And we would never have to see each other again if we did not want to.

We were married nine months later, and the past four years have been the happiest, most rewarding and settled of my life. The institute suggests that this may be because at our age – my wife is eight years younger than me – we are "more attentive, patient and altruistic" than couples normally are when they marry earlier.

It is true that we are both hypersensitive to signals that we may be getting on each other's nerves and quicker – certainly than I was in previous relationships – to take avoiding action, or to apologise immediately if a collision occurs. We are much readier than when we were younger to give the other space and accept it in return. And there is a lot more to talk about: we had lived for a total of 110 years before we met.

None of this, of course, is to be taken as an argument against monogamy, the institute being careful to point out that it is perfectly possible for men to fall in love with their wives again when they are 50 – that, too, counting as a "genuine resurgence".

What, though, of the biological determinism? Among my friends are a couple in their fifties who were sweethearts at school, and many who have been faithfully and, what's more, happily married since they met in their twenties. And if I know many more who have been divorced and libertine, I suspect that is mostly to do with like calling to like.

But, having said all that, it is undoubtedly chastening to find one's life, in all its complexity, reduced to a recognisable formula. It makes you feel like one of a row of butterflies with a great pin through your back. Thanks a lot, fellas!

22 **to pall** [pɔːl] to become less interesting
31 **panache** style and confidence
38 **jaundiced** critical because one has had bad experiences
62 **like calling to like** people prefer friends with similar interests

Do you find the cartoon below funny? Why, why not?

"Why yes, I am fun-loving 40ish Mel Gibson look-alike. Are you 30ish Julia Roberts look-alike with a sense of humour?"

By John Robert, Electronic Telegraph, *August 23, 2000.*

Exploring the text

1 Take notes on the results of the study conducted by the institute in Rome. Then do **one** of the following tasks:
   - Sum up the results in the role of a representative of the institute who gives a press conference about the survey.
   - Write a news item either for a popular or a quality newspaper in which you summarise the results of the survey. [Cf. skills file, "Newspaper texts, p. 188]

2 a) To what extent does the writer's biography confirm the results of the study?
   b) How does he feel about his life?

3 Discuss the language of the text (syntax, tone) in terms of readability and entertainment value.

Close-up: if-clauses

a) In groups, prepare questions for the writer of the article which:
   - explore alternatives in his past life, e.g. What do you think would have happened if you had (done) … ?"
   - look to the future, e.g. "If you met / saw / could decide …, (what) would you … ?

b) One student takes the 'hot chair' and answers the questions in the role of the writer.

A step further

- Write a response to the findings of the study from the point of view of a woman who, like the writer, is also about 55 years old. Try to copy the light-hearted tone and structure of the article you have read.
- Do **one** of the following:
   - Write the text of the lonely hearts advert which attracted the writer's attention ("Well educated", line 39).
   - Write and act out the dialogue of the first "halting phone conversation" (ll. 40–41) between the writer and his present wife.

Meet the media

- Television show

  The writer of the article is invited to be the star guest on the British TV show "This is your life". The presenter introduces the writer and explains why he was invited. Then, in an informal interview situation, the writer outlines events in his life in chronological order. In the course of the interview the presenter welcomes surprise guests from the writer's past for an unexpected, and in most cases, happy reunion. For a time the new arrival is the focus of attention as he / she recalls memories and anecdotes relating to the writer.

  The rest of the class can also get involved in the programme, e.g. as follows:
  - spectators who ask questions during the show;
  - journalists from a TV magazine. These students take notes about the highlights of the show and write an assessment of its entertainment value;
  - programme planners at the TV station whose job is to assess the quality of the moderation and the success of the TV format;
  - language observers whose tasks need to be clearly defined in advance.

Reading in groups

The following method can, with small adaptations, be applied to a variety of text formats. Try it out on the text below, then evaluate its advantages / disadvantages and suggest improvements.

- Work in groups of five or six. Scan the text for a first impression. Then distribute the roles below and prepare them at home.
  Chairperson Prepare a list of general questions about the text that the group can discuss. The best questions usually come from your own thoughts and feelings, which you should note down while or after reading the text.
  Make sure that all group members contribute to the discussion. At the end of the discussion, get the group to agree on which results / questions / activities are to be suggested for a class discussion.
  Summarizer Prepare a 1 – 2 minute, oral summary and a poster / diagram which presents the key ideas in the text (visual anchor).
  Passage master Locate interesting / important passages for the group to discuss. You can read these passages aloud, ask someone else to read them, or have people read them silently and then discuss. Explain why you chose that particular section.
  Investigator Find information on the topic and feed it into the discussion at suitable points. Visual material such as photos, graphs or statistics are welcome.
  Vocabulary enricher Be prepared to provide definitions of unknown words on demand and suggest a number of words / phrases which are worth learning. You could also correct any serious language mistakes – as politely as possible.
  Secretary Note down the main conclusions the group comes to and be prepared to give short summaries during the discussion. You will have to report back to the class about the work done in the group and suggest activities for classwork.

  Once the secretaries have reported to the class, decide which aspects to deal with. Conclude the lesson with a final assessment of the results and method.

Active reading

Scan text
↓
Choose roles
↓
Read text individually
↓
Explore text in groups
↓
Do classwork
↓
Evaluate results and method

The way of the Wodaabe

Only a few thousand strong, the nomadic Wodaabe clans live in the West African country of Niger. Every three or four days they move camp, looking for food for their sheep and cattle. For eleven months of the year the Wodaabe live in near-drought conditions until the rains come. For one month, the desert blooms and the Woodabe hold their annual festival, the Geerewol.

Note: Only look up words if you need them to understand the text. The vocabulary enricher in your group will answer any further questions about unknown words.

For the Wodaabe, personal relationships are the essence of being human, which is why they take them so seriously. They cherish them with a rich etiquette of intimacy and reserve. Men hold hands with their male friends as women do with their female friends. Yet men may not look each other in the eye when they meet, and a man and a woman (even a husband and wife) are never seen holding hands or otherwise displaying affection in public. Wodaabe believe that you should respect those you love and should not make public demonstrations of affection for those you respect. [...]

Yet women talk a great deal among themselves about which men are the best lovers. A man may be known as a good lover because he is "as strong as a horse", but more importantly – and here perhaps is the key to Wodaabe notions of foreplay and the erotic impulse – because he is a beautiful *Yakke* dancer and he has lots of

Members of the Wodaabe tribe at the Geerewol celebrations

togu or "charm". It is togu that Wodaabe cultivate, not just physical beauty (which is called *bodem*), and it is this charm that attracts lovers and kindles romance. A man's togu is enhanced by *magani*, a potion or medicine, and most men go out to collect fresh magani for the Yakke dance, which is a well-known occasion for romantic liaisons. [...]

Wodaabe philandering takes place within an elaborate set of rules that allows for romantic sexual passion while preserving the stability of the family. Within one's lineage – and there are fifteen separate lineages among the Wodaabe – a man may only marry one woman, and this marriage is arranged at childhood. It is called the *kobgal* marriage. Affairs are not outlawed within one's own lineage, but they can never lead to marriage. It is considered dangerous and disruptive to the entire lineage to carry on one of these affairs for too long, and while it is going on, it must be very discreet. Wodaabe etiquette says, "What the eyes do not see did not happen," which means that rumors and suspicions have to be ignored. Unless the couple is caught in the act, the affair is not reckoned to have taken place.

A far more common source of romantic adventures is the practice of wife-stealing between different lineages. This occurs throughout the year when lineages meet at marketplaces or common wells, but again the biggest opportunity is at the annual Geerewol celebrations, the great festival that includes the Yakke dance. This dance competition lasts for a week and may involve as many as a thousand young men who compete to be chosen as the most charming and beautiful. The competition is judged by three unmarried girls, also chosen for their beauty, but it is watched by everybody who can get to it. The men therefore perform before a critical and appreciative audience of women, with members of both sexes on the lookout for possible liaisons. A woman has to indicate her interest in a dancer very subtly. If he is interested, he will wink at her. At that she is supposed to lower her eyes demurely but, if he has not made a mistake and winked at the wrong person, she will not lower them all the way. She is now watching for him to indicate, by a slight twitch of the mouth, the bush behind which he wants to meet her.

A couple may meet each other for trysts, where they lie "invisible" under a blanket and make love. They may eventually decide to elope. What is extraordinary from the Western point of view is that the decision to run away together, made "from the heart" as they say, is often reached very quickly. A Wodaabe couple may arrange a meeting, sleep together once, and decide to marry. If they are already married to others, as is often the case, and her husband is anywhere near, he will give them chase. But this is a ritual, strictly for show. He usually accepts that if his wife wants to leave, there is no point in trying to stop her. His best bet is to go off and use his togu to persuade another woman to join him. The runaway wife goes to live with her new husband and his other wives. Why would a woman want to leave the formally sanctioned kobgal marriage within her own lineage to join another wife or wives in the foreign camp of another lineage? Such a union is considered a marriage all right – it is called a *teegal* marriage – but it is a secondary one. The kobgal wife

is a man's principal spouse and takes precedence over teegal wives. She has the largest dowry of calabashes and animals. Above all, she stays with her children. A woman who runs away has to leave her children behind to be raised in her husband's lineage.

A woman who is a kobgal wife is unlikely to be deterred from leaving her marriage by material considerations. There is not a lot of material wealth among nomads anyway. One person may have a few more animals or calabashes than another, but the differences are insignificant. A man might be deterred from taking a teegal wife by the additional strain she will put on the resources of his camp. She will need her own milk cows, donkey, and goats. This, in addition to any feelings of personal jealousy that might arise, is the reason why a new teegal wife usually gets a frosty reception in her new husband's camp. He leaves her at some distance from his camp, where she sits under her blanket, socially "invisible", until the other women of his household are willing to accept her. The process may take a few days and cannot be pleasant for the newcomer.

In spite of the drawbacks, Wodaabe are regularly willing to take the plunge in teegal marriages. Accustomed to getting by with little and to sharing what little they have, they do not measure their comfort or success in terms of material possessions. What they do value, almost above all else, is personal relations. So men are constantly on the lookout for lovers, and women are often willing to leave the stability of their arranged marriages and go for love into the household of a man whose togu has charmed them. But life goes on, even if they do. Their children are not uprooted, and the orderly relations of Wodaabe society, which are built around the kobgal marriages, are unaffected. The Wodaabe have dealt effectively with the age-old problem of trying to reconcile marriage with passion by instituting these two kinds of marriage. The sensible kobgal marriages form the foundation of their social institutions while spontaneous teegal marriages allow a freer rein to passion and personal whim.

From Millennium: Tribal Wisdom and the Modern World *by David Maybury-Lewis, Viking Penguin: New York, 1992, pp. 101–103.*

A step further

- Panel discussion: "What can we learn from the Wodaabe?"
  A panel of five or six speakers discusses the above topic. Panellists may either voice their own views or take on a role which was agreed on beforehand in class, e.g. a professor of African studies or a traveller who lived with the Wodaabe for a time.
  The panellists Work in groups. Prepare statements about the topic for one panellist. One member of each group is then chosen to take part in the discussion.
  The moderator Prepare his / her role in a group. Think of useful phrases to call on speakers and direct the discussion. Decide how to introduce the themes given below. Again one member of the group is selected to be the moderator. This role should be evaluated carefully after the main discussion.
  The audience Students who are not on the panel may still be involved in the discussion as questioners, journalists or language observers.
  Themes the way of the Wodaabe versus Western (or other) cultures – social stability versus individual freedom – passion and romance versus marriage / raising children – domination by one sex versus equality between the sexes.
- **Essay** Write an essay on the topic of the panel discussion above.

Panel discussion

Compile a list of guests
↓
Allocate roles
↓
Prepare roles in groups
↓
Hold the panel discussion
↓
Evaluate the results and method

Using your skills

Love story: writing a twenty-minute script

Before you start

- Telling a story through images
  Write a script for a self-contained scene in which two very different people meet in an unusual setting.
  - Limit the dialogue to not more than 55 words.
  - Use extensive stage directions to describe what you can see in the scene, e.g. the setting, the characters' appearance and body language. (Show, not tell!)
  - Look at the screenplay extracts on pp. 143 – 145 for conventions in scriptwriting.

Step 1 Finding an idea

- In groups of five or six, brainstorm ideas until you have three possible storylines for a short film. Describe the main characters and plot in a few sentences. An unusual beginning or an unexpected twist will help to create suspense.
  Possible starting points for a film idea could be:
  - a photo (see below and opposite page);
  - a text in this book, e.g. "The four stages of love" (pp. 152 – 153);
  - a short story you have read.

  Present your film ideas to the other groups and invite comments. Choose the most promising idea based on their reactions.

Step 2 Creating character profiles

- Start a character profile for the *protagonist* and the other characters in your film. Keep the plot in mind. Record the following information on a sheet of paper.
  - Basic information: name, age, profession, living conditions, family background, short biography, interests;
  - Personality: main traits, habits, values, aims, idols;
  - Initial situation: a crisis or a conflict with an *antagonist*, an important event or challenge in the protagonist's life;
  - Type of character: Is he / she a flat or a round character? Does he / she remain unchanged during the film or does he / she undergo a learning process?;
  - Twists in the plot: The best / worst thing that could happen to him / her.
- As you work on the scenes and the characters develop, add any new details to the profile. You may also need to add extra categories to the profile.

Characters
The **protagonist** is the main character. If a viewer identifies with the protagonist, he / she will follow the plot with greater interest.
The **antagonist** is a character who is opposed to, or in conflict with, the protagonist.

Using your skills

Step 3 Preparing a plot outline

- Describe the sequence of scenes in your film. Store the information on computer so that you can add changes, such as new columns, more easily later. Make notes in a grid like this:

scene	setting (= place and time)	characters / action
1		
2		

Step 4 Writing dialogue

- Add a fourth column to your grid for the dialogue. Use dialogue to:
  - explain the present situation and the back story, i.e. the invention of past events necessary to understand the present situation;
  - show the crisis or conflict (A quick exchange of remarks should be enough.);
  - hint at what will happen next (and where) in order to establish context and facilitate understanding.
- Reduce the dialogue to what cannot be shown by body language. Only use voice-over narration if necessary.

Step 5 Choosing cinematic devices

- In a fifth column of your grid, add any important cinematic devices, e.g. key camera operations (cf. page 184 for ideas), music or special effects. Say briefly what effect you wish to create with the device.

Step 6 Writing the screenplay

- Turn your grid into the screenplay format. Cf. the box on the right for abbreviations often used in screenplays.
  - Give each scene a number and indicate whether it will take place indoors by using INT. (= interior) or outside by using EXT. (= exterior), e.g. 18. INT.
  - Define the location and time of day in a few words, e.g. JOHN'S HOUSE – DAY.
  - Anything to do with music is also usually written in capitals, e.g. MUSIC BEGINS. Use capitals for a character's name the first time you use it and whenever he / she speaks.
  - Check the extracts from *Shakespeare in Love* (pp. 143 – 145) for various types of film directions (in italics) to accompany the dialogue (in normal print).

Characters ctd.
A **flat character** can be described in a few words; his / her behaviour is predictable as he / she does not change.
A **round character** is a life-like, complex individual. He / she may be shown in different moods, is able to surprise the viewer and may change in the course of the action, e.g. as the result of a learning process.

Screenplay abbreviations

APT.	apartment
BGD.	background
O.S.	off screen
POV	point of view
V.O.	voice-over
CU	close-up
LS	long shot
MS	medium shot

City lights

Aspects of the city

Looking and thinking

a) What aspects of city life do you associate with the photos below? Collect your ideas in a mind map.

b) As you work through the chapter add any new terms you come across to the mind map.

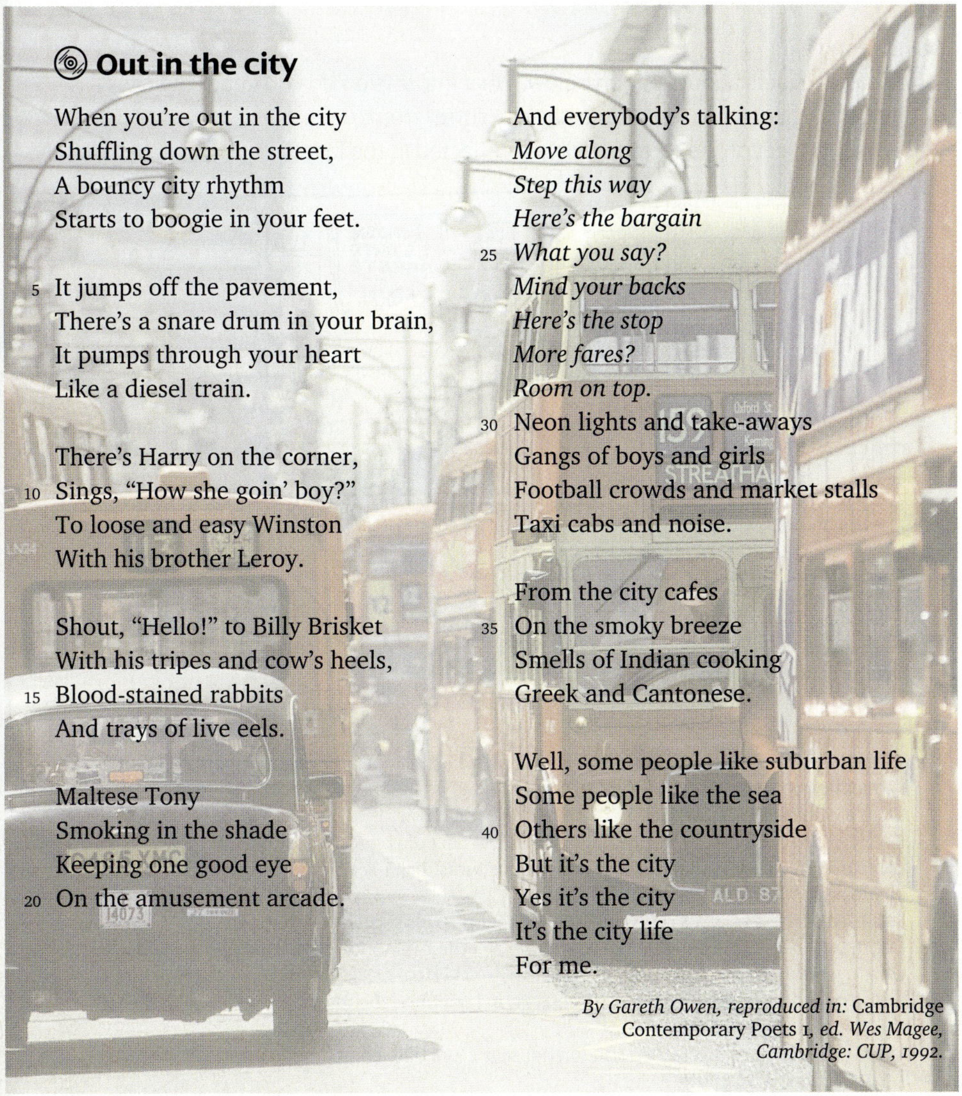

Out in the city

When you're out in the city
Shuffling down the street,
A bouncy city rhythm
Starts to boogie in your feet.

It jumps off the pavement,
There's a snare drum in your brain,
It pumps through your heart
Like a diesel train.

There's Harry on the corner,
Sings, "How she goin' boy?"
To loose and easy Winston
With his brother Leroy.

Shout, "Hello!" to Billy Brisket
With his tripes and cow's heels,
Blood-stained rabbits
And trays of live eels.

Maltese Tony
Smoking in the shade
Keeping one good eye
On the amusement arcade.

And everybody's talking:
Move along
Step this way
Here's the bargain
What you say?
Mind your backs
Here's the stop
More fares?
Room on top.
Neon lights and take-aways
Gangs of boys and girls
Football crowds and market stalls
Taxi cabs and noise.

From the city cafes
On the smoky breeze
Smells of Indian cooking
Greek and Cantonese.

Well, some people like suburban life
Some people like the sea
Others like the countryside
But it's the city
Yes it's the city
It's the city life
For me.

By Gareth Owen, reproduced in: Cambridge Contemporary Poets 1*, ed. Wes Magee, Cambridge: CUP, 1992.*

2 **to shuffle** to walk without lifting o.'s feet
3 **bouncy** full of life
6 **snare drum** small military drum
11 **loose** *here:* very relaxed
14 **tripe** the wall of a cow's stomach *(Pansen)*
29 **room on top** there are free seats in the upper deck of a double decker bus
30 **take-away** small shop which sells food to eat elsewhere

Exploring the text

1. Describe where the characters in the poem are and what they are doing. What impression of the city is conveyed by the poem?
2. What hints are there in the poem to suggest that it is an English city?
3. Comment on the form of the poem and give examples of the poetic devices used by the poet.
4. Describe the *tone* of the poem. You could refer to the box on the right for ideas.
5. Which of the senses does the poem appeal to? Refer to examples in the text in your answer.

Talking about tone II

neutral – naive – critical – biased – exaggerated – down-to-earth – serious – balanced – provocative – light-hearted – cynical

New York

Listen to the song entitled "New York" by U2. How does the singer perceive the American city?

Before you read

- a) Read the facts about London below. What impression do you get of the city?
  b) What particular problems does the city suffer from?
  c) Which aspect of the cartoon below is reflected in the fact file?

"There's a couple here who only have £ 200,000 to spend."

Two countries in one land?

- If London were a nation, it would rank above Sweden, Finland and Hungary in terms of economic output. Its Gross Domestic Product would be £ 2,500 higher per person that in the UK as a whole.
- Financial and business services account for 38 per cent of London's economic activity, compared to 25 % nationally. Manufacturing accounts for 11 % in London, against 21 % nationally.
- Fourteen of the 33 London boroughs are in the top 20 most deprived in the UK.
- One in four people in central London are from an ethnic minority, compared to one in 20 in the UK as a whole.
- House prices have been rising twice as quickly in London as the rest of the country for the past five years.
- The average price of a detached London house is £ 293,000, compared to a national average of £ 145,000, and £ 94,000 in Wales.
- The Government spends £ 677 per head on public transport in London, compared to £ 75 in the West Midlands.

While you read

As you read the text write down a heading or short sentence summing up the main point in each paragraph. This will help you to understand the text better and concentrate on the most important points.

It's London vs Britain

The capital is the dynamic engine driving the UK. But the shires are growing weary of its irresistible force. Richard Reeves and Andy McSmith report

Question: What has Europe's eighth biggest economy, 77 floodlit artificial football pitches and the world's most ethnically diverse population? Another clue: if you own a house in this place, it's worth nearly twice the national average for homes in Britain.

The answer, if you haven't already guessed, is London. If it were a country, the capital would rank above Sweden in terms of economic power; within a couple of years it will have overtaken Switzerland.

London has always differed from the rest of Britain – but political, economic and social trends are conspiring to drive the wedge deeper. Londoners and other Britons look at each other with growing suspicion across the concrete border between the two worlds, the M25.

A beer commercial starring two pointy-headed aliens drinking through their snouts featured a rural barman asking politely: "Up from London, are we?" [...]

Economic output is £ 13,000 per head in London, compared to a national average of £11,000. The gap between GDP per head in London and the rest of the country has increased sixfold in the past 15 years. The pay gap, already 30 per cent, is set to widen to 35 per cent by 2003 according to the Centre for Economics and Business Research. House prices continue to soar in the capital. And with London's service-based, international economy booming, the level of subsidy from London to poorer regions is more than £ 20 billion a year – or £ 8,000 for every metropolitan household.

So while Britain complains about the political dominance of the capital, the capital moans about being used, in the *London Evening Standard*'s phrase, as a 'giant cash machine'.

But the real differences between the two nations, London and Britain, are not measured by Gross Domestic Product or fiscal transfers. The differences are visible to anyone who walks around Soho, Brixton or Brent.

(Tony) Travers (London School of Economics) says the ethnic diversity of the capital is the most important difference from the rest of Blighty. Half of the UK's black and Asian citizens live in London. "Look at it this way," he says. "There are more black and Asian people in Brent, in just one of London's 33 boroughs, than in the whole of Scotland."

London absorbs between half to two-thirds of immigrants to the UK every year – refugees from Kosovo, nurses from South Africa, bartenders from Australia, bankers from America. It is now the world's melting pot. "London is becoming a Manhattan-upon-Thames," says Travers. "Sustained economic growth, a flexible labour market and a reputation for tolerance are all making London a magnet." Young Europeans are flooding in to be 'baristas' in the mushrooming coffee bars in the capital. A London bus typically echoes to the sounds of three or four languages. And even when immigrants are 'dispersed' – think of the Vietnamese population – follow-up studies show a drift back to the capital.

Travers says that the revival of urban 'chic' is part of the attraction, too. "Fifteen years ago the talk was all of people retreating to the countryside, and working down the phone lines. Now the population of London is rising, and the loft apartment culture is on the rise."

Reinforced by the media, of course – which is strongly focused on urban issues. Series such as *This Life*, and US sitcoms, add to the glamour of city living. "Programmes about the countryside tend to be about vets or rural detectives," says Travers. "All the exotic, high-powered, trend-setting images are urban ones, while rural images reinforce the image of thatched cottages, of an Agatha Christie Britain." [...]

London is also young: four in 10 Londoners are aged between 20 and 44, against 36 per cent in the rest of the country; and central London has the highest proportion

11 **wedge** piece of wood or metal used to keep things apart
17 **GDP Gross Domestic Product** *Bruttosozialprodukt*
31 **Blighty** *(BE slang)* England
40 **barista** *(from Spanish)* barperson who works in a coffee bar
42 **dispersed** *here:* relocated in towns outside of London

60 **hip** *(slang)* fashionable
65 **desertification** movement of inhabitants to the towns which leaves the country empty
66 **to up sticks** to gather one's things and leave

of all. London is liberal: 37 per cent of capital-dwellers believe that people should not be prosecuted for possessing small amounts of heroin, compared with 21 per cent in the country as a whole.

Of course the London / non-London divide is far from clear-cut. Manchester, Leeds, Glasgow also brand themselves as trendy urban centres. Birmingham is ethnically mixed. And London is far from a uniformly wealthy, hip place: 94 per cent of the poorest council estates in England are in London; 75,000 families live in overcrowded conditions. And London supports – and welcomes – 50,000 destitute asylum seekers each year.

But the debates about the place of London in Britain will only intensify. Pessimists point to France, where the metropolitan bias is still stronger, and the 'desertification' of the French countryside and rural economy. Maybe Westminster should up sticks itself, and meet as Travers suggests, in village halls around the country [...]. "What a difference that might make to policy!" he says.

By Richard Reeves and Andy McSmith, The Observer, *February 6, 2000.*

Exploring the text

1 a) In what ways does London differ from the rest of Britain?
b) According to the writers, what function does the M25 have?

2 Explain what is meant by the following phrases from the text:
the level of subsidy (l. 21) – fiscal transfers (l. 28) – urban chic (l. 44) – working down the phone lines (ll. 45 – 46) – an Agatha Christie Britain (l. 52).

3 What economic trends do the writers mention to illustrate the gap between London and the rest of the country?

4 a) Explain the following *metaphors* used in the text:
to drive the wedge deeper (l. 11) – mushrooming coffee bars (l. 40).
b) Find further examples of metaphors in the text and explain them.

Talking about trends

to fall behind
to decrease by six times
to plummet
to go into a recession
a decline
going downhill

Close-up: vocabulary

Find expressions in the text describing upward / positive trends which are the opposites of those in the box on the left. Check any unknown words in a dictionary.

A step further

- In groups, choose **one** of these cities: Manchester, Leeds or Glasgow and use the internet to find out:
  a) how it is presented by its city council or tourist board;
  b) the kind of problems it faces.

Using your skills

Project: a trip to London

Working in a group, plan a trip to London.

- Find out about accommodation which is suitable for young people (hostels, guest houses, etc).
- Draw up a letter booking accommodation for the group. Cf. sample letter, page 111 for ideas.
- Find out about sights and events in London and plan activities for one week.

Before you read

- a) Which buildings in your community do you like / dislike?
  b) Say how the building(s) which you find unattractive could be improved.
- Describe the block of flats in the photo on the right. What social problems could develop there?

Can you hear me at the back?

In the following play extract Philip Turner, Chief Architect of a New Town called Feltonly, is delivering a speech to a group of senior, grammar school students. Also present is his wife Sarah and son Colin and the headmaster Jack Hartnoll and his wife Margery.

(A projection screen is flown in.)

Philip Firstly, may I say how pleased I am to have the opportunity to open this Sixth Form Conference. *Art and the Community,* the programme says. And for once somebody has realised that the basis of the community is its environment. The houses it lives in, the schools it goes to, the shops it buys from, the halls of all sorts it meets in. Without building, there is no community. Without community there is no art. The questions are, do buildings automatically make for community? Does a community automatically make for art? We know the answers. In both cases – no. Let's look at some buildings.

(He flicks his slide changer. On the screen comes a picture of a typical high rise development: tall blocks of flats, widely spaced on grass surroundings.)

If a bright young architect, straight out of college, had seen this drawing twenty-five years ago, he would have drooled with delight. "Look," he would have said, "high density development, no sprawling over the landscape. A sense of openness, freedom. Grass and trees. And each living unit, a 'machine for living in'." Now we know he was wrong. You can stack flats one on top of the other, and the pre-stressed concrete can stand the pressure. But, until someone discovers a way of pre-stressing people, the strain breaks them down. Now, some planners may say, "That's very inconvenient of people. After all, this is a very economical solution. Why do they have to have their feet on the ground. We don't." As if we didn't know!

(He clicks again and there is a slide of the centre of a city, full of wide roads and office blocks.)

The centre of a British city. Now, and as it used to be.

(A click: we see the centre of a medieval city.)

I have never heard a convincing argument why it is a good thing to fill the centres of cities with office blocks. And there are dozens of reasons against. The roads are jammed twice a day. The leisure life of city centres is killed. Theatres, cafes, can't exist in the high rated area, and the people can't afford to live there. So, why does it happen? Because a very few people make a great deal of money and the rest of us are all too spineless and weak-kneed to say, "This is our city, not yours. Go away." It happens because a few people have the energy and drive to take away our community and we are too lazy to stop them. Now, to our community. I've prepared the slides with loving care. We may as well see them now they're here.

(A click: the town centre.)

7 **to make for** to have as a result
10 **to flick** *here:* to switch on
13 **to drool** to let liquid come from the mouth
14 **sprawling** spreading out
16 **to stack** to put one thing on top of another
27 **jammed** *here:* blocked with cars
30 **spineless** weak

47 **shrine** *(fig.)* place one goes to worship
49 **mould** container used to give its contents a shape *(Form)*
50 **harness** *here:* set of wires
54 **farce** light comedy
55 **Gilbert and Sullivan** refers to comic operettas by these two composers
56 **damp squib** wet firework which does not explode; *(fig.)* disappointment
69 **to plonk** to put down carelessly

There. The town centre. I'm very proud of that. A study in cubes, I called it when I designed it. In fact, it's a brown study of boring boxes.

(A click: a multi-storey car park.)

The car park.

(A click: a housing area.)

And this is very important. A people filing cabinet. The only way of telling the contents of each file is the colour of the front door.

(A click: a community hall.)

The Community Hall. You can do all sorts of things here, badly. Plays, painting, music. Always knowing, of course, that if you had a real job that satisfied you, you wouldn't need the therapy.

(A click: the factory estate.)

Which brings us to this twentieth-century shrine. The plastics factory, the transistor assembly plant, the glossy printing works, the potato crisp factory, and the place where they make moulds to press the cases which will hold the clips that will fasten the wires forming the harness of the output side of the distributor, which is part of the ignition system that sparks the engine, which drives a car – nowhere at all worth going. So, what price Art in this community? At a rough guess: your body; your soul; your past; your future. And for this, you receive a box to live in, a box to move about in, a box to work in, a box to look into, and a box to die in. Three farces, two revivals of classical plays, ten folk concerts, a Gilbert and Sullivan, three exhibitions of Sunday paintings, a string quartet, and a damp squib on carnival night. If you think it's worth it – that's up to you. Me? I've had enough.

(PHILIP comes forward away from the screen.)

And I'll tell you why. I am fed up with Lego. That's what this town is – Lego Land. A group of us, all middle-class – and, incidentally, living up on the hill, in the only private estate – we draw plans, and rearrange the groups of houses and roads and schools and factories. Of course, we ask questions about your welfare, but we don't ask *you*. We ask the psychologists and sociologists at the Ministry of Housing and the County Council. We make a whole town *for* you, not *with* you. We have enormous energy at our disposal, and we use it to play toy towns, and the only thing left to the toy people to do in it to make it their own, is to squirt aerosol obscenities on the walls. There is nothing in this town that's crazy. Plenty that's stupid – but nothing that's just crazy – human, ridiculous. It hasn't grown out of the landscape, it's been plonked on it. Christopher Wren's memorial in St Paul's reads: "If you want his memorial – look around you". But he didn't want that to apply to just the church, but to the whole of London. Thank God he didn't get his way. London grew up crazily and today there are still left some of the little streets and tiny shops and theatres, and all the other absurd and uneconomic use of space that makes a real city. Even though the Lego Land builders are trying to destroy that too. Don't let them do it.

(Spot on MARGERY.)

Margery Great, Philip. Marvellous.

(Spot on Jack.)

Jack Emotional. How do you think that will help us to get the sixth form thinking positively?

(Spot on Colin.)

Colin It was all true enough – but superficial.

In the text, Philip criticizes Christopher Wren, the architect of St Paul's Cathedral, London, which is shown below. Why do you think he does so?

(Spot on Sarah.)

Sarah Self-indulgent ... what are you going to do now?

Philip ... Resign, I suppose.

From "Can you hear me at the back?" *by Brian Clark, Ashover: AmberLane Press, 1979, pp. 38–41.*

Exploring the text

1 a) Which aspects of the town does Philip criticize?
b) Why does he feel that planning mistakes have been made?

2 Explain the "Lego Land" image in l. 59, taking its *denotative* and *connotative* meanings into consideration.

3 What rhetorical devices does Philip use in the talk? What effect do they probably have on the audience?

Denotation
what is actually described by a word (e.g. the sun is a planet)

Connotation
the ideas and feelings associated with a word (e.g. the sun is warmth, energy, light, desire, love)

A step further

- What are the implications of Philip's statement "we make a whole town *for* you, not *with* you" (l. 64)?
- Choose **one** of the following topics and write an essay of about 300 words. (Refer to skills file, page 187 for ideas.)
  - The town where you live has been nominated "the world's most ... town" in a competition. Decide which superlative is most appropriate and explain why your town should win the title.
  - An international airport is to be built within 10 kilometres of your home. Give reasons why you are in favour of / against this development.

Using your skills

Project: A talk on improving your town

You have applied for a position as an urban planner with your local council. As part of the application process you have to prepare a talk about ways of improving the quality of life in your town. Cf. skills file, "Presentations", pp. 182–183.

- Compare the situation in your town / city with that in an ideal town. You could record your ideas in a table like the one below.

	your town	ideal town
shopping facilities	huge supermarkets in town centre, no shops in suburbs	...
schools	...	
public transport		
sports facilities		
entertainment...		

- Decide which areas are most in need of improvement. Note down the reasons why you think this and concentrate on these in your talk.
- Brainstorm for ways of improving these areas.
- Make a note of key words and phrases on cue cards.
- Collect and / or develop materials to use in your talk, e.g. a transparency listing your main points; charts with facts / statistics; maps or photos showing the current situation in your town; an illustration showing the difference improvements would make.

Before you read

- a) What problems can the presence of ethnic minorities in a city cause?
  b) How could these problems be solved?

The Language of the Streets

The subject is vast – that is the only way I can put it. I can't imagine anyone being able to do justice to it. I will improvise, but I have more questions, as I have indicated, than answers because it is a great question and I am a city boy.

For example, I am trying to figure out what I am doing here. I thought – and I suppose this is insignificant, but this is how I began to think about the subject. Many years ago I was out of the city – that is the only way to put it – I was in the country, walking along a country road to go to the store, to do this or that, and a woman passed me – a white woman, by the way – and she said, "Good morning," and I thought, "Who is this nut!" No one in the city, except your immediate family – not always they – says good morning. I thought about it because it meant something, it meant something enormous, that I had grown up or I had become accustomed to such an incredible silence. Or again in New York, when it is immobilized by some natural disaster like snow. New Yorkers don't believe in snow. I have been there during a couple of blizzards when the city is completely immobilized: subways can't go, buses can't go, taxis can't go, people have to walk, and for the first time they talk to each other. They are like children at a fair: delighted by the snow, delighted by the fact the subways aren't moving, buses aren't moving, they can't get to work. All they got is each other. But when the snow melts and things go back to what we call "normal", nobody says a word to nobody. [...]

It may be interesting to suggest that, apart from our other addictions, the city is probably the most visible product of the industrial revolution. People left the land to come to the city because they had no choice.

Now, I am not a sociologist, and I am not equipped to discuss in any detail the implications of the creation of the city, but I can say that that creation has had devastating effects on human life everywhere.

I have, for example, a typewriter somewhere else in the country, and I spend a lot of my time living in the country trying to work, trying to write, and in the country there is this: You wake up whenever it is that you wake up, and you look at the sky. It is there, and it gives you some idea what kind of a day you are going to have, and you walk on the ground. It's there. It gives you some sense of yourself, and you go about your duties: You have your lunch, you take a walk, you know that at a certain moment the sun is going to go down, and you prepare yourself to deal with that. Close the shutters, turn on the lights, have a drink, make love, go to sleep. And every day in the country is a little like that.

Every day in the city, on the contrary – and I grew up in the city – involves a subtle divorce from reality. There is something a little terrifying about being forty stories in the air and looking around you, and you see nothing but walls, other skyscrapers, and you don't dare look down. And if you are on the ground, if you want to see the sky, you must make an effort of the will and look up. And if you do that, you are likely to be carried off to Bellevue – but that is another story.

Now, if I am right, the tremendous noise of the city, the tremendous claustrophobia of the city is designed to hide what the city really does, which is to divorce us from a sense of reality and to divorce us from each other. When we are divorced from each other, we have no way back to reality, because even in this democracy people cannot live without each other – something Americans are going to have to discover again.

1 **vast** wide ranging
2 **to do justice to s.th.** *here:* to analyse s.th. properly
20 **addiction** obsession
36 **divorce from s.th.** *here:* being in a separate state
42 **claustrophobia** fear of being cut off from the outside

50 **slaughter** killing
56 **captive** unable to move freely
70 **repercussion** consequence of some action

Now, for example, the European immigrants coming through Ellis Island is a very important matter. They had gone to the cities before I did; and once they had become white Americans, part of their function, part of their action, was to keep me out of the city. When I got to the city, I met slaughter. But more important than that, the reason my father left the land and came to the city was because he was driven by the wave of terror which overtook the South after the First World War when soldiers were being lynched in uniform, slaughtered like flies. So, daddy came to New York – others went to Chicago, others went to Detroit – and we know what happened when we got there. We immediately became, from an economic point of view and from another point of view, a captive population. We immediately were herded into the ghettoes which the immigrants were trying to get out of; and, you see, part of the hidden thing – part of the hidden thing which Americans again are going to have to think about and confront – I know, historically speaking, what drove me to these shores, and I may be the only American who can say, quite candidly, "I know I never meant to come here." Never. A friend of mine, Judge Bruce Wright, says I am the only immigrant who never got a package from home.

Now, if that is so, and that is so, it says something about what I would call the price of the ticket, the price Americans paid for the ticket to cross all that water and to become Americans – and the price of the ticket was high. The price of the ticket was to become white. Americans failed to realize that they were not white before they got here: They were Greek, they were Russian, they were Turks – they were everything under heaven, but they were not white. They were being white because they had to keep me black; and there are economic reasons for that, and the economic reasons have moral repercussions and moral results.

The life of the city, watching it – I watched – well, I grew up in Harlem, and when we were able, when we made a little money, enough to put something aside – and do not underestimate that effort; it is hard for everybody, but, baby, try it if you are black – we began to move across the river to the Bronx. When we started moving across the river to the Bronx, all those people who had lately become white fled in terror, and one of the results of that is the present disaster called the South Bronx where nobody can live. The motion of the white people in this country has been – and it is a terrifying thing to say this, but it is time to face it – a furious attempt to get away from the niggers.

From "The Language of the Streets" by James Baldwin, Literature and the Urban Experience, *ed. Michael C. Jaye/ Ann Chalmers Watts, New Brunswick, New Jersey: Rutgers University Press, 1981.*

Exploring the text

1 How does James Baldwin illustrate his fascination with silence?
2 a) How does a day spent in the country differ from one in the city?
  b) What conclusions does the writer draw about city life?
3 The writer uses different modes of presentation: description, narration and argumentation. Find examples of each in the text.
4 What criticisms of American society does he voice?

A step further

- Considering that the essay was published in 1981, can James Baldwin's views and criticisms still be applied today, or not?
- To what extent can the development of US cities be compared to that of German cities?

Which issues in the text are mirrored in the Harlem billboard below?

THE WALL STREET JOURNAL

What's News–

Iraq Unlikely to Spur Shift in OPEC Quota

For Auto Makers, Diesel No Longer Is a Dirty Word

'New' U.S. Allies Struggle to Fill Role

Before you read

- What kind of reader does the *Wall Street Journal* (see left) probably appeal to?
- What problems might an immigrant have in making a living in the host country?
- The following text is a short play entitled "The Cabbie from Calcutta" (cabbie = taxi driver). Speculate as to what the play might be about.

The Cabbie from Calcutta

Production Notes

Players 1 male; 1 female.

Playing time About 10 minutes.

Costumes RAGGI wears jeans and Bruce Springsteen T-shirt. MRS. HARTFORD has on a gown, lots of diamonds and jewels. She also wears a lot of make-up and a gray wig.

Properties The *WALL STREET JOURNAL*, a quarter.

Lighting effects None.

Sound effects Sound of screeching brakes, revving engine, honking horns, and traffic.

Characters RAGGI, a young cabbie from India; MRS. HARTFORD, a rich widow from Fifth Avenue.

Scene 1

Time Today.

Setting Four chairs facing audience form the front and rear seats of RAGGI's cab.

At rise RAGGI sits reading The WALL STREET JOURNAL as he waits for a fare.

Raggi Look at this. Once more Polaroid and IBM are up. This is up, that is up. Good, great America. The land of much wondrous opportunity. Raggi, the cabbie from Calcutta, will be a very, very rich man someday. I don't spend all my life driving this hick … or is it hack? Well, whatever it is, it's a necessity for Raggi now. True, it is also one big pain in the buttock, but then so was riding that blinkin' water buffalo back in Bombay. At least here you get paid. There all I got was bites by that infernal beast. *(Paging through paper.)* And does Raggi see any water buffalo stock in this wondrous paper of the great American dream? No. Thank the great lord Rama. But Raggi sees much stock in many interesting things. Many. My heavens! Look at Sony. Sony is truly no baloney. *(Just then MRS. HARTFORD enters.)*

Mrs. Hartford *(She walks up to RAGGI's cab and peeks in.)* Cabbie? Yoo-hoo. Hello. *(Annoyed, she shouts)* Cabbie!

Raggi *(Jumps and puts down his paper quickly.)* Oh, yes, dear lady. That is my middle name.

Mrs. Hartford Cabbie is your middle name?

Raggi Well, actually my middle name, it is Gandhi, after the great one. But in America, dear lady, it is Cabbie. You can call me Fred, you can call me Red – but when you need a cabbie, please, dear lady, call me anytime cabbie.

Mrs. Hartford *(In a hurry, bored.)* Yes, yes. How nice. *(Shakes her head.)* Another alien. Good lord, the country is full of them.

Raggi You telling, Raggi. In India we have your basic Indian. But not in America. Here one person can never tell from where the other is coming or to where he or she is going. It's a very curious place America, but very great. I am proud to be an

16 **fare** *here:* paying passenger
17 **Polaroid and Kodak are up** the companies' share prices have risen
20 **hick** *(AE slang)* foolish person
20 **hack** *(AE)* taxi
21 **pain in the buttock** Raggi misuses the phrase **pain in the butt** *(slang)* s.th. annoying
25 **Rama** Indian god
26 **baloney** *(AE, informal)* nonsense
37 **alien** *here:* foreigner

alien in this great, wondrous land of America. God bless the Grand Canyon and Bruce Springsteen, who I hear was born in the U.S.A.

Mrs. Hartford Yes, well some seem to think so. As for me, I'd just like to get this trip over with as soon as possible. Do you understand my meaning, cabbie?

Raggi Oh, yes. Very well, misses. Yes, dear lady. And where can Raggi take you?

Mrs. Hartford I'm on my way to Wall Street –

Raggi Good golly! Ah! Yes! Oh, how wonderful. The great Wall Street. *(Holds up paper.)* It is all here in black and write.

Mrs. Hartford That's black and white.

Raggi Oh, yes, to be sure. That, too. Is it not amazing how IBM and Polaroid are always up? *(Holds up the paper.)*

Mrs. Hartford Oh, good heavens, not another one.

Raggi *(As he starts up his cab, we hear sound of engine revving up.)* Another what?

Mrs. Hartford Another dirt-poor alien overly impressed by our capitalistic system.

Raggi Oh. Well, one is truly amazed by such things when one's family and friends live on a very few rupees a year, and who must eat – but who have no money to buy food. Slow, fast, or microwaved. And, dear lady, as a result, you don't want to know what we poor folk must eat. It is not a pretty sight, I assure you.

Mrs. Hartford I'll bet.

Raggi This would be a good bet. Truly our daily bread, it is not what you call your microwave gourmet variety.

Mrs. Hartford Yes, yes. Well, so you've picked yourself up by the proverbial bootstraps and have come to America for our microwave TV dinners and our *(Fans herself.)* non-air-conditioned taxi cabs? Is that it?

Raggi Oh, the air conditioner is on full bust, but it's as hot as buzzards out there. New York is worse than Calcutta in summer.

Mrs. Hartford I'll agree with you there. So you've come to America to make your fortune? Is that part of your great American dream? Besides the TV dinners.

Raggi That is, indeed, part of what you call it, my American dream. But there is also McDonald's and the Great Cornell.

Mrs. Hartford The Great Cornell? What Cornell is that?

Raggi Cornell Sanders.

Mrs. Hartford I should have guessed.

Raggi Finger lickin' good, you know. Yes, indeed. And in two very pleasant styles – regular and crispy. Truly remarkable. And one is also entitled to a creamy rich mashed potato treat and one amazingly good biscuit. Is this not truly amazing?

Mrs. Hartford If you're into fast food.

Raggi Oh, yes. In India there is only fast food.

Mrs. Hartford There is? Really?

Raggi Oh, truly. One must run very fast to catch it, or one has no fast food. Here the Cornell catches it for you.

Mrs. Hartford How interesting. Are we almost there? *(She mumbles the next words.)* I hope.

Raggi Look!

Mrs. Hartford *(Braces herself in a panic, thinking she's about to be in a tremendous crash – we hear brakes screech and horns blow.)* WHAT?

Raggi Foot-long dogs sold right in the street!

Mrs. Hartford Foot-long dogs? Oh, you mean the Sabret stand there?

65 **full bust** *here:* as high as possible
65 **as hot as buzzards** extremely hot
72 **Cornell Saunders** *pun on* Colonel Saunders founder of Kentucky Fried Chicken restaurants
74 **finger lickin' good** slogan used by Kentucky Fried Chicken
76 **biscuit** *(here AE)* flat, dry (potato) cake
87 **dogs** *short for* hot dogs
88 **Sabret stand** *(AE)* small stall selling hot dogs

Raggi Yes, yes. They even have a truly wonderful umbrella for the monsoons. In India we have many monsoons, but no truly delicious foot-long sabret dogs with chili, mustard, relish, sauerkraut and such wonderful umbrellas.

Mrs. Hartford It's a darn shame.

Raggi Yes, yes. Did I tell you about my trip to see the lady?

Mrs. Hartford What lady is that?

Raggi The great lady. The statue.

Mrs. Hartford In the Metropolitan Museum of Art?

Raggi No, no. In the truly wonderful harbor of the great metropolis. The lady Liberty.

Mrs. Hartford Oh, that lady.

Raggi Yes, that lady. *(Long pause, then.)* So aren't you going to ask me about my trip to see the lady?

Mrs. Hartford I wasn't planning to. But if you insist … So how was your trip to see the lady, cabbie?

Raggi I'm glad you asked. And please call me Raggi.

Mrs. Hartford Ragoo?

Raggi No. *Raggeeee. (Spells it.)* R-A-G-G-I. The good old boys down at the garage, at the pepper mine –

Mrs. Hartford Salt mine.

Raggi Huh?

Mrs. Hartford You mean salt mine. It's salt mine, not pepper mine.

Raggi It is?

Mrs. Hartford It is.

Raggi This English is a very big pain in the buttock.

Mrs. Hartford Butt.

Raggi But what?

Mrs. Hartford Butt. *(Spells it.)* B-U-T-T. Butt. The idiom is not pain in the buttock, but rather pain in the butt. Another bit of America's gift to the free world.

Raggi So that's what it is …

Mrs. Hartford That's what what is?

Raggi An idiom. I know many of America's great idioms.

Mrs. Hartford I know many of America's great idiots.

Raggi You do?

Mrs. Hartford You're darn tootin'.

Raggi *(Turns and points to her.)* Yes!

Mrs. Hartford *(Bracing herself – as we hear brakes screech and horns blow.)* Look where you're going! You're not driving an ox cart now!

Raggi *(Looking at the road ahead, dodges a truck – loud screech of brakes and horns.)* Hit the dock!

Mrs. Hartford You mean hit the deck!

Raggi Deck, dock. Here one has a wondrous variety of possible obstacles to hit. In India the only thing you hit is a sacred cow or a water buffalo.

Mrs. Hartford Don't they have any cars?

Raggi Oh, yes. But in my little village outside of Calcutta we have no cars, no roads. We barely have any villagers. Fortunately we are very lucky to be in walking distance of the great city.

92 **darn** *(slang) here:* terrible
123 **darn tootin'** *(AE, slang) here:* absolutely right

Mrs. Hartford Just a few blocks out of town, are you?

Raggi No, walking distance.

Mrs. Hartford That's what I meant. Walking distance. A few blocks.

Raggi Oh, no, dear lady. In India walking distance is any distance one can walk and not get trampled by a sacred cow or eaten by a man-eating tiger. I lived thirty-seven miles out of town.

Mrs. Hartford Good heavens! What do you do if you run out of milk in the middle of the night?

Raggi Yes, telling me about flit.

Mrs. Hartford Not flit, it. Tell me about *it*.

Raggi I'm telling you already. Hold your haunches. This could be a real boomer.

Mrs. Hartford I think you mean it could be a real bummer.

Raggi Truly.

Mrs. Hartford Very dangerous walking in the Indian jungle at night for a container of milk, huh?

Raggi No. Very dangerous milking a sleeping water buffalo.

Mrs. Hartford You're serious.

Raggi I'm joking, dear lady. But we manage.

Mrs. Hartford I guess. But to be perfectly honest, I am not at all happy by all you foreigners coming to my country to rip us off.

Raggi Raggi rips no one. I keep this cab clean, and not even one lady has ever torn or ripped her famous, fabulous Leggs or silky soft, sheer –

Mrs. Hartford That's not what I mean! I was not talking about pantyhose!

Raggi You said Raggi rip off people.

Mrs. Hartford I meant cheat them! As in take their money unfairly and illegally! Cheat!

Raggi *(A bit annoyed.)* Cheat? Raggi never cheat a single person. I am an honest man! My father was an honest man and his father before him. We are good people. We are not cheats.

Mrs. Hartford Then you're not much of an American. Here it's dog eat dog.

Raggi In India it's man eat dog, occasionally lizard. Now *that* is *very* fast food.

Mrs. Hartford I think I'm going to be sick.

Raggi If you have to eat dog, you'd be very sick.

Mrs. Hartford *Stop talking about food!*

Raggi OK. What do you want me to talk about? Perhaps the future of pork belly options on Wall Street? Maybe margin buying and selling? Securities and Muni Bonds are good. Or, perhaps, we can rap right on about ... my favorite ... insider trading scandals. Very shifty, you Americans. You do that in Calcutta, they cut off more than your credit.

Mrs. Hartford Look, Rummie or Ronnie, or whatever your name is, just get me to Wall Street. OK?

Raggi It's Raggi. With two g's.

Mrs. Hartford Just get me to Wall Street!

Raggi In a gipsy!

Mrs. Hartford What? This is a gypsy cab?

Raggi No. A fast cab. You know: in a gypsy. Pronto.

Mrs. Hartford Good gracious! You mean in a *jiffy*, not gypsy.

146 **haunch** *pun on* hold your horses (= take your time); **haunch** = upper part of the leg
147 **bummer** *(AE, exclam.)* s.th. unpleasant
157 **Leggs** *(trademark)* tights
158 **pantyhose** *(AE)* *Strumpfhose*
166 **lizard** *Eidechse*
171 **margin buying and selling** buying shares (= *Aktien*) using borrowed money
180 **gypsy cab** *(AE)* unlicensed taxi
182 **in a jiffy** *(informal)* quickly

Raggi Oh. I see. A jiffy. Like peanut butter? Is Jiffy peanut butter fast food?

Mrs. Hartford I have no idea.

Raggi It sounds like a fast food.

Mrs. Hartford You're kidding, of course. Tell me you're kidding.

Raggi Of course.

Mrs. Hartford Another bit of Indian humor?

Raggi Another bit of Raggi's humor.

Mrs. Hartford So Raggi, how does an immigrant from Calcutta make his fortune in the Big Apple?

Raggi One works his B-U-T-T off. It is no picnic this Big Apple.

Mrs. Hartford I'm sure. Do you plan the cabbie business as your life's work?

Raggi No, no. I am enrolled at Columbia University. I am some day becoming a system analyst.

Mrs. Hartford YOU … you mean you're a computer programmer?

Raggi You bet! Yes. I am very well knowing of *Cobol, Fortran, APL* and *Focus*. I'm even good at Space Invaders.

Mrs. Hartford I didn't even think they had computers in India – let alone video games.

Raggi Of course we do. And here, too. I'm not going to be driving this hick –

Mrs. Hartford Hick?

Raggi This cab.

Mrs. Hartford You mean hack – H-A-C-K.

Raggi I knew it. Hack. Anyhow, someday I'll be working on Wall Street in the electronic data processing section of Whitney, Wainwright, Wagner and Hartford.

Mrs. Hartford *My ex-husband's company?*

Raggi *(Ironic.)* No?

Mrs. Hartford YES!

Raggi Imagine that. Only in America. Small world, huh?

Mrs. Hartford Too small.

Raggi They say it's a global village. Soon we'll all be one.

Mrs. Hartford How thrilling.

Raggi Yes. Soon I'll be raking in the big shmucks.

Mrs. Hartford I think you mean big bucks.

Raggi Yes, that, too.

Mrs. Hartford You couldn't do that in India?

Raggi In India a person of my cast can do only two things.

Mrs. Hartford And what are they?

Raggi Milk the water buffalo and feed the water buffalo. It is a very limited job market with no IRA fund, no major medical and absolutely no dental plan.

Mrs. Hartford Good heavens! What if you should get kicked by a water buffalo? What do you do?

Raggi You kick him back.

Mrs. Hartford In America if you get kicked by a water buffalo, you sue the owner and buy a condo in Beverly Hills on the settlement.

Raggi Is this not truly the land of opportunity?

Mrs. Hartford Truly.

Raggi God bless America.

214 **to rake in** to make a lot of money
214 **shmuck** *(Jewish slang)* stupid idiot
221 **IRA fund** *(AE)* old-age pension plan
226 **condo** *(AE) short for* **condominium** apartment in a housing estate or block of flats
226 **settlement** *here:* money one receives as a result of a court case

Mrs. Hartford Yes, I, too, love America. In my own way.

Raggi Well, here we are, dear lady.

Mrs. Hartford *(Getting out, hands RAGGI money and a quarter tip.)* My fare, and here's a quarter tip for you.

Raggi Truly God bless America. A whole two butts!

Mrs. Hartford That's two *bits.*

Raggi Right, no butt's about it.

Mrs. Hartford You mean you're not offended by such a small tip?

Raggi Small? Listen, this is better than what you get for driving a rajah on an elephant to Delhi.

Mrs. Hartford You're all right, Rags old boy. *(She exits.)*

Raggi *(Puts the quarter in his pocket, then opens the paper.)* Now let's see how many penny stocks I can buy for a quarter. Good golly. That last penny stock I bought took a real flying leap. Bought this cab company on that one. *(Curtain falls as RAGGI laughs and reads the* WALL STREET JOURNAL.*)*

"The Cabbie from Calcutta" by Robert Mauro, Plays for Student Actors, *Colorado Springs: Meriwether Publishing Ltd, 1988, pp. 91–100.*

Exploring the text

1 Outline what happens in the short play.
2 How are Raggi and Mrs Hartford characterized by their language, appearance and actions?
3 What do the stage directions and production notes contribute to the presentation of the short play?
4 How is humour created in the play? Refer to specific examples in the text.
5 What typical features of a *short play* do you notice? (Cf. "Talking about short plays" on page 29 for ideas.)

A step further

- Collect the cabbie's language mistakes in one column of a table. Then explain and correct each mistake in the second column.
- Which aspects of American society and the American dream does the play satirize?
- Raggi writes a letter to his parents in India telling them about his life in New York. He also describes his meeting with Mrs Hartford. Write this letter.

Projects

Using your skills

- Radio play
  In groups of four, turn the short play into a radio play. In your script you should outline the necessary changes for this kind of medium. One person in the group directs the action and another is responsible for the sound effects. The other two group members are the actors. Act out and record the play.
- Two short plays
  Compare *The Cabbie from Calcutta* and *Los Vendidos* (pp. 22–29) as regards: the topic – the order of events – the presentation and type of characters – the ending.

low rent – garden – nice view – access to public transport – work / shops in walking distance – small / large community – leisure facilities

Before you read

a) Imagine you have accepted a job in a town 150 kilometres away from home and you have to find a new place to live. Which of the factors in the box on the left would influence your choice? Rank them in order of importance.
b) What other factors would affect your choice?
c) How might your criteria change later in life, for example, if you had a family?

Surviving without a dictionary

As there are only a few annotations with this text, concentrate on the gist, rather than trying to understand every word. Work out the meaning of new words from the context, word families, or similarities to German words or other languages you know.

Power to the cities

Around the world, political power is shifting to the cities. Right now, many of them still have no power to levy their own taxes or allocate funds; fiscal policy and major public works are still the province of national and state governments. This may well change. Bruce Katz, director of the Brookings Center on Urban and Metropolitan Policy in Washington, D.C., notes that in the United States (where metropolitan areas do have tax power) cities are taking on infrastructure responsibilities that once belonged to states. "Cities and suburbs will band together to have more power, and states will have less," he predicts.

Cities may even manage to chip away at national authority. Last summer, at a U.N. meeting of cities and local authorities, Barcelona Mayor Joan Clos urged U.N. Secretary-General Kofi Annan to grant cities an official role in U.N. policymaking. Across Europe, cities have put similar pressure on the EU, resulting in a greater allocation of regional funds to urban areas. "There's an understanding now that if a city is healthy, it can make an entire region healthy," says Rudolf Niessler, head of the urban-affairs section of the EU's Regional Policy and Cohesion Division.

Urban trade alliances now go well beyond a smile, a photo op and a friendly "sister city" proclamation. Helsinki has opened incubators in Moscow and St. Petersburg, which help its own small and midsize businesses set up in the region (perks include introductions to local power brokers and temporary office space). Barcelona, a founding member of the influential urban networking group Eurocities, is currently plugging its publishing sector to the Latino market in New York. [...] The implications are clear. "Successful cities need a foreign policy," says Michael Parkinson, director of the European Institute for Urban Affairs in Liverpool.

They also need to avoid the perils of growth. The number of cities with populations above 10 million has risen from six to 19 in the past 40 years, and continues to rise. These "megacities" include some of the most notoriously overcrowded: Lagos, Karachi, Mumbai. Even in less populous cities, like Nairobi (population: 2.4 million), the growth has created a situation in which 75 per cent of the residents live in slums without running water, electricity or sanitation. The risks are not lost on cities of fewer than 1 million inhabitants, which will absorb nearly half the world's increase in urban population over the next three decades. "Most big-city problems started when cities were smaller," notes Christine Kessides, an urban-economic adviser for the World Bank.

There is now an active global market for ideas on how to answer the challenges of growth. Eastern European cities in countries hoping to enter the EU are being "mentored" by Western European cities. Cities within close proximity to each other, like Manchester and Liverpool, or Glasgow and Edinburgh, are coming together around issues of urban planning and business development.

9 **to chip away at s.th.** *here:* to gradually reduce s.th.
16 **photo op** *short for* **photo opportunity** chance to have one's photo taken
19 **power broker** s.o. who uses his / her political influence in return for financial support
30 **not to be lost on s.o.** to notice s.th.
36 **to mentor** to advise and guide

One of the most interesting models is Curitiba, a city of 1.6 million people in Brazil's southern farm belt that has rejected many of the standard trappings of urban development. In the 1970s, as Curitiba became a magnet for farmworkers displaced by mechanization, a handful of young architects, including the city's 31-year-old mayor, Jaime Lerner, sat down to discuss the needs of the growing city. At a time when most Third World cities mimicked America's love of skyscrapers and bigness, Curitiba went another way. Many big Latin American cities have become monochrome symphonies in gray concrete, but Curitiba is a harmonious mix of nature and architecture, with nearly 52 square meters of greenery per resident – twice the open space recommended by the World Health Organization. Rather than gut the streets to build a subway, the city devised a bus system that works like a metro. Raised platforms allow the system to move up to three times as many passengers as a normal bus service. Some 78 percent of the Curitibanos now commute by bus, one of the highest rates in the world. Urban planners from as far away as Boston and Johannesburg have come to study the Curitiba bus system, and last year Los Angeles opened a replica in the San Fernando Valley.

40 **trappings** outward signs

Curitiba also avoided the demolition of old buildings to make way for wider streets and highways. At the same time that American cities were sacrificing entire neighborhoods to a car culture, Curitibanos were building Brazil's first downtown pedestrian walkways, planting millions of trees and lining older streets with flowerpots. In an attempt to avoid congestion, the city has even turned away factory proposals from companies like Renault and Volkswagen, steering them to smaller satellite cities. In place of factories, Curitiba has set up apprentice workshops, providing work space and venture capital to small merchants and industrialists.

A raised bus stop in Curitiba, Brazil

The small-is-beautiful philosophy is harder to apply in the megacities, but they are trying. Tokyo, the world's largest city, plans to introduce a system under which cars entering crowded areas will be taxed. In Berlin, where streets and car parks take up more space than apartments, planners are trying to reclaim some of the prewar shape of the city in a major redesign allowing for more pedestrian walkways and public spaces. Likewise, many cities are renovating abandoned "brown fields" (industrial zones) that have become a magnet for crime. [...]

Perhaps the biggest danger in all this interchange between cities is in a certain degree of homogenization. But as urbanist Jane Jacobs noted years ago, the one thing all cities share is uniqueness; one is never a complete model for another.

By Rana Foroohar, Newsweek, *December 2001–February 2002.*

Exploring the text

1 What evidence does the writer give that cities are becoming more powerful?
2 What lessons can be learned from the problems faced by megacities?
3 How have the problems resulting from growth been avoided in Curitiba?
4 a) What does the writer mean by the "small-is-beautiful philosophy" (l. 63)?
b) What effect could this type of policy have on town planning?

Close-up: vocabulary

Explain the following words and phrases from the text: province (l. 3) – infrastructure responsibilities (l. 6) – proximity (l. 36) – to mimic (l. 44) – to gut (l. 49)

A step further

- a) "Successful cities need a foreign policy" (l. 22). What are the implications of this?
  b) Draw up a foreign policy for a city of your choice. What might its aims be and how might these be achieved?
- What factors cause traffic and transport problems in cities? How could these factors be dealt with? Record your ideas in a table like the one below.

Causes of transport problems	Solutions
– too many people use their cars	– introduce a tax to enter the town ...

- In groups, think of ways to apply the "small-is-beautiful" concept to big cities. Then draw a plan of your ideal city including the features you thought of.

A Los Angeles suburb from the air

Before you read

- What do you know about the city of Los Angeles? Collect your ideas in a mind map.

Los Angeles sprawl bumps angry neighbor

SANTA CLARITA, Calif. – This is the last frontier, the place where the suburban sprawl of Los Angeles meets a peaceful patch of live oaks, rolling hills and quiet back roads along the Santa Clara River, one of a tiny handful of wild waterways left in Southern California. It is also a battle zone, the future home of Newhall Ranch, the largest housing development ever approved by Los Angeles County, with 21,600 units for 70,000 people to be built over the next 20 years.

To its critics, including neighboring Ventura County, which has filed a lawsuit seeking to block it, Newhall Ranch is a symbol of all that is wrong with California's decades of catch-as-catch-can development, in which suburbs sprang up in ever-widening, ill-considered rings.

To its backers, Newhall Ranch is a sensitively planned community, the vision of a responsible developer with a long track record of building affordable slices of the American dream.

But big and controversial as it may be, Newhall Ranch is nothing compared with the projected need for new housing in Los Angeles County: about 25,000 units a year, according to the Southern California Association of Governments.

By 2025, the state's population of 34 million is projected to grow by 18 million more (a whole New York State) and that of the Los Angeles region by 6 million (or two Chicagos). [...]

"What are you going to do?" asked Mr. Fulton, the author of *The Reluctant Metropolis: The Politics of Urban Growth in Los Angeles*. "Build 200 Newhall Ranches? The truth is, with six million people, growth has got to be both up and out."

That is easier said than done in a place where even residents of modest means have long viewed a patch of yard and sky, a lemon tree and maybe even a swimming pool as all but a birthright, and the fight over Newhall Ranch is proof positive of how hard it will be to change the paradigm. Planners and politicians may talk of "urban infill" and "downtown redevelopment," but Los Angeles has been steadily sprawling for more than 80 years.

0 **sprawl** unplanned housing development
7 **to file a lawsuit** to bring a claim before a lawcourt
9 **catch-as-catch-can** *here:* not having an order
11 **backer** s.o. who gives financial support
12 **affordable** which one has enough money to pay for
26 **paradigm** ['pærədaɪm] pattern
27 **urban infill** providing housing in deserted city centres to attract residents

Since at least the mid-70's, residents of established neighborhoods have consistently opposed construction of higher-density apartment complexes, leaving developers little choice but to build in fringe areas like those near Santa Clarita, a collection of old farming towns northwest of Los Angeles that have been consolidated into the fourth largest city in the county, with nearly 150,000 people.

"In Los Angeles, it's part of our culture to aspire to live in open spaces in single-family homes," said Supervisor Zev Yaroslavksy of Los Angeles County, a Democrat who acknowledged that it pained him to vote for a project as big as Newhall last year but who felt he had little choice, given his own constituents' opposition to living any closer together. "People don't want to live in skyscrapers like New York. People fled New York to come here, and once you've lived in a single-family house with your own backyard, you're basically not interested in moving back to what amounts to a Holiday Inn-like existence." [...]

"Despite all that you would hear, and the outcries about development a house is still the American dream," said Thomas L. Lee, chairman and chief executive of Newhall, which expects that about half the buyers for new Newhall Ranch houses will come from the Santa Clarita Valley itself. "We're providing homes to people who just want a piece of the American dream like everybody else. The large majority of people want to live that way."

Mr. Lee added: "The people are going to be here, whether the housing is here or not. They already have a serious problem in Los Angeles."

But critics of Newhall's plans point out that much of the demand for housing in the region is among the growing Hispanic and immigrant populations of urban Los Angeles, where families are doubled up in apartments and cannot yet afford suburban houses. (Hispanic residents were the only group in the recent Public Policy Institute survey that said the state would be a better place to live in 20 years). At the same time, Newhall's opponents note that some 40,000 additional housing units have already been approved but not built in Santa Clarita, and they would like to see these developed before builders encroach on pristine land.

"You're just vaporizing your open space and watershed and indiscriminately paving it over for something that I can't see as a genuine need," said Lynne Plambeck, first vice president of the Santa Clarita Organization for Planning and Environment. [...]

"I sort of feel like sometimes it's a situation where if you don't build it, they won't come," Ms. Plambeck said.

By Todd S. Purdum, The New York Times, *February 13, 2000.*

31 **fringe** *here:* outer
34 **to aspire to s.th.** to have an ambition to do s.th.
37 **given** *(preposition)* taking into account
52 **to double up** *(informal) here:* two families live in an apartment for one family
57 **to encroach** *(negative) here:* to build in areas where one should not

Exploring the text

1 Describe the Newhall Ranch project in your own words.
2 What arguments are put forward for and against this development?
3 Why is the demand for housing difficult to meet in Los Angeles county?

Close-up: vocabulary

1 Explain the ideas underlying the phrases in the text: the last frontier (l. 1) – a battle zone (l. 4) – affordable slices of the American dream (ll. 12–13) – a Holiday Inn-like existence (l. 41) – to vaporize your open space (l. 58).
2 Find antonyms in the text for: well-planned – to support – trivial – in a planned way – supporters – rejected – to deny – unreliable.

Before you read

- a) Read "The Language of the Streets" (pp. 168 – 169). How does the writer feel about life in the country?

  b) In pairs, discuss where you would prefer to live – in the city or the country. Make notes about your partner's view and report back to the rest of the class.

Why I live where I live

I live in the Red River Valley. I grew up in a small prairie town, moved on, and lived in several others. You know the type: one grain elevator, railroad tracks, abandoned train station, general store, and a curling rink with eight sheets of artificial ice. The kind of place about which people say that if you blink when you drive by, you'll miss it. Now I live in Winnipeg, and I suppose some may say the same comment applies. But these are just tourists skimming across the valley in their boats or trolling with empty hooks. Valley, they say. Where are the hills?

True, one must travel far to find them – but they're here. Comforting little brown humps on the shoreline. Why do I continue to live here in Winnipeg in the Red River Valley? It's God in a cbc T-shirt, calling to make me think.

I've contemplated moving to Vancouver, where they tell me that the difference between Vancouver and Toronto is that in Toronto people dress up in bizarre costumes and pretend they're crazy, while in Vancouver they really are crazy. I don't mind the crazy people in Vancouver. They're like wildflowers on the side of a mountain, pretty to look at from a distance but never meant to be picked and taken home. But I find when I'm in Vancouver that after three days I no longer see the mountains. All I want to do is find a quiet place, huddle down in the sand, and stare at the ocean. And the same thing happens to me when I'm on the east coast. Why do I live here?

I ask a friend. Grasshoppers and crickets sing from either side of the dirt road. It's not quite a full moon but bright enough for long shadows. Perfect night to play Dracula. It's my turn to wear the cape. The question eats at me, interferes with the game. On the horizon Winnipeg shimmers pink and still. You live here, he says, because you're short. You're close to the ground and if a big wind should come along you'd be safe. And yet you feel tall. Naw, that's not it, my daughter says.

It's Sunday, and the question rankles as I make my weekly trip through the forest where thick dark trees wrestle the granite boulders for soil. I push the speed limit to get to the lake before all the others, and finally I find my spot, huddle down into the sand, and stare out across the water. I think: Why do I live here? The answer comes to me. It's because when I live in the Red River Valley, I'm living at the bottom of a lake.

When you live at the bottom of a lake you get cracks in your basement walls, especially in River Heights, where they can afford cracks and underpinning and new basements. I like the cracks. The wind whistles through them, loosens the lids on my peach preserves, makes the syrup ferment, and the mice get tipsy. In the potato bin, sprouts grow on wrinkled skin, translucent, cool sprouts. They climb up the basement walls, push their way through air vents and up the windows in my kitchen. I don't have to bother about hanging curtains.

1 **Red River Valley** area south of Winnipeg, Canada and north of the US border
4 **to blink** (!) to open and close one's eyes
10 **CBC** *short for* Canadian Broadcasting Corporation
20 **cricket** *Grille*
25 **naw** *(slang)* no
26 **to rankle** to stay in one's mind and make one feel uncomfortable
27 **to push the speed limit** to go faster than is allowed
28 **to huddle** to sit with one's legs and arms near one's body
33 **underpinning** support
36 **sprout** green leaf when it first appears on a plant

And time is different here. The days piled on top of lake sediments shift after a good storm so that yesterday slips out from beneath today. Or even last Friday with all its voices will bob up from the bottom and it's possible to lose track of tomorrow. You can just say to hell with tomorrow and go out and play Dracula.

When you live here at the bottom of a lake you can't pin your ancestors down with granite monuments. They slide out of their graves. They work themselves across the underground on their backs using their heels as leverage, they inch their way back into town until they rest beneath the network of dusty roads, and they lie there on their backs and read stories to you from old newspapers.

Now, this is something tourists can never discover as they roar across the valley in their powerboats, churning up the water with their blink-and-you'll-miss-it view of my place. Sometimes a brave one will leap from the boat, come down, and move in next door. I've seen it happen. They become weak and listless, like flies trapped inside a house at the end of summer. And you'll see them walking along the highway in scuba gear muttering to themselves or rowing across the lake in search of a hill. I'll admit, sometimes it's nice to surface, to take off the cape and put on my respectable prairie jacket and boots and do a walking tour of Halifax, sniff a wild mountain flower in Vancouver, get a stiff neck looking up at all those skyscrapers in Toronto, or a three-day party headache in Montreal. But inevitably my eyes grow tired, glazed, and like a sleepwalker I awake to find myself crouched down beside an ocean, a lake, a river, and I know it's time to get back there – to get down in the basement and breathe the wind in the cracks of my walls where, nestled up against the foundation of my house, is the pelvic bone of an ancestor.

From "Why I Live Where I Live" by Sandra Birdsell, Writing Home – a PEN Canada Anthology, *ed. Constance Rooke, Toronto: McClelland & Stewart, 1997.*

45 **leverage** ['li:vərɪdʒ] *here:* object which one uses to lift s.th.
57 **inevitably** *here:* always
60 **to nestle up** to lean against
61 **pelvic bone** bowl-shaped bones at the base of the backbone

Exploring the text

1. Describe the writer's attitude towards Vancouver, Toronto and Montreal.
2. What does life in Red River Valley mean to Sandra Birdsell?
3. To what extent does her attitude to the country differ from that of the tourists?
4. How would you describe the tone of the text?

A step further

- Would you describe the writer's attitude to her ancestors as being unusual, or not? Give reasons for your answer.
- Look at the notes your partner made in task b) on page 180. Has your opinion about city and country life been influenced by the text you have read, or not?
- Write a descriptive essay entitled "Why I live where I live". Refer to the vocabulary list you put together as you worked through the chapter.

Imagine the conversation between the couple in the photo. The girl wants to go to the city but the boy would prefer to stay in the park.

Presentations

Step 0 Research your subject and prepare the presentation / talk carefully. Keep in mind the knowledge, interests and expectations of the audience.

Step 1 Write key words on prompt cards. Then arrange the cards in a logical order, e.g.

- from the least to the most important idea (or vice versa)
- in chronological order
- all arguments for and then all those against an idea
- arguments for and against a certain idea one after the other.

Note: Use one card for each point. Give each card a title. Note down references to visual aids. Use different colours.

1 Introduction
- note on points of talk
- key words for quotes / examples, etc.
- useful phrases

2 Point 1
- key words
- cf. transparency / Powerpoint slide no. ...
- useful phrases

3 Conclusion
- note on points of talk
- key words for examples / quotes, etc.
- useful phrases

Step 2 Make a prompt card for your introduction (see above). After greeting the audience and stating the title of your talk and the time available, catch the listeners' attention with:

- a provocative statement or question,
- a surprising fact, discovery or experience,
- a short anecdote, joke or quotation,
- a picture or cartoon on a transparency.

Then outline the aim and structure of the talk / presentation so that listeners know what to expect.

An example:
Good morning everybody.
As some of you know, since my early childhood I have taken a special interest in ... and so it will not come as a surprise that today I would like to talk about ...
As you know I have been allotted 20 minutes but I will try to finish in 15 to allow time for questions and comments.
[Pause – Look at your audience.]
Ladies and gentlemen, by the time I have finished speaking to you today, 30 children will have died of ... in ... This terrible statistic can be reduced by..

Step 3 In order to hold your listeners' interest:

- use examples to support your statements
- use short, clearly-structured sentences and divide your talk into clear units
- link the parts of your talk (cf. "Presenting an argument", p. 193), repeat and emphasize important ideas; say how many more points you have to make and when you are going to finish.
- use visual aids such as transparencies and Powerpoint slides. For example, it is useful to present the structure of your talk on a transparency.

We remember only...
10 % of what we read
20 % of what we hear
30 % of what we see
50 % of what we see and hear.

Step 4 With your final prompt card, come to a convincing conclusion, e.g. in the form of a short summary, a quotation, a call for action, a look to the future, a rhetorical question or a promise.

An example:
That brings me to the point where I would like to briefly review the arguments. We have seen that although there are advantages to ..., there are also problems which ...
We have had a close look at the facts and figures ... and drawn the conclusion that ...
The question remains: if ...
Let me suggest a possible answer in the words of ...
Thank you for your attention.

Step 5 Decide if you want to give the audience photocopies of transparencies or a summary of the main points to take home.

Step 6 To improve your presentation you could do the following ...

- at home: Practise your talk or presentation out loud either in front of a mirror or ask s.o. to listen to you. Learn your opening by heart. Be sure to stay within the given time frame.
- in the classroom: Practise using overhead projectors and beamers. If necessary, change the seating so that everyone can see the board or screen.

While speaking

1. Body language
   – Be confident, stand firmly but relax, too. Keep your hands out of your pockets and smile!
2. Voice
   – Speak as freely as possible.
   – Vary your tone, volume and emphasis.
   – Speak clearly. Make pauses to let information sink in or signal the transition to a new idea.
   – Talk to your audience in a friendly way. Be natural!
3. Contact with the audience
   – Face your audience at all times.
   – Make eye contact by moving your gaze across the entire audience. Just look at your notes from time to time to make sure you are keeping to your plan.
   – Make sure that all of the audience are able to hear you and see any visual aids clearly (ask them at the beginning of the talk if they can).
   – Use the pronouns 'you' and 'I'.
   – Finish by thanking your audience for their attention. Invite questions and feedback on the content and the quality of the presentation.

Visual aids

A visual aid such as a transparency or Powerpoint slide has two purposes:

– to make, explain, emphasize or summarize a point to support your point of view;
– to remind the audience of a point.

In general, avoid

– unnecessary visual aids which take attention from you the speaker;
– long lists and complicated charts / graphs;
– print which is too small to read;
– talking to the screen or blackboard and losing eye contact with the audience;
– reading out every word on the transparency / slide;
– giving the audience too little time to read the same;
– leaving a transparency / slide visible when you have already moved on to the next point;
– blocking the view of the screen or blackboard.

Media management

– Transparencies: Use 16 point plus print size for a legible text. Headings should be at least 6cm high.
– Overhead projector: Stop talking – pause – place your first transparency on the projector – switch on the machine – give people time to read – face the audience, not the screen – explain your points – use a pointer to refer to certain points or use an overlay to uncover the transparency point by point – stop talking – place your next transparency on the projector – face the audience – continue talking…
– Blackboards / posters / flip-charts: Use generous spacing and large print; use no more than three colours and leave plenty of white space; do not talk and write at the same time; stand beside the chart when you are writing on it and / or talking.
– Videos: Wind the video to the beginning of the piece you wish to show; find out how the equipment (including remote controls) works before the presentation and check that the screen is large enough to be easily seen from the back.

Group presentations

– Before you begin, decide who is going to do what. Involve all group members in the presentation.
– Make sure that your presentation is well-structured and easy to follow. Choose a moderator to introduce the topic, link the various contributions and make a concluding statement.
– Rehearse your presentation, especially the links between the contributions and the use of visual aids.
– Only group members who are playing an active part should be 'on stage' at one time.

A bad dream

a) Watch the sequence, "A bad dream" and make a note of the mistakes the speaker makes.
b) What advice would you give him / does he give himself?

Glossary of film terms

The nos. refer to the page the term appears on.

Basics

shot unbroken piece of film from one point of view 85
cut (fast c.) (fast) switch from one shot to the next 148
segment, sequence, scene increasingly larger units in a film composed of a number of shots
setting time and place which characterize a film 148
special effects artificial effects, e.g. computer-generated imaging, slow motion and voiceover narration used to create an illusion. 87
storyboard Key scenes are visualized in drawings by the director and illustrators before the scenes are shot. The drawings are collected on a board. 78

Types and functions of shots

establishing shot camera is at eyelevel and shows a particular scene; sets the scene for the next scene(s)
fast motion a shot in which time appears to move more quickly than normal; increases suspense 89
overhead shot gives an aerial view (bird's-eye view) e.g. of a town or an area; sets the scene as viewers are given an overall impression of the setting 148
over-the-shoulder shot the camera is behind one speaker and is pointed at a second speaker; viewers feel involved in the dialogue
reverse-angle shot camera is placed behind the second speaker and focuses on the first dialogue partner; often used with the over-the-shoulder shot to give viewers both sides of a dialogue
eyelevel shot camera is placed at a subject's eyelevel; gives the impression of authenticity and directness
high-angle shot camera is placed above s.o. / s.th.; can make a character seem vulnerable
low-angle shot camera is positioned below a subject or object; enlarges s.th. and stresses its importance

Field size

long shot camera is at a great distance from the subject or object being filmed; presents an entire setting
medium long / full shot shows all of a subject and his / her surroundings; gives a complete picture of s.o. / s.th.
medium shot shows s.o. from the knees upwards; brings viewers closer to the action
close-up camera is very close to the subject; concentrates attention on s.o. / s.th. specific or reveals feelings by showing s.o.'s facial expression 148
detail shot / extreme close-up camera is extremely close to s.o. / s.th. to show importance in a scene

Camera movement

to tilt up / down camera moves up or down a vertical plane; shows the subject in his / her full length
to pan left / right camera moves horizontally; follows an action or moves attention from one thing to another
to zoom in / out camera moves quickly towards / away from s.o. or s.th. to focus attention or move it away
hand-held camera the camera movement seems to follow the rhythm of s.o. who is moving; pictures are often unclear; a scene seems more authentic.

Types of montage

flashback a scene shows past events often to provide background information or recall a past event
flashforward a scene shows future developments 148
cross-cutting mixing shots from different scenes to show links between events
split screen the screen shows one or more pictures at a time; shows different aspects of a scene or character
jump cut a cut in a scene which leaves out some action; maintains suspense or cuts out irrelevant action

Film scene analysis

In the course of three viewings, take systematic notes. Cf. p. 30 to help you arrange your notes on one page.

First viewing – focus on the action
Try to understand the gist of the action. Include key phrases from the dialogue in your notes. Consider...

- setting: What is the time and place of the action? What atmosphere is created?
- plot: What happens, and why?
- suspense: What questions remain unanswered? Why do you want to keep on watching?

Second viewing – focus on characters
Describe and then comment on your impression of the character(s). Consider ...

- appearance: hair, cleanliness, clothes;
- body language: facial expression, gestures, posture, movements;
- language / communication: diction, syntax, tone, interaction with others.

Third viewing – function of the scene in the film
- Place the scene in the context of the film. Does it move the action forward, build suspense, provide a turning-point, reveal a trait in s.o.'s character, introduce a character or (re)define a relationship?
- How do cinematic devices (camera operations, music / sound, visual symbols, types of montage, cf. glossary, page 184) serve the main function of the scene?

Documentaries

Documentaries are non-fiction films, mainly broadcast on television. They inform and draw attention to issues of social, cultural, historical and political interest. They usually include real people, authentic locations / on-location coverage and natural lighting and sound. The viewer takes on the role of an eye-witness. Camerawork is generally unobtrusive with few camera operations, mainly eye-level shots, long takes and few cuts. Special effects are seldom used, unless they are necessary to show scientific phenomena.
The format of the documentary – observational, expository / argumentative, narrative / dramatic or investigative – depends on its purpose (cf. table below).

Analysis
Consider the following points:
- What is the main **topic** of the documentary? Which aspects of the topic are dealt with?
- How effective is the **film material** (= footage)? (you could watch sections of the documentary without the sound.)
- What is the function of the **voice-over**? E.g. to give extra information, to explain the footage ...
- How much background **information** is included? Are complicated facts visualized onscreen or explained by the voiceover?
- To what extent are **expert opinions** integrated?

	observational	**expository / argumentative**	**narrative / dramatic**	**investigative**
Purpose	• presents reality as it occurs	• focuses on aspects of the topic	• shows plot development	• exposes scandals (undercover filming)
Features	• camera as 'eye-witness' • little planning of footage, intensive planning of camera location	• intensive planning of sequences • re-enactment of situations, real people 'play' themselves	cf. expository	• camera as 'eye-witness' • intensive planning of how to get access to material
Camera	• usu. static • often a number of cameras used to get a variety of footage	• on-location filming • some (unobtrusive) camera operations • studio interviews, statements	cf. expository	• on-location filming • usu. one static camera • 'talking heads' in the studio
Sound (usu. authentic)	• voice-over, usu. by reporter on location, describes events as they happen	• voice-over explains, comments on, etc. a point of view • 'talking heads' (= experts comment)	• voice-over links scenes or highlights the plot (as in a feature film)	• voice-over and talking heads critically analyse material
Editing	• selection of most typical scenes	• selection of best footage • shots are assembled into logical units	• as in a film, shots are put in chronological sequences, have a storyline, create suspense	• usu. little material so most of it is shown

Music video clips

Music video clips are short sequences which connect a song with a set of images or scenes. They have to appeal to their target group quickly as the viewers of music channels tend to move quickly from one channel to another and often do not pay close attention to the video.

Step 1 Based on the information in the table below work out how the criteria in **bold print** apply to the clip you are analysing.

entertainment
- enable the viewer to escape everyday life
- evoke an emotional response

Do you watch clips to relax? When and how do you watch them, e.g. actively or when you are doing s.th. else? Do they change your mood?

part of youth culture
- allow the audience to identify with other young people
- mirror (and influence) the tastes of the target group

Do you discuss music video clips with friends? What type of music do you prefer? How is your favourite singer / band often portrayed in music videos?

advertisement
- promote a CD or film
- compete with other clips

What dreams / wishes are fulfilled? What emotions does it appeal to? What locations are shown? What lifestyles are presented?

'work of art'
- are innovative
- offer food for thought

What special effects are used? Does the video reflect trends in the media?

Step 2 Classify the clip based on the information below.

Performance clip (singer / band perform song)

performance documentary
- format: live concert
- interaction between singer and band

enhanced performance
- studio performance plus outdoor locations
- usu. song and dance number

Concept performance (singer / band as actor(s))
- action usu. illustrates lyrics
- performance may include associative visual elements (cf. concept clip)

Performance clip / Concept performance:
- moderate use of camera operations and editing techniques
- focus on singer / band (appearance, personality)

- effective if singer / band are already well known

- adequate, if fans want to escape into a dream world or identify with the singer / band
- usu. love songs

Concept clip (voiceover of singer / band)

narrative
- illustrates lyrics
- chronological order of action

or
- a sequence of short scenes

abstract
- no plot
- reflects mood of lyrics
- visuals usu. independent of lyrics

frequent cuts, changes of camera position, extreme camera angles, digital processing (= editing of images on computer), special effects

- high intensity, all-senses approach
- most likely to attract viewers by quickly-changing images and moods

Adverts

When you analyse printed adverts, like the one on the right, consider the following points:
- What kind of **product** is being advertised?
- What **brand image** (positive characteristics / associations) is the product given?
- Who is the **target audience** the advertiser wants to reach? Consider age, gender, income, level of education, life-style, political leanings.
- How does the **AIDA formula** apply to the advert?
  How does the advert attract **A**ttention?
  How does it arouse **I**nterest in the product?
  What **D**esire does it appeal to?
  What kind of **A**ction should the reader take?

You should also examine:
- the **layout** (the position of the product, headline, slogan and product information, the use of visuals such as photos, the effect of the size and colour of the different elements)
- the **language** (choice of words, sentence structure and length, tone, use of rhetorical devices)

Don't forget your **personal reaction** to the advert! Do you like it, or not? What would you change to make the advert more interesting / effective?

Essays

The two most common essay types are expository (present a situation or explain an idea) or argumentative (discuss a controversial topic).

Tip: Make sure that you respond correctly to the instruction in a set essay such as "**Discuss** what measures should be taken to avoid discrimination" or "**Describe** the process of ghettoisation in Northern England". The most commonly used instructions are:
- analyse (break a subject into its components),
- compare (point out similarities and differences),
- describe (say what s.th. is like by providing details),
- discuss (comment in a general way),
- evaluate (judge the effectiveness / usefulness of s.th.),
- illustrate (provide examples to support an idea),
- interpret (explain the meaning / importance of s.th.),
- respond (give your personal reaction to s.th.).

Planning
- Take five minutes to write down relevant ideas.
- Decide on the position you want to take.
- Put your ideas into a logical order, e.g. you could number them.

Writing
- Begin with a thesis statement, i.e. a sentence / short paragraph that presents the main idea of the essay and helps you to focus on one central point.
- In an expository essay…
  • present two or three stages of a development or aspects of a problem.
  • write one paragraph for each point and use examples to explain what you mean.
  • write a conclusion in which you summarize your findings or outline possible consequences or further developments.
- In an argumentative (persuasive) essay…
  • state why the problem is controversial.
  • present a few views that are opposed to / different from your own position (cons) and try to oppose them.
  • define your position and put forward arguments to support it (pros). Use examples.
  • write a logical conclusion based on your arguments.
  • convey your ideas as clearly as possible.

Comments

In a comment you pass judgement on events or ideas by expressing your personal thoughts, values or beliefs. A comment is subjective and contains elements of the argumentative essay (cf. page 187). An extended comment (= a commentary) can be found in the views section of newspapers, esp. as a leading article.

Step 1 Begin by stating the problem / issue.

Step 2 Outline the rejected view and present your own.

Step 3 Continue to structure your text by giving your view as compared to the facts and using constrastive words and expressions such as: *however, yet, still, all the same, conversely, by contrast, in spite of …, for all that.*

Step 4 In your conclusion you could:
- sum up your results using expressions such as: *Thus – Altogether – To sum up … – In conclusion … – To summarize my arguments ….*
- point out results and consequences using phrases such as: *Thus – Therefore – Consequently – As a consequence / result … – That is why …*

Newspaper texts

Step 1 Decide if the text is going to be …
- a full-length, detailed **news article** that answers the questions, 'who', 'what', 'when', 'where', 'why' and 'how', and gives further background information, or
- a **news story**, which gives your personal impression and / or quotations from eye-witnesses / experts, or
- a short **news item** which is usu. no longer than one paragraph and focuses on the most important information only.

Step 2 Ask yourself the following questions:
- Is the text intended for a quality newspaper (to inform) or a popular newspaper / tabloid (to appeal to readers' emotions, entertain, influence opinion)?
- What style is appropriate? When writing a text for a quality paper, avoid slang and colloquial English and try to use a factual style. Lots of adjectives and exaggeration are more suitable for a tabloid text.
- What kind of layout should you choose? It should correspond both to the type of article and the newspaper you are writing for (cf. below). You could also include pictures with suitable captions.

Step 3 Organize your material. If your article is based on a text you have read in class, make sure that you have understood it properly. You should refer to its main ideas or central problem in your text.

Step 4 If you want to make your article more colourful, entertaining or even sensational, add more details, observations and quotations. If you want your article to be concise and informative, cut your material down to the most relevant aspects.

Step 5 A full-length article should include:
- an introduction (usually answering the five "w's" and "how")
- paragraphs, each of which deals with one piece of information. Paragraphs in tabloids tend to be short.
- a conclusion or prediction in the last paragraph.

Step 6 Think of a headline to arouse interest. In a popular paper, this often appeals to the readers' love of sensation. Tabloid articles are also often subdivided by crossheads (= headlines for sections of a text).

Step 7 Finally check your spelling and grammar.

UN staffers and AIDS expert die

7 MINUTES FROM SAFETY

Brave captain almost made it.. then came the plunge to disaster in the Atlantic

Mystery blaze is the No 1 suspect

Tennis star Marc safe

Mystery of crash pilot's last message

The captain of Swissair flight 111 seems to have had no inkling of disaster. **Nick Hopkins** and **Martin Kettle** report

Mark Tran on the chequered history of a relatively new airliner

Term papers

A term paper demands long-term preparation.

Step 1 Choose a topic to write about. It may deal with issues or texts discussed in class, or a topic, book or film that is of personal interest to you. If you choose a topic based on classwork, it should explore a new aspect rather than copying what you have already done. Narrow the topic down to one central aspect and check with your teacher.

Step 2 If you write about a book or film, try to find reviews and information about the writer / director, characters / actors, by typing key words into a search engine. If you use study aids, do not just copy out of them and do quote them in your bibliography!
For current or historical issues, try your school library for relevant materials or again use a search engine. Visual materials such as photos, drawings, maps or diagrams will help to support your ideas.

Step 3 Choose the texts and visual materials which are the most relevant to the theme.

Step 4 Draw up a table of contents to see if you have included all of the aspects necessary to deal with the topic in depth. You could discuss the table with your teacher. Your table of contents should include:
- an introduction (in which you may give your reasons for choosing the topic),
- a main part with a well-structured development of your arguments,
- a conclusion which summarizes your observations and findings,
- a reference section with a bibliography and copies of all the texts and materials used in your term paper.

Step 5 Plan carefully so that you will have enough time for each stage of the paper. You could discuss your time plan with your teacher.
While writing your term paper, you should:
- develop your ideas from one chapter to the next and refer to the title of your paper,
- guide the reader through the paper in a logical way, by using connectives and dividing the chapters into paragraphs,
- support your ideas by referring to other texts and materials,
- make it clear whether you are analysing material or stating a personal opinion,
- give a critical, personal analysis of the topic,
- follow your school's formal requirements as regards the layout and length of the term paper, the structure of the table of contents, the way of referring to or quoting texts, etc.

Step 6 Before you hand in your term paper, check it carefully.
- Have you developed your train of thought logically?
- Have you quoted your sources correctly?
- Is your bibliography complete?
- Have you used the appropriate register, i.e. avoided colloquialisms? Have you used technical terms correctly, varied the sentence structure?
- Use your dictionary or the spelling function of your computer to eliminate spelling mistakes. Check word order and punctuation.
- Does your term paper have a complete title page?

Film reviews

A film review should provide the potential viewer with information about a film which will help him / her to decide whether to go and see it, or not.
When you write a review, you could include the following points: the genre and theme – a plot summary (do not give the ending away!) – the main characters and their relationships – memorable quotes – descriptions of cinematic devices (cf. page 184) – comparisons with other films or the novel on which the film is based – information about the director and cast – an analysis of excessive displays of violence, sex or melodrama – the message of the film – your reaction and evaluation / recommendation.

Step 1 Decide which of the above aspects, or any others, you wish to include in your review.

Step 2 Organize your material so that your review has a logical train of thought.

Step 3 Write a first draft of your review. Your opening sentence should catch readers' attention.

Step 4 Check your draft for content and correctness. Write your final draft and check again.

The glossary contains all the literary terms introduced in *Password to Skyline Plus* and *Skyline Advanced Level – Ausgabe C.* The terms in italics refer to main entries in the glossary. The numbers refer to the page where the term appears in a box.

alliteration [-ˌ--ˈ--] the repetition of consonants at the beginning of words or within words. 19
allusion [əˈluːʒən] a reference to historical or fictional characters, places or events or works which the reader may recognise 35
anecdote [ˈənɪkdəʊt] a simple, short and usually amusing or thought-provoking story about a real person or event, usually passed on by word of mouth 98
antagonist [-ˈ---] character in a fictional text or drama who is opposed to, or in conflict with, the *protagonist.*
assonance [ˈæsənəns] the repetition of vowels in stressed syllables, used for emphasis. 19
atmosphere the tone or mood of a *novel, short story or play* created by setting, description and characters.
characters see *characterization.* 158–159
characterization [ˌ----ˈ--] characters in a narrative text can be presented in two ways. The *narrator* or a figure in the text tells the reader what a person is like (direct characterization). Alternatively, the reader has to find out what a person is like through what this character does, says, thinks or feels (indirect characterization). A flat character can be described clearly in a few words. His / her behaviour is predictable, as he / she does not change. A round character is a life-like, complex individual. He / she may be shown in different moods and may change in the course of the action.
connotation associations and emotions a word may evoke. 167
couplet [ˈkʌplɪt] a *stanza* of two lines.
denotation *literal* meaning of a word. 167
drama a play or drama may consist of several acts which can be subdivided into scenes. The roles or parts are played by actresses and actors, who make up the cast. The characters talk to each other in dialogues. The director helps the actors to put the stage directions (where to stand, how to move and speak) into practice and decides about the use of props (= objects on the stage). A public performance is prepared through a number of rehearsals. The people who watch the play are called the audience. The author of a play is called a playwright. In English, the term drama also refers to the art of writing and performing a play.
dub poetry a form of Caribbean oral *poetry* which originated in Jamaica and Britain in the 1970s. 36
euphemism [ˈjuːfəmɪzəm] a more gentle expression used instead of the more usual one to express unpleasant, frightening or embarrassing facts, e.g. The old dog was put to sleep (i.e. killed).
exposition the first part of a play or story. It gives the information necessary to understand the conflict and events which follow.
figurative using images and pictures that must be 'translated' to be understood.
free verse a form of poetry which is 'free' of metre and does not usually rhyme.
hyperbole [haɪˈpɜːbəlɪ] a statement which is exaggerated for effect. 18
imagery images express a thought indirectly, that is *figuratively* rather than *literally.* See also *simile, metaphor, symbol* and *personification.* 35
irony [ˈaɪrənɪ] saying one thing but meaning another. 19
literal using words in their everyday meaning.
metaphor [ˈmetəfə] a comparison between two objects or ideas, without a word of comparison ('like', 'as' or 'as if'), e.g. "Holidays are heaven".
metre the regular pattern of stressed and unstressed syllables.
mini-saga a story of exactly 50 words. 115
mode of narration see *narrator* 54
narrator [nəˈreɪtə] the person or voice who tells the story in a *novel* or *short story.* The narrator is not identical with the author. The narrator can be a *character* in the text who tells the reader what he / she experiences, thinks and feels, ("I"). This first-person narrator is always limited in his / her view of the events (limited point of view). A third-person narrator is not a character in the narrative but stands outside it. He / She refers to the characters in the story as "he / she / they". A third-person narrator may be an omniscient [ɒmˈnɪsɪənt] narrator who knows everything about characters and events (unlimited point of view); a 'selective' third-person narrator who presents the story through one character's eyes (limited point of view) or an unobtrusive third-person narrator who describes the action but not characters' thoughts, etc.
novel a long fictional prose text. It often has many *characters,* different *settings* and a complex *plot.*

parody ['pærədɪ] speech, text or music that imitates and exaggerates the style of a well-known text in order to be amusing.
personification [ˌ----'--] a kind of *metaphor* in which human characteristics or feelings are given to an object, an animal, an abstract idea or a plant, e.g. the door screamed. 11
poetry a *poem* is usually a fairly short piece of writing, divided into single lines. It often expresses the speaker's experiences. Traditional poetry makes use of four very important poetic devices: *metre, stanza, rhyme, rhythm.* Modern poetry often does not have a regular *rhythm* or a *rhyme scheme.*
play see *drama*
plot the sequence of events as arranged by the author. It says what happens, and why.
point of view the position or perspective from which the *narrator* presents the story to the reader. 35
protagonist [-'---] the main character in a *novel, play* or *short story.*
quatrain ['kwɒ'treɪn] a *stanza* of four lines.
rhyme similarity of sounds in two or more words. Words rhyme when their accented vowels and all following sounds are identical. This often occurs at the end of lines (end rhyme). The pattern created is called a rhyme scheme. It is represented using small letters (see Herrick: abab cdcd…).
rhythm ['rɪðm] the flow of language created by the arrangement of unstressed and stressed syllables. It is mainly based on *metre.*
sarcasm *irony* which is cutting and meant to hurt. 19
satire ['sætaɪə] combines humour and criticism in order to expose and ridicule evil and stupidity. It attempts to correct and reform. 69
setting the time and place that characterize a work of literature.

"What the hell is 'I heart NY' supposed to mean? I see it everywhere."

short story a short story is a short fictional prose text which is meant to be read in a single sitting. It can be as short as 500 and as long as 15,000 words. A lot of short stories follow different patterns but the following points apply to many of them. There may be one main *character* (*protagonist*) or a group of equally important *characters.* There is a single *setting* (i.e. the time and place of the action does not change). However, longer short stories might have more than one setting. The setting also helps to create a certain *atmosphere.* The reader may be led into the story through an *exposition.* In modern stories the action often starts immediately in the first sentence. In some stories the action can develop logically through conflicts or crises and finally reaches a climax or turning-point near or at the end (emphasis on action and suspense). Some stories concentrate on a decisive moment in the life of the main *character* (emphasis on character and psychology). There is often a surprise ending, a happy / unhappy ending or an open ending.
simile ['sɪmɪlɪ] a comparison between two objects or ideas, using 'like', 'as' or 'as if', e.g. "Holidays are like heaven".
sketch a short, humorous scene often as part of a theatre or television show.
sonnet ['--] a sonnet is a very traditional *poem* consisting of 14 lines. It is usually written in iambic pentameter (i.e. five beats per line, each beat consisting of an unstressed and stressed syllable). A sonnet often deals with subjects such as love or death. Its most common form in English literature is the English (or Shakespearean) sonnet. It consists of a logical sequence of three *quatrains* and a final *couplet* in which a well-worded, general insight or truth is given as a conclusion. Its *rhyme scheme* is abab cdcd efef gg. 136
speaker the speaker is the voice speaking to us in a *poem.* He / she is not necessarily identical with the author, even if "I" is used.
stanza ['stænzə] the usually regular number of lines which form a unit in a *poem.*
suspense the feeling of expectation or excitement aroused in the reader about what is going to happen.
symbol ['sɪmbl] an object, a place, etc. which stands for an abstract idea, e.g. a heart is a symbol of love.
understatement opp. of *hyperbole;* s.th. that is represented as being less important than it really is. 19

Acknowledgements

The editors wish to thank all authors, publishers and literary agencies who have given permission to use copyright material. Sources are given next to the texts. The following list acknowledges copyright holders who are not identical with the publishers quoted and also gives specifications requested by copyright holders. Every effort has been made to locate owners of copyright material, but in a few cases this has not proved possible and repeated enquiries have remained unanswered. The publishers would be glad to hear from any further copyright owners of material reproduced in this book.

Pp. 7–9: Copyright 2001 U.S. News & World Report, L.P. Reprinted with permission; pp. 10–11: "Mexico's Children", from DAYS OF OBLIGATION by Richard Rodriguez, copyright (c) 1992 by Richard Rodriguez. Used by permission of Viking Penguin, a division of Penguin Group (USA); pp. 20–21: Copyright 2000 U.S. News & World Report, L.P. Reprinted with permission; pp. 70–72: Bulibasha was first published by Penguin Books (NZ) Ltd. in 1994. Permission is granted by Witi Ihimaera and Penguin Books (NZ) Ltd.; p. 75: Text: Buffy Sainte-Marie (c) 1968 by Gipsy Boy Music Inc., für D: Rondor Musikverlag GmbH, Berlin; p. 82: By Daniel B. Wood. This article first appeared in The Christian Science Monitor on February 19, 1998 and is reproduced with permission. ©2001 The Christian Science Monitor (www.csmonitor.com <http://www.csmonitor.com>). All rights reserved.; pp. 118–119: This article first appeared in Salon.com, at http://www.Salon.com. An online version remains in the Salon archives. Reprinted with permission; pp. 143–145: From SHAKESPEARE IN LOVE by Marc Norman & Tom Stoppard. Copyright (c) 1999 Marc Norman & Tom Stoppard. Reprinted by permission of Hyperion; p. 150: "Unfortunate Coincidence" from DOROTHY PARKER: COMPLETE POEMS by Dorothy Parker, copyright (c) 1999 by The National Association for the Advancement of Colored People. Used by permission of Penguin, a division of Penguin Group (USA) Inc.; p. 151: From *Serious Concerns* by Wendy Cope. Publisher Faber and Faber Ltd; pp. 176–177: From Newsweek, December 2001–February 2000 © Newsweek, Inc. All rights reserved. Reprinted by permission; pp. 178–179: Copyright © 2000 by The New York Times Co. Reprinted with permission.

Picture credits

Cover photos: t-l, PhotoDisc, Seattle, WA; b-l, b-r, MEV, Augsburg; p. 1: PhotoDisc, Seattle, WA; p. 6: background, pp. 7–31, t-r and t-l, p. 21: Getty Images, München; p. 6: centre, Corbis / (Sohm), Düsseldorf; b-l, Corbis / (Bettmann), Düsseldorf; pp. 12, p. 23: Corbis / (Joseph Sohm; ChromoS), Düsseldorf; p. 17: Corbis / (James Leynse), Düsseldorf; p. 18: Corbis / (Sygma/McDermott), Düsseldorf; pp. 17–18: Corbis / (Bernd Obermann), Düsseldorf; p. 19: Reprinted with Special Permission of King Features Syndicate; p. 20: Corbis / (Diltz), Düsseldorf; pp. 22–24, 26–29: Corbis Digital Stock / (RF), London; p. 25: Corbis / (Bettmann), Düsseldorf; p. 30: Cinetext, Frankfurt; p. 31: defd / (pwe), / Hamburg; p. 32: l Corbis / (Chris North; Cordaiy), Düsseldorf, r, dpa, / Frankfurt; p. 37: Bloodaxe Books; p. 39: Concerto / (Sergio Salma), Brüssel; p. 42: AFP, Bonn; p. 45, pp. 33–49: Corbis, Düsseldorf; p. 50: t-r, National Geographic, Vol 173, No. 2 Feb. 1988; pp. 50: t-l, pp. 51–62: t-l and t-r: Yothu Yindi Foundation, Archerfield, QLD: Steve Parish Publishing; p. 50: t-r, p. 57: National Geographic / Belinda Wright, b, National Gallery of Victoria; pp. 51, 52: Corbis / (Penny Tweedie), Düsseldorf; p. 53: Okapia, / Frankfurt; pp. 55, 82, 108, 136, 161, 171: MEV, Augsburg : MEV, Augsburg; ; 61: Klett-Archiv, Stuttgart; pp. 62, 112, 113, 130, 153: The Spectator Limited, / London; p. 63: t-l Corbis / (Rabinowitz), Düsseldorf, b Corbis / (Catherine Karnow), Düsseldorf; p. 63: t-r, pp. 63–74: E-Lance Media GmbH, / Gauting; p. 71: Corbis / (Roberts), Düsseldorf; p. 72: Corbis / (Bettmann), Düsseldorf; p. 73: Corbis / (Paul A. Souders), Düsseldorf; p. 75: t-l, Corbis / (Bettmann), Düsseldorf; b, pp. 75–83: Corbis / (Fleming), Düsseldorf; p. 77: Jim Crowson; p. 78: l defd, Hamburg, r Miramax; p. 79: Corbis / (Fleming), Düsseldorf; p. 80: Corbis / (Gandert), Düsseldorf; p. 83: Corbis / (Essel), Düsseldorf; p. 84: Cinetext, Frankfurt; p. 84: b, p. 85: t, pp. 85–93: t-l and t-r, Cinetext, Frankfurt; p. 84: t-r, p. 85: centre, p. 87, p. 89: Corbis / (Sygma), Düsseldorf; p. 85: b, p. 88: Corbis, Düsseldorf; p. 91: Corbis / (Sygma), Düsseldorf; pp. 94, 94–113, t-l, t-r: Topham Picturepoint, Edenbridge Kent; p. 95: Atlantic Syndication / (Emmwood), London EC1R; p. 96: Whiteway Publications Ltd; p. 98: By kind permission of Bill Caldwell and the *Daily Star*; p. 105: l Cinetext, Frankfurt, r REX Features LTD, London; p. 106: Ernst Klett Verlag, Stuttgart; p. 109: Jerry Swaffield; p. 110: Copyright=(C) Corel Corporation, Unterschleissheim; p. 119: Corbis / (Richard Cummins), Düsseldorf; pp. 120, 124: CartoonStock / (Daryl Cagle), London N5 1XL; p. 122: Cinetext, Frankfurt; p. 126: ActionAid, London N19 5PG; pp. 132: background, pp. 140–141, p. 141: Cinetext Frankfurt; pp. 132, 133, 146–147: Corbis / (Hellier), Düsseldorf; p. 133: Corbis / (Morris), Düsseldorf; p. 134: Corbis / (Ergenbright), Düsseldorf; p. 135: Corbis / (Wheeler), Düsseldorf; p. 138: Cinetext, Frankfurt; p. 142: Corbis / (Bettmann), Düsseldorf; pp. 143: Corbis / (Sygma), Düsseldorf; pp. 143, 145: Corbis / (Sygma), Düsseldorf; p. 152: Klett-Archiv, Stuttgart; p. 156: Corbis / (Baldizzone), Düsseldorf; p. 158: Corbis / (Vogt), Düsseldorf; p. 159: l, pp. 158–159: background Corbis / (Jean-Pierre Lescourret), Düsseldorf; r, Corbis / (Prince), Düsseldorf; p. 160: b, t-l, pp. 161–181, t-l, t-r Corbis / (Schein), Düsseldorf, t-r Corbis / (Maze), Düsseldorf; p. 162: Ken Pyne; 163: Getty Images, München; p. 165: Corbis / (Gillian Darley), Düsseldorf; p. 166: Corbis / (London Aerial Photo Library), Düsseldorf; p. 169: Corbis / (Lee Snider), Düsseldorf; p. 170: Klett-Archiv, Stuttgart; p. 172: Corbis / (Michael Freeman), Düsseldorf; p. 173: Corbis / (Bojan Brecelj), Düsseldorf; p. 177: Jonas Rabinovitch, New York; p. 178: Corbis / (Jonathan Blair), Düsseldorf; p. 180: DigitalVision / (Digital Vision), Maintal-Dörnigheim; p. 183: Private Eye, London W 1D 3 BN; 187: Klett-Archiv, Stuttgart; p. 188: MIRROR Syndication International, London; Guardian & Observer News Services, London; p. 191: Punch.